Making Matters

Clare Hunter has been a banner-maker, community textile artist and textile curator for over twenty years and established the community enterprise NeedleWorks in Glasgow. Her first book, *Threads of Life*, won the Saltire First Book Award, was a Waterstones Scottish Book of the Month and a Radio 4 Book of the Week. Her second book, *Embroidering Her Truth*, described by Hilary Mantel as 'a charmed feat of imagination and learning', was a source of inspiration for the Christian Dior 2024 Cruise Collection in Scotland.

Also by Clare Hunter

Threads of Life: A History of the
World Through the Eye of a Needle

Embroidering Her Truth: Mary,
Queen of Scots and the Language of Power

MAKING MATTERS

In Search of Creative Wonders

CLARE HUNTER

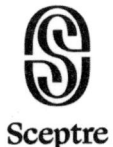

Sceptre

First published in Great Britain in 2025 by Sceptre
An imprint of Hodder & Stoughton Limited
An Hachette UK company

The authorised representative in the EEA is Hachette Ireland, 8 Castlecourt Centre, Dublin 15, D15 XTP3, Ireland (email: info@hbgi.ie)

1

Copyright © Clare Hunter 2025

The right of Clare Hunter to be identified as the Author of the Work has been asserted by her in accordance with the Copyright, Designs and Patents Act 1988.

All rights reserved. No part of this publication may be reproduced, stored in a retrieval system, or transmitted, in any form or by any means without the prior written permission of the publisher, nor be otherwise circulated in any form of binding or cover other than that in which it is published and without a similar condition being imposed on the subsequent purchaser.

A CIP catalogue record for this title is available from the British Library

Hardback ISBN 9781529346299
Trade Paperback ISBN 9781529346305
ebook ISBN 9781529346312

Typeset in Sabon MT by Manipal Technologies Limited.

Printed and bound in Great Britain by Clays Ltd, Elcograf S.p.A.

Hodder & Stoughton policy is to use papers that are natural, renewable and recyclable products and made from wood grown in sustainable forests. The logging and manufacturing processes are expected to conform to the environmental regulations of the country of origin.

Hodder & Stoughton Limited
Carmelite House
50 Victoria Embankment
London EC4Y 0DZ

www.sceptrebooks.co.uk

To all makers of wonder

Contents

	An Introduction	1
1	Paper Boats	7
2	Paper-cuts and Pop-ups	34
3	Paper Theatres	64
4	Snow and Sand	92
5	Bubbles, Blow Books and Kites	115
6	Dressing Up	142
7	Puppets	174
8	Pinholes and Peepshows	205
9	Lanterns	233
	An Ending	259
	Notes	263
	Acknowledgements	271
	Bibliography	273
	Index	281

hopes for the child's future. Flown by family members, the kite's string is cut as it rises so that their petition for the baby's wellbeing can be carried to the gods above. While in Mexico, for the Day of the Dead, people make and display loops of delicate tissue-paper flags with cut-out images of death to remind revellers of the fragility of life.

Most of the objects people make at home are short-lived. The snowman melts, the sandcastle is washed away, a costume, once worn, is discarded. And yet something of their quality persists. Our experience of them has an afterlife, remembered as part of a cherished moment of fun and fascination to kindle a lasting affection. Their very ephemerality endows them with a preciousness so that they linger in our memory as intangible keepsakes.

I have always been a maker, someone who relishes creative possibilities in the unlikeliest of forms. The home I grew up in housed an abundance of salvaged oddments – bits of string, scraps of cloth, coils of wire and a plentiful supply of paper and card. Making in our house was something you did whenever you happened upon something that might become something else: a foil biscuit wrapper would be pounced upon to fashion a tiny silver chalice; yesterday's newspaper commandeered, cut into strips and – with each strip rolled, glued and painted – threaded as beads on a necklace; a length of cardboard could be notched at each end to fashion a makeshift loom. At theatre school, under the tutelage of a prop master from the Royal Shakespeare Company, I was taught how to replicate a commedia dell'arte mask by disguising latex as old leather with a surfeit of shoe polish, and I constructed a wooden toy theatre, styled in homage to the celebrated Glasgow architect Charles Rennie Mackintosh, in stark white paint with a proscenium adorned with the Glasgow rose motif.

When I became a community artist, making with others became my full-time job. Craft workshops abounded and with them came puppets, pinhole cameras, pop-up books and a plethora of miscellaneous, crafted diversions. This was making as co-creation, passing on the knowledge and confidence I had acquired to others so they could realise their own original, creative expression, where the process – not just the product – was an essential part of our co-operative journey.

I discovered that making offers both physical and mental stimulation. It is a sensory and tactile pursuit. With hands acting as mediators between the intimate self and the external world, a maker can feel the potential of different materials, experiment with their pliability or strength and be responsive to touch. And making is therapeutic, providing a distraction from anxiety. It is soothing to settle into concentration, into the rhythm of creativity. The colouring in of tiny figures to grace the stage of a paper theatre is mindful; the snipping out of small pieces of paper to fashion an intricate paper-cut might not seem taxing but it still demands vigilant attention. And what we make is autobiographical, it marks our presence at this time in this place. It captures our personality.

In our fast-moving, algorithmic world of sophisticated technology, there is a growing appetite for simpler forms of imaginative creativity, a yearning to embrace a more personal, more ecologically sensitive way of registering and expressing our humanity. But there are also ways in which

An Introduction

The great doesn't happen through impulse alone, and is a succession of little things that are brought together
Vincent van Gogh

Every day across the world, in every community, people are making myriad things as totems of celebration or loss, as talismans of luck and happiness, as harbingers of hope or simply to delight. Yet many of the things they make – paper boats and lanterns, eccentric costumes and colourful kites, sentinel snowmen and turreted sandcastles and more – are excluded from the panoply of what we call crafts. Such things do not necessarily require honed artisanal skills. They are simple objects, usually created at home from basic or found materials, most often for a local participatory event. Their makers seldom receive any formal guidance on how to construct them. Rather they learn by watching others, replicating their methods, being shown the rudiments of design and structure by a father or grandmother, a schoolfriend or sibling: shape, size and symbolic iconography passed on from one generation to the next as a form of material legacy to become, in time, a tradition.

What is made, while individual and sometimes personalised, often has a public purpose as a contribution to an age-old ritual or annual festival, evoking a potent expression of shared energy and spirit. Such events connect the makers to their history, their culture and their distinct identity in a memorable way. It is mesmerising to watch a flotilla of paper boats inscribed with people's hopes drift out to sea, to encounter a nighttime city street glowing with illuminated lanterns made by one's own community, to witness the mass release of hundreds of dancing kites into a summer's sky. And it is the public presence of these individually crafted objects that endows such events with special meaning, that invests them with emotional, sometimes even spiritual, resonance. Through them participants and spectators can, for a little while, transcend their everyday lives and experience a moment of collective wonder.

It is curious, therefore, that such common and widespread creativity is generally overlooked: its history rarely explored, its significance scarcely discussed, its contemporary practice barely considered. Along with many other things we now think of as mere playthings – puppets, toy theatres, kaleidoscopes and dress-up dolls – such artefacts have been deemed to be of negligible cultural value. Yet most have a surprisingly rich history, rooted in shamanic rites, in scientific experiment, in religious devotion or in social change. These are artefacts made with an altruistic intent: to share and preserve material memory, keep faith with local traditions, maintain cultural continuity and curiosity, and replenish community spirit. For the Obon festival in Japan, floating lanterns decorated with personal messages are sent out to sea to convey the souls of loved ones back to their afterlife. In Korea, the birth of a baby is marked by the making of a special kite inscribed with digital media is supporting this new enthusiasm for making, with platforms such as TikTok, Instagram, Pinterest, Facebook and YouTube all enabling people to discover and exchange creative ideas and techniques more widely: multiple online sources to inspire and support would-be makers. More than this, there is a revival of interest in participatory events: an increasing enthusiasm for kite festivals, lantern processions and costumed gatherings around the world. People are coming together and contributing something they have made themselves.

All this heralds a growing recognition of the value, both individual and collective, in the simple things we create, not just because of the pleasure we experience in their making but because, in this increasingly grim world of ours, any small delight feels like treasure. The small things we make are unique. They are intimate, creative expressions of celebration, commemoration and connection; imaginative, tactile markers of our human existence. Through them we can journey beyond the humdrum of our everyday lives to embrace, however fleetingly, a moment of mesmeric enchantment.

I
Paper Boats

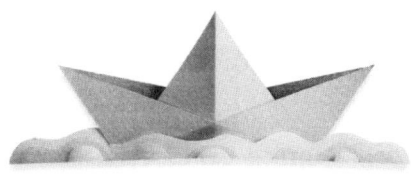

For whatever we lose (like a you or a me)
it's always ourselves we find in the sea
'maggie and milly and molly and may',
e e cummings

It is the evening of 31 December 1999, the brink of a new century. In our small glen, we have reached the climax of what has been a year of community workshops and events. Now we are gearing up for the grand finale. A huge digital clock has been installed outside the village hall to flash through the last minutes of the twentieth century and, in the hall, our oldest resident, ninety-year-old Jessie, has already sliced through a home-baked millennium cake to enthusiastic applause. On the loch-side of the building, a large wooden boat – hewn by a local builder – lies waiting, its sails writ large in golden script with the dates of the departing and arriving years. It will be set alight just before midnight in a spectacular visual hurrah. But, before that, before the countdown of the clock and the burning of the boat, there is to be another mesmeric event.

Over the previous week I have been helping local children make tiny boats from silver card. Toothpicks have been requisitioned as masts; printer paper appropriated to serve as billowing sails on which the children have penned their hopes for the future. A tealight has been carefully placed in each boat, each one safely secured by a liberal dollop of Blu-tack.

Now, as darkness falls, the children process from the hall to the old bridge. It is a route they know well but, while they have been devouring cake, it has been transformed and turned magical with verges of candlelit lanterns that spill streams of gold across their path. And nature has lent a hand, providing the unexpected enchantment of a sky studded with stars. The procession is led by a local piper playing a sonorous lament. It endows the event with gravitas, as its haunting skirl and drone harbour age-old memories. The children encounter an elsewhere world. Our glen is said to be a place of thin air where the separation between heaven and earth is more fragile than in other places. Ours is a land where fairies dwell and spirits lurk, where ancient beliefs are mapped out in standing stones and silver streams. Here, we are thought to share our lives with beings beyond our ken. And tonight, on the eve of the new millennium, that claim feels more plausible than ever.

At the bridge the flotilla of our children's hopes lies nestled in the dark of the water. Earlier that evening, anxious lest a boat be toppled by the current and a child's dream washed away, I had arranged for a wooden pallet to be anchored to the riverbank and had my husband lower me down to it on a makeshift harness. It was a challenging enterprise, given the steepness of the bank and my less-than-sylphlike frame, but it allowed me peace of mind. I crisscrossed the pallet with double-sided tape to ensure that each little boat was fastened firmly to its wooden surface so that the armada could float down the river. And, at the first wheeze of the pipes, I had my husband lower me again so that I could ignite each tealight with a shaky hand.

As the children, families and neighbours reach the bridge we unloose the pallet from its moorings and launch its cardboard fleet. It floats downstream, claimed eagerly by the river, following its curve, speeding on and on until it reaches the arch of the bridge, where it disappears. Everyone rushes to the other side, awaiting its re-emergence. There is a whoop of triumph as a quiver of reflected light appears, followed by the palleted fleet illuminated in starlit, candlelit glory. We watch to the end of its flickering gleam, holding vigil until the river's bend takes it on its course, on to its end, carrying the hopes of our children far from home and out to sea.

Well, that's how it should have been. Real life, however, is never as reliable as we plan. On its reappearance the pallet is abruptly grounded. Quick-minded onlookers snatch up fallen branches to prod it onwards, but their efforts are in vain. We placate the anxious children by reassuring them that the river will urge it on, that later its current will tug their boats free and send them on their way. In truth it is a local farmer who, very early next morning, clambers down and sends the pallet bobbing off to sea.

Paper boats represent improbable but possible survival. While a boat symbolises the journey of the soul, each fold made in a paper boat is thought to strengthen its capacity to carry that soul, or the wish a boat carries, safely to its desired destination. Paper boats are harbingers of hope: each sailing an act of faith. Our trust in water to carry us – and what we give it – somewhere else is an ancient tryst but it is one tinged with risk and misgivings. Water symbolises the power of life – regenerative, cleansing and redemptive – but it also threatens. It is both a creator and destroyer.

It was in Japan that the first illustrations of origami boats appeared, their existence recorded when they featured as repeating motifs on a *kosode* (the predecessor to the kimono) depicted in a pattern book of 1713.[1] The secret of how to make paper from plant fibres had been safeguarded in China for over 500 years until it spilled out to other parts of Asia, reaching Japan in AD 610. While the Japanese might have gained knowledge of the process of making paper, it remained a complex and labour-intensive process, and paper was a valuable and treasured commodity reserved for ceremonial purposes, such as the making and wrapping of offerings to deities. It was used with reverence, with an awareness of its preciousness.

Origami originated in Shinto/Buddhist practice, where small, folded simulations of nature – butterflies and birds – were created to boost the efficacy of temple blessings. The use of a single sheet of uncut folded paper ensured that there would be no openings for evil spirits to slip through and, because of its spiritual purpose, the art of origami evolved as an intricate, mindful craft with its own etiquette to become a unique feature of Japanese culture. Over the following centuries, as paper technology and production expanded in Japan, what is now called 'recreational origami' emerged. Made as gifts to warriors, as favours for weddings or as festive decorations, many recreational origami models still hold symbolic meaning: a crane for long life, a dragon for wisdom, a swan for tranquillity, a frog for thrift and a paper boat for hope. By the eleventh century, both origami and the techniques involved in making paper had migrated to Europe. The earliest European record of a paper boat is found in the medieval *Tractatus Sphaera Mundi* (On the Sphere of the World), written in 1230 by the English scholar, monk and astronomer John Holywood.[2] His illustrated treatise includes a small drawing of a town lying huddled along a shoreline as a tiny, folded paper boat drifts through the waves.

Today we view paper as a basic material: utilitarian, cheap and plentiful. But until the early nineteenth century and the advent of paper-making machinery, paper was produced one sheet at a time by manual workers and was a highly valued material. Letters, inventories and reports were penned with words crammed tightly together to make the most economic use of the paper they were written on. And paper was recycled, reused, stuffed into walls to act as insulation, slipped between the cloth layers of a quilt to provide extra warmth, and utilised to stiffen ecclesiastical vestments. A vintage textile retailer told me that she once found, in the remnants of a sixteenth-century vestment, the fragments of a musical notation for a canticle that would have been sung at a Catholic mass, a hymn forbidden by the Reformation. Here was a melody not destroyed but repurposed and safeguarded as a lining for a costly, embroidered ecclesiastical cope. Its surprising rediscovery unearthed music that had been unheard and unsung for hundreds of years.

Experimentation with the use of wood pulp and the industrialisation of paper-making processes in the early nineteenth century made its mass production viable and its cost more affordable. As supply increased and prices were reduced, the use of paper became more playful. Paper was adopted as the craft material of choice for fun pastimes in family parlours. These became hives for the domestic manufacture of paper novelties: dainty Valentine cards, silhouettes of relatives, decoupaged boxes pasted with an exuberance of paper scraps, concertinaed paper fans, lampshades made from paper that had been delicately pricked out with winsome designs, and pretty paper garlands and bouquets.

This enthusiasm for paper crafts included the making of paper boats. They became a common sight on Britain's boating ponds in local parks: a popular recreation. As an island nation, with a proud naval history, not only were Britain's seas and rivers thick with commercial shipping, but its canals, lakes and ponds were all sites ripe for public pleasure. It is no surprise, therefore, that the construction and sailing of paper boats became a widespread diversion. The novelist Jane Austen cites paper-boat making as one of the entertainments she organised to distract her newly motherless nephews from their grief. Writing to her sister, Cassandra, in 1808, she reports, 'We do not want amusement . . . spillikins, paper ships, riddles, conundrums, and cards . . . while I write now George is most industriously making and naming paper ships.'[3]

A decade on and it is the radical, English Romantic poet Percy Bysshe Shelley who has become enamoured of paper boats, enthusiastically launching his miniature fleets on the Serpentine in London's Hyde Park, on the ponds of the city's Kensington Gardens, and setting more adrift on Oxford's waters. His 1848 biographer, Thomas Medwin, left us an image of the poet excitedly engaged in a flurry of paper-boat adventuring:

> He took as great an interest in the sailing of his frail vessels as a ship-builder may do in that of his vessels – and when one escaped the dangers of the winds and waves, and reached in safety the opposite shore, he would run round to hail the safe termination of its voyage.[4]

Shelley's friend Thomas Jefferson Hogg also attested to what he called the poet's 'unaccountable passion' for paper boats, remembering that 'all wastepaper was rapidly consumed, then the covers of letters, next letters of little value; [then] the most precious contributions'.[5] Given that Shelley used redundant missives for his boat construction, it is not inconceivable that some of these boats might have been crafted from discarded drafts of his poems. Perhaps Shelley watched to see if his words prevailed, if they could weather the ripples of a pond or the current of a river, and – if they reached a shore safely – exulted in the successful trial of their poetic persistence. In one of his poems, 'Letter to Maria Gisborne', written in 1820, Shelley even makes reference to his paper-boat sailing:

> . . . the breeze
> Is still – blue Heaven smiles over the pale seas.
> And in this bowl of quicksilver – for I
> Yield to the impulse of an infancy
> Outlasting manhood – I have made to float
> A rude idealism of a paper boat[6]

And Shelley was not the only poet to seize on the image of a paper boat as a potent metaphor. For the Indian writer Rabindranath Tagore paper boats were harbingers of promise. His were boats of dreams:

> Day by day I float my paper boats one by one down the running stream
> In big black letters I write my name on them and the name of the village where I live.
> I hope that someone in some strange land will find them and know who I am.[7]

Tagore was writing about his own childhood experiences in India, when the monsoon season sheeted the streets in rain from June to September. For centuries, Indian monsoons have heralded a rush of children escaping outdoors to float their home-made paper boats on rivers and streams, launching them on overflowing gutters and deep-watered puddles. Some children, as Tagore recalls, inscribe their little boats with their name and the name of their village: each casting off their boat in the hope that not only will it survive the journey but that, should it be stilled on a faraway shore, it will be found by another child who, on discovering the name and whereabouts of its creator, will make contact. Their paper boats are imbued with the possibility of connection.

By facing their fate in mercurial waters, fragile paper boats make optimism, courage and possibility tangible. And for those unable to explore wider horizons, a paper boat travels as a cipher for their spirit. It represents their future. This is the sentiment behind the India-based Paper Boat charity, which chose a paper boat for its name and its logo. It is committed to supporting children who face economic and educational barriers to progress. Following its mantra, 'Imagine, Create, Play, Share and Reflect', the charity works to equip children with the skills, confidence and ambition to journey beyond their current limitations and realise their potential. To this end, it has established child-centred, community-owned creative spaces and has designed a programme of events to inspire children to overcome their present difficulties and discover new opportunities.[8] And it was in the spirit of future possibility that members of the Youth Congress in Hubballi, Karnataka, organised a paper boat race in 2020, not in a local river but in the city's puddled potholes, as an imaginative way to draw attention to the tardiness of the municipal corporation in tackling its much overdue programme of road repairs.

It is India that holds the 2022 Guiness World Record award for the greatest number of people making paper boats in the least time when, in Cuttack in the eastern state of Odisha, over 2,000 students made 23,000 paper boats in 35 minutes.[9] And also in India, that same year, twelve-year-old Nesto Biju from Kerala won the national record for the smallest paper boat, just 4mm long, to be fashioned by a child.[10] Paper boats are an intrinsic part of devotional practice in India, tactile markers designed to appease and appeal to its many water-bound deities: Varuna, the god of the Ocean; Narmada, the river goddess; and Ganga, the goddess of purification and forgiveness, to name but three. And it is to honour Ganga and placate her spirit, that people fill their paper boats with incense and marigolds on a daily basis and float them on the Ganges River as a sacred act of veneration and penitence.

*

Paper boats were a mainstay of Victorian entertainment and they feature in the 1896 edition of *Pleasant Work for Busy Fingers; or, Kindergarten at Home* by Maggie Browne, which sits on a bookshelf in my writing shed. It is an adaptation from a German publication and features a paper boat on its cover. Its fictional protagonist, Aunt Pollie, has been appointed guardian to her young nephews and niece – Bob, Bessie, Bertie and Baby – as their mother is ill. She tackles her mission with an alarmingly energetic zeal. Through 322 pages, Aunt Pollie steers her charges away from any possible slide to idleness by guiding them through multifarious edifying projects. The making of a paper boat is included in her relentless schedule of creative activities:

> 'It is quite simple,' said Aunt Pollie. 'Do as I tell you, and you can manage it easily for yourselves. Fold down each triangle, so that all three lie in a square . . . Let us call the top angles of the triangle *a*, *b*, and *c*, the centre of the square *d*, and this part *e*,' said Aunt Pollie. 'Fold the paper so that *a*, *b*, and *c* lie on *d*. . . . Double the square in half, then,' said Aunt Pollie, 'so that the top of it lies on *e*, and you will have a single boat on one side and a pocket on the other.'
> 'It is the jolliest thing we have made yet,' said Bob.[11]

Despite the accompanying diagrams, Aunt Pollie's method and explanation of how to make a paper boat would bamboozle an adult boat-builder, never mind a child. But making a paper boat should be a simple, straightforward process. It demands a minimum of materials and a modicum of dexterity and there are, for those uncertain of how to progress, an astonishing number of manuals and

YouTube videos devoted to the subject. The three-pointed boat is the simplest and most popular model, requiring a single sheet of paper and a small number of folds. More sophisticated models are crafted by those with a surfeit of patience, time and engineering skills – pirate vessels, canoes, yachts, full-rigged sailing ships – but, for most of us, a basic boat will suffice.

With that in mind, I confidently embark upon construction. Sitting at the kitchen table one Saturday afternoon I equip myself with some sheets of paper. Eschewing Aunt Pollie's complicated instructions, I fold my paper as I think it ought to be folded and fold again. I turn down an edge here and a triangular flap there, but nothing remotely like a paper boat emerges. I resort to YouTube and carefully watch a pair of disembodied hands crafting a paper boat. When I try to copy them I get confused as to which way the paper is to face and how to execute the final pull of what is now a multi-folded piece of paper to reveal the boat itself. I watch the YouTube video again, this time pausing at each step, paying closer attention to every crease, checking and double-checking my progress, but I still find that the final abracadabra moment, the transformation from two-dimensional folded paper to a three-dimensional paper boat, evades me. I rewind, replay, rewind, replay until, finally, I have made my ten folds correctly and I have tucked in my edges and tugged my paper bundle open. And I discover that, at last, I have a paper boat cradled in my hands: a perseverance rewarded, a paper boat created.

It was this simplest version that George Wyllie, the Scottish artist, sculptor and performer, decided to emulate in

1989 – albeit on a much larger scale. George Wyllie was the great-great-grandson of a Corsican mariner. He spent much of his childhood beguiled by the sea, living for a while in Dunbarton, holidaying in Dunoon and making small boats to sail on the ponds of his local parks, including a mini-galleon that he called *The Merry George* made from scavenged offcuts of wood and cloth. As an adult, George Wyllie continued to follow the call of the sea and went to work for a company of ship owners and stevedores, delivering letters to and collecting reports from vessels docked along the River Clyde. At the age of eighteen, with the Second World War underway, George enlisted and was assigned the role of petty officer in the Royal Navy. His wartime experiences saw him traverse the world – Gibraltar, Algiers, Sicily, Greece, Sydney – evading bombardment and capture, experiencing the terror of artillery fire on the D-Day beaches and witnessing the emaciation of the POWs liberated from Japanese prison camps, some of whom boarded the ship George served on to return home. A short time after the first nuclear bomb destroyed the Japanese city of Hiroshima, killing over 100,000 of its inhabitants, George visited the city and witnessed first-hand its awful devastation.

When the war ended, George returned to Scotland, found employment as a Customs and Excise officer, reclaimed his role as husband and embraced mischief and delight by making eccentric art from scrap materials. He became a father, built a rowing boat, then a dinghy, joined a yachting club and sailed around the coast of Scotland. He also took delight in devising large, ironic sculptures as visual puns, built from salvaged paraphernalia and named with characteristic playfulness: *A Dancing Lamp Post,*

Mortgage Climbing the Wall and *A Canary with Its Foot Stuck in a Girder*. He found artistic empathy and encouragement in the company of Richard Demarco, then the *enfant terrible* of the Scottish art scene and a promoter of international avant-garde events and exhibitions. Joseph Beuys, the provocative German artist and art theorist, was another creative soulmate. When George decided to take a leap in the dark and make visual arts his profession, he applied to the Arts Council of Scotland for support but his application was rejected. He realised that he was viewed as an amateur outsider, destined to be relegated to the fringes of the art world. But he carried on regardless, making his own idiosyncratic art.

This is a fate experienced by many other outsider artists, those self-taught creatives who make works that are not modulated by a mainstream arts culture but stand alone as singular, self-expressive statements. Within its ranks are artists such as the American Judith Scott who, born deaf, used wool and thread to fashion abstract cocoon-like forms that evoked her sense of isolation and separation. A fellow American, the preacher Howard Finster, filled his garden with over 40,000 paintings and sculptures as personal visions of human inventiveness and nature's bounty. While the Russian artist Eduard Bersudsky created monumental kinetic sculptures from redundant wheels, metal scrap and old furniture, incorporating exquisitely carved human figures and animals as visual commentaries on social repression and the abuse of political power. In time the work of these artists became noticed, reviewed, exhibited, collected and acclaimed. They, and other self-taught artists, eventually found themselves acknowledged as significant by an art world that had excluded them, recognised as a separate artistic genre, as a self-styled cultural force.

So it was with George Wyllie. He was nearly sixty years old when he took early retirement and devoted himself to creating artworks that, in his own words, were 'plain, clear, open and visible': art that was dubbed quirky by some but that resonated with community relevance. This was art that emanated from the heart, from George's sense of emotional connection to the places and people he knew and cared about. In 1987, for the Glasgow festival of Mayfest, George finally won his artistic spurs when he conceived and engineered a vast straw locomotive as a homage to Glasgow's long-lost engine-building prowess, a poignant symbol of the past skills and spent spirit of the city – both a commemoration and a lament.

The decline of what had been a nineteenth-century industrial boom, which had seen Glasgow celebrated as the second city of the British Empire, brought mass unemployment. Poverty and drug addiction stalked the city's streets. George crafted his locomotive as a metaphor for past community strength and present civic fragility. For six weeks it dangled from the huge Finnieston Crane on the River Clyde, the last landmark of a lost industry, hung high like an urban mascot in the spring sunshine, appearing as a sombre silhouette in the dark of the night. And it was loved. It seemed a heartfelt symbol representing what the people of Glasgow feared their city had become, a place of frail fortune. After six weeks, the straw locomotive was lowered, put on a low-loader lorry and driven through the streets of Glasgow to the former site of the North British Locomotive Works, where it was set alight. As his giant sculpture turned to ash, its steel skeleton revealed another symbol secreted within its depths, a giant question mark that hovered in the last of the flickering flames like a portent of what lay ahead.

It was two years later that George launched his giant paper boat, nearly 24 metres long. It too made visible – made palpable – the tragedy of community loss. Its ambiguous name, 'QM', was pondered over by many, although George, ever mischievous, failed to enlighten. Did it stand for the *Queen Mary*, one of the largest ocean liners ever built on the Clyde, or for George's own cryptic trademark signature stamp, his ever-present question mark? George Wyllie voyaged with his paper boat down the Clyde, the river that had harboured maritime traffic since the fifteenth century. It was the shipyards, established along its length three centuries later, that fostered a dynamic industry which became the lifeblood of the city. Thirty thousand ships had been constructed in its yards by the 1960s, when the privatisation of shipbuilding coupled with increased competition from overseas manufacturers forced a downturn. By the 1970s the designers and draughtsmen, tracers and engineers, joiners and riveters, who had won international renown for the quality of their workmanship, found that their talents had become redundant when Glasgow's shipbuilding industry collapsed. With its demise came unemployment and demoralisation. Civic pride was decimated. The spirit of the city was eroded.

George Wyllie's paper boat was a statement not of protest but of dismay. At dusk, lit from the inside, it lay like a ghost ship on the silent dark of the river. And George took his paper boat into deeper waters, first to London where, on reaching the Houses of Parliament, it opened up to display his question mark. The following year the paper boat was transported to America, with George boarding a plane to fly ahead. Reunited with his boat, he sailed it up the Hudson River and into the World Financial Center, with members of the Duke Ellington Orchestra trumpeting his progress. But when he docked it was to the patriotic swell of the bagpipes and the unfurling of the Scottish Saltire, which fluttered from his paper boat's mast. Keeping his Scottish credentials to the fore, George recited to the assembled crowds the first sentence of *The Theory of Moral Sentiments* by the Scottish economist and philosopher Adam Smith, the precursor to his classic text *The Wealth of Nations*:

> How selfish soever man may be supposed, there are evidently some principles in his nature, which interest him in the fortune of others, and render their happiness necessary to him, though he derives nothing from it except the pleasure of seeing it.[12]

And George's paper boat continued its journey. It sailed down the east coast of Scotland. It sailed to Antwerp and Liverpool. And, wherever it went, George went with it, treating the gathering crowds to a rousing chorus of 'The Paper Boat Song' he had composed himself, to the accompaniment of his ukelele.

I knew George a little, if not well. I first met him when he kindly agreed to open an exhibition in Glasgow that featured work by aspiring artists, a small group of people of different ages and backgrounds who, lacking the necessary qualifications, had been excluded from art school but who harboured artistic talent and dreams. With the support of the Collins Gallery, under the guidance of the artist Kim Paterson, and with the mentoring encouragement of other practising artists, the group had assembled an astonishing array of powerful work that George was happy to admire. His presence, and his enthusiastic endorsement of their achievement, lent them confidence.

Later, George invited me to his seventy-fifth birthday party, where Liz Lochhead, later Scotland's Makar (national poet), recited a poem she had written in his honour, 'A Wee Multitude of Questions for George Wyllie':

> In the dark space of our heads
> divers, multitudinous, unmarked, the questions float
> above a straw locomotive and a paper boat.[13]

And, in his last years, a friend brought George to visit me in my small glen and we walked to the bridge where, years before, local children had sailed their hope-inscribed paper boats. When I suggested a game of pooh sticks (racing small twigs down the river), George acquiesced with glee. We dropped our sticks over one side of the bridge and waited, watching on the other side for them to re-emerge – as the small boats had done that Millenium evening – willing our own to lead the race, to slip into the fastest current and find itself victorious.

George spent his last days, appropriately, in the Sir Gabriel Wood's Mariners' Home, where his room was called a 'cabin' and where the walls displayed pictures of seafaring adventures. He died in 2012, aged ninety, but his paper boat lived on. It inspired new songs to be written, one by Karine Polwart, the celebrated Scottish singer-songwriter, and another by the Irish composer, Gareth Patrick Wiliams. It was also immortalised on one of the twelve community-created textile panels made as a fabric calendar of Glasgow for its year as European City of Culture in 1990. There, on the May panel, 'Paint the Town Red', which traces the city's political history, is George Wyllie's paper boat, reprised in crisp white cotton, floating across a sunset-hued Clyde River. It takes its place on the textile alongside other significant landmarks of Glaswegian subversion: the Rent Strike of 1915, the raising of the red flag in the city's George Square in 1919 and the Glasgow Upper Clyde Shipbuilders' work-in of 1971. And, in Greenock, a harbour town on the Clyde estuary where George built his paper boat, a new gallery named The Wyllieum has opened, dedicated to George Wyllie's work and legacy. Exhibiting his original sketches, an assemblage of his artworks and showing archive film of him at work, it stands as a testimony to the originality and popularity of a playful maker and ensures that George Wyllie's indomitable spirit will live on.

Paper boats have become the metaphor of choice for others using their voices to comment on social and ecological malaise. For the 56th Venice Biennale in 2015, the Brazilian artist Vik Muniz launched *The Lampedusa*, a 14-metre-long paper boat whose hull was imprinted with a magnified headline that had appeared in an Italian newspaper on 3 October 2013: 'Migranti, centinaia di morti . . .' (Migrants, hundreds dead . . .). This was the day that 366 migrants drowned in their attempt to reach safety on the Italian island of Lampedusa. Muniz's paper boat was intended to be both a memorial and a rebuke: a call for more care and compassion for those fleeing desperate circumstances by desperate methods. But his artwork attracted controversy. Made to commemorate those who had died and raise awareness of the plight of migrants, Muniz was accused of trivialising the escalating horror of such drownings by encapsulating their tragedy in a plaything made of paper.

Undaunted, other artists have followed, choosing paper boats to illustrate the vulnerability of sea-crossing migrants. In 2017, the artists Patricia Silva and Lyall Harris published a limited edition of their book *Paper Boats*, featuring 100 photographs of people's hands holding a small paper boat. Some have it lying on their outstretched palm, some have it nestled in their cupped hands, while others hold it gently between their fingertips. When I emailed Patricia Silva to ask if she might tell me more about the process of creating the book, she was generous with her response.

She wrote of how she had sent Lyall Harris some origami paper and, within a fortnight, received back 200 tiny paper boats made not only from the paper she had sent but also from pages of Italian-language textbooks and maps of countries beset by war, famine or ethnic persecution. She described how she placed the boats in a box and walked the streets of Florence, asking strangers if they would be willing to choose a boat and allow her to photograph their hands as they held it. She not only stopped passers-by but also enlisted family, friends and colleagues, consciously involving people from different backgrounds, ages and genders. Having equipped herself with a blank book, she asked those she photographed if they would write a few words in it, to register their thoughts on the migrant crisis, taking care to keep her voice neutral so as not to influence their response.

What Silva and Harris produced was a moving visual documentary and a poetic commentary on the loss of identity experienced by displaced people. The boats symbolised, in Lyall's words, 'the collective voyage': both the shared physical perils experienced by migrants and the emotional and social displacement they all encountered. Since time immemorial, people have sought refuge from fear by fleeing the country of their birth on dangerous waters, hoping to find a safer future over the seas. While too many have died, even those who have managed to reach a safe harbour often remain adrift, severed from their families, their homelands, their cultures and traditions, forced to make what they can of their lives in a place that is not home.

More recently paper boats have been used by other artists as a metaphor for the jeopardy facing our natural world from global warming and ecological carelessness. In 2010, the German conceptual artist Frank Bolter inveigled volunteers to help him construct a giant paper boat that he launched on the River Thames in London in a project called *To the World's End*. This was a boat designed to sink, its sinking deliberately orchestrated to demonstrate the environmental threat posed by our throw-away society.

Bolter continued his campaign, sailing and sinking outsized paper boats in Leipzig in Germany in 2011 and in Galway in Ireland in 2016. Then, in 2022, Bolter changed tactics and ramped up his visual declaration of the need for change. In Procida, a small island in the Bay of Naples, as part of the city's programme as the Italian Capital of Culture, he launched the Procida Paper Fleet (La Flotta di Carta). It was led by Bolter in a 9-metre-long paper boat that he had built in collaboration with the island's community.

The boat carried the slogan 'Children Will Save the World'. Following it were over 2,000 other paper boats made from recycled paper, created by local children who had illustrated and inscribed them with messages that voiced their embrace of cultural diversity and inclusion and expressed their fears for the world they would inherit. The children's boats were launched along the eight beaches that curve around the island's coast, each small fleet making its own journey before joining one to another and another to become an armada of the next generation's humanitarian unity and concern.

The symbolic use of paper boats to promote public concern at climate change also galvanised a group of Scottish writers to take action, as I discovered when I was visiting the Edinburgh Book Festival in August 2023. Popping into the Writers' Tent to catch a friend, I spied a paper boat, made from a map, lying on the table and pounced upon it with unseemly zeal. I was just beginning to research paper boats, so to find this one, encountered in the unlikeliest of places, seemed a talisman of sorts. On asking what it was doing there, who and what it was for, I learned of the Scottish writers who had begun a campaign to urge members of the Scottish Parliament, and others with national and civic power, to honour their pledge and undertake the measures they had promised to safeguard our natural world. Through social media and live events, they were encouraging people to make 1,000 paper boats from recycled paper and write on them their own ecological concerns. The boats were to be sent to political and environmental representatives, and more were to be brought to the Scottish Parliament in November for a collective display of disquiet. This was a call to action inspired by the Japanese belief that if 1,000 origami paper cranes are made with hopeful hearts then whatever is wished for will come true.

When I got home I looked up their website: paperboats.org. Under a drawing of a paper boat was the tag line 'We will rise'. The group's mission statement demanded that MSPs (Members of the Scottish Parliament) take urgent action in the face of accelerating climate breakdown. There was a poem by the current Scottish Makar, Kathleen Jamie. Its last verse read:

> I heard the beautiful promises . . .
>
> and, sure, I'm a river,
> but I can take a side.
> From this day, I'd rather keep afloat,
> like wee folded paper boats,
> the hope of the young folk
> chanting at my back,
> fear in their spring-bright eyes
>
> so hear this:
>   fail them, and I will rise.[14]

I decide to join the campaign, to contribute, and I buy a second-hand copy of the selected writings of John Muir, the Scottish-born naturalist, environmental advocate and philosopher who, having emigrated to America in 1849, ultimately won the accolade of 'Father of the National Parks'. Feeling somewhat guilty at the desecration of a book but reassuring myself that it is for a very worthy cause, I cut out its pages one by one and begin to construct twenty-five paper boats, one for each year of my twins' lives. I write 'Hope' in red felt pen on each boat.

On 23 November 2023, I leave home at 6.30 a.m. in the winter's dark to get to Edinburgh for the launch three hours later. Rain is scudding horizontally across the sky, pummelled sideways by a fierce wind. It is tempting to turn for home but I drive on, despite the alarming whooshes of water that punctuate my journey.

When I arrive at the Parliament building there is a small huddle of campaigners shielding from the rain under its eaves and I hand over my clutch of paper boats. The rain leaves off and I find a small stone tussock to squat on until the event begins. I watch as a couple in the distance round the base of Arthur's Seat, the ancient hill that looms over Holyrood. Their heads are bent down against the wind and they are gripping a large cardboard structure tight between them, wrestling against its struggle for freedom. They gamely steer themselves and their burden towards the crowd and when they reach their destination they unloose their wayward parcel and undo its wrappings. It is a 1.5m-long boat made of cardboard which, once opened, acts as the repository for all the small paper boats people have made.

Along the piazza edge of the Parliament building, a textile frieze of brightly coloured panels is being laid out on the ground. Curious, I wander over to discover an exuberant display of stitched and knitted protest. Made by groups and individuals from different parts of Scotland, the panels voice their care and anxiety about the human cost of climate change, the lack of political will, the urgent need to protect the earth. Here is the natural world textured in cloth, thread and yarn: seas crocheted in rivulets of wool, trees branched in fabric leaves, flora and fauna animated in patterned patchwork, a materialisation of our threatened universe. Slogans proliferate: 'Dare to Care'; 'Restore, Respect, Repair, Renew'; 'Love Life'; and, more expansively, 'We Don't Inherit the Earth from Our Ancestors, We Borrow It from Our Children'. In the drab grey of a November morning, the vibrant panels are uplifting.

With a large crowd now assembled, there is a frisson of activity. A microphone rasps and, with a choir especially recruited for the event and schooled that morning under the direction of Karine Polwart, the singing begins. Voices are raised soulfully to sound out the 'Unst Boat Song', a song sung in ancient Norn, a language that came from Scandinavia to Scotland's Shetland Islands centuries before. It is a prayer for protection of those at sea and as the harmonies rise and fall, they fill the air with a lilting rhythm that traces the ebb and flow of tides.

There are speeches. Kathleen Jamie reads her paper-boat poem and others recite their own poetry. This is, after all, an event organised by Scottish writers where, for them, words are as important as deeds. The choir strikes up again, this time with a song written by Karine for the Paper Boat writers' campaign:

> These boats are made to dream
> These boats are made to wonder
> These boats are made to hope
> And they're not going under.[15]

It is Karine who places the first boat on the Parliament pond. Press photographers crouch down for the media snapshot. Other people pluck paper boats from the large boat container and lower them gently, sending them skimming over the pond's surface. I follow suit, fishing one out and setting it down on its watery bed, where it hugs the pond's edge in a shy protest. When later the Scottish writers' collective post online images of the event, it is possible to see, close-up, the handwritten messages that people have put on their paper boats: 'You are Never Wrong to Do the Right Thing'; 'Save the Earth Today to Survive Tomorrow'; 'Protect Our Future'; 'Save the Earth'. Many of them are signed. There is power and potency in the simplicity of these hand-made, autographed tokens of protest. This gathering of small creative acts is both heartfelt and purposeful, and the launching of 1,000 paper boats – of 1,000 Climate Hopes – has honest concern on its side. It might not carry the blare and bluster of larger political rallies but, in its own poetic way, it makes its point.

When I strolled away from Holyrood, back up the hill to Edinburgh's city centre, I thought about the people who had made all these little paper boats. What were they thinking as they folded them into shape, what were they feeling as they laid them down on the still water of the pond? Is it different to make something with a public purpose, with a cause in mind, than to make it for private delight?

I found myself thinking back to China where, thirty years earlier, I had visited remote hilltop villages that could only be accessed on foot and were culturally different and disconnected from mainland China. I was there courtesy of a Winston Churchill Memorial Fellowship, searching out story cloths, the complex embroidered narratives of the Miao people, one of China's minority clans: textiles that, over centuries, had documented their history and beliefs. I found that I had stepped into not just an ancient way of life but a different sensibility. The Miao are animists. They believe that each person, every creature, each element of nature and all objects have a distinct spirit: a spirit that they have a responsibility to shield and nurture. They therefore strive to manifest a harmonious spirit in everything they make – in the baskets they weave, the doors they carve and the embroideries they stitch.

What astonished me then was the exquisiteness of their craftsmanship. These were people who survived on what they could grow, on the livestock they raised, on the little they might sell at market and what they could make themselves from local materials. The villagers operated collectively, sharing labour, skills, tools and materials, heaping up wood, stone and dyestuffs in communal stores for anyone's use when the need arose. Yet, despite their isolation, despite the fact that what they created would only be seen and appreciated by their own community, each and everything they made was beautiful and meaningful. Theirs was a making imbued with altruistic intent. What they created added to the intangible store of community good, marked with talismanic symbols of protection and good fortune to safeguard those they lived amongst and those who would come after.

As I meandered my way through the grey streets of Edinburgh, I pondered on whether the contributors to the paper-boat event were propelled by an innate animist instinct. When they were folding and refolding their paper, were they thinking that they were helping to reshape their own future and the future of the generations who would follow? Did they believe that their hopes and concerns could reside in the boats themselves, be somehow absorbed, trapped within their folds? The value of making does not lie solely in what is made but *why* it is made, its context. We make such meaningful artefacts to connect to something beyond ourselves: a tradition, another person, a cause, a different culture or a faith. The children in our glen that Millenium Eve, the children in India who set their paper boats afloat under a monsoon sky, the myriad artists who created paper boats to register dismay, all trusted that their fragile vessels would reach a wider world. And the makers of the paper boats that were launched in November at the Scottish Parliament believed that they were creating a visible, tangible petition that would touch the conscience of those in power. It might be a small act, a simple symbol, but a paper boat has emotive strength. It has potency.

Paper might seem like the dullest of materials, ordinary and featureless, but its transformative potential cannot be underestimated. It is through the crafting of paper that diverse cultures throughout the world have sought to protect, protest, preserve and promote the wellbeing of their families and communities; to commemorate the dead and celebrate the living. Accessible and adaptable, paper has been used in a plethora of ways to carry human dreams to distant shores.

2
Paper-cuts and Pop-ups

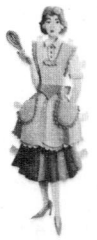

*I trust my hand. If I go into a space with a roll of
paper, I can make a work, some kind of work,
and feel pretty satisfied.*
Kara Walker

When I was a child, I made my own paper dolls, inventing an array of characters and their interchangeable – usually totally impractical – wardrobes: a fantasy of outlandish, glamorous and extravagant garments that were far removed from my post-war serviceable hand-knitted jumpers and home-made frocks. When I was old enough to be doled out pocket money that stretched beyond a single sugar rush, I invested in dress-up-doll books. They introduced me to the haute-couture glamour of yesteryear and the sartorial finery of historical luminaries. Colouring them in, dressing them as I saw fit, mixing and matching their outfits and accessories bred in me an aspiration to become a dress designer or a theatrical costumier: an ambition that, once voiced, was quickly quashed by my teachers. But dress-up paper dolls fanned in me an interest in the art of fashion and the history of costume that has never left me.

Much later in life, I decided to concoct my own series of paper dolls on a Scottish theme. It was to be a commercial venture, producing a quirky range of Scottish icons that could add a dash of humour to the more sedate gifts found in most museum shops. My prototype was based on Bonnie Prince Charlie, that Young Chevalier, the ill-fated Charles Edward Stuart, who was foiled in his attempt to reclaim the Stuart crown and was ignominiously defeated at the Battle of Culloden in 1746. My paper version of Charlie had him modestly garbed in long johns and simmit (a Scottish undershirt). Using extant portraits as my inspiration, the cut-out of Charlie was to be accompanied by three different outfits: what he wore as the swaggering prince, resplendent in a blue velvet jacket and frilled lace cravat, skirted and swathed in red tartan; the fugitive attire he was depicted in on a satirical 'Wanted' poster of the time, still elaborately dressed but in more subdued shades of green and ochre; and his Betty Burke disguise – the persona he adopted to escape to the safer shores of France under the protection of Flora MacDonald – garbed in a drab gown of grey with a frilled bonnet framing his white curled and powdered wig.

My dress-up doll of Charlie never went into production. Other distractions prevailed. But I still have my artwork and, from time to time, I take it out and consider his revival. It would not take much to prepare him for public sale, to team him up, as I had originally intended, with another doomed Scottish monarch – his female predecessor, Mary, Queen of Scots. I had planned for her to be dressed in the iconic black gown and cascading gossamer white veil she wore for her execution, which, once removed, would reveal an undergown of blood red, the colour of Catholic martyrdom. It was what the Scottish queen wore for her final public appearance as her last defiant declaration. With her dress-up doll designed with a retractable head, Mary's fate could, as I imagined it, be thrillingly re-enacted by purchasers with a penchant for the macabre.

Perhaps there might still be a market for my imagined Scottish dolls since, in current popular culture, there lurks a sentimental attachment to paper dolls. The demand for them is buoyant and today's enthusiasts and collectors can purchase a wide range of dress-up-doll books. Not only that, but now they can download paper personifications of their favourite icons and what they wear at the touch of a keyboard button. They can also access online tutorials and find a variety of paper-doll templates should they wish to create their own. In the privacy of their own homes, fans are attiring Taylor Swift and Harry Styles in their most celebrated stage costumes; American voters could choose which clothes Kamala Harris or Donald Trump should sport for the primaries; and feminists are keeping faith with the sisterhood through such publications as *Rebel Women, Awesome Women Who Changed History, Famous African American Women* and *Great Women Paper Dolls*. There are paper-doll drag queens and paper dolls inspired by role models from the LGBTQ+ community. The diversity and range of contemporary paper-doll fandom, of dress-up-doll publications, aimed at adults not children, is not just surprising but staggering to the uninitiated. Vampires, literary greats, Russian revolutionaries, glam-metal rock stars, legendary baseball heroes, famous painters and torch singers are all available as paper men and women. This ephemeral panoply of the great and the good continues to fascinate, even if most cultural critics seem impervious to its charms.

Paper mannequins first appeared in Germany in the mid-seventeenth century. These were hand-painted jumping jacks with moveable limbs, which boasted expansive wardrobes of different clothes, hairstyles and accessories. The fact that paper dolls have maintained such a steady, if undocumented, presence for over four centuries and that they continue to be a source of recreation and amusement is intriguing. Despite the seismic social and political shifts that have taken place since their invention, paper dolls have endured, shifting their appeal to suit the prevailing social mores century by century. In eighteenth-century France they were produced as a promotional ploy by French dressmakers to tempt their fashion-conscious clients to greater modish indulgence. While, in nineteenth-century England, they were designed to underpin the moral education of children with, in 1810, the appearance of the first named paper doll.

The History of Little Fanny, Exemplified in a Series of Figures, published by S. & J. Fuller of London, was not devised as a fashion appetiser but as a cautionary tale for children. Hers is a piteous story told in rhyming couplets. Fanny, a wilful child, denied the dress she wants to wear, runs away from home only to find herself lost in the city. She has to beg for food before finding ignominious employment as an errand girl, delivering fish and dairy products to grand houses. When a delivery leads her back, miraculously, to her own home she is joyfully reunited with her family. In Fuller's book the fate of Fanny is a sartorial drama. Accompanying the text is a single coloured plate that contains various illustrations of Fanny's head adorned in different headgear to accompany the seven outfits that the book's owner is to cut out and paste onto card, leaving a slot for Fanny's head to be inserted.

Her attire mirrors her changing circumstances. Fanny is first shown in a pretty, pink-sashed dress and makes her escape in a very fetching coat trimmed with ermine. Downfall brings us a bare-footed Fanny clutching a begging bowl. Employment sees her donning an apron and shoes but now burdened by the basket of wares she carries on her head. Happily, family reunion restores Fanny to fashionable finesse. She appears demurely attired in a dainty frilled frock, pictured primly reading a book. Fanny's story would have been read or narrated as the little paper doll was dressed and re-dressed to provide a visual commentary that accentuated the moral tale. Its message was clear: disobedience not only risked abject poverty but, worse, sartorial disgrace.

Fuller followed this publication with another aimed at boys. *The History and Adventures of Little Henry* proved particularly popular in America, fanning an American ideal of gung-ho masculinity. In it Henry, stolen from his fine home by a gypsy, becomes first a chimney sweep, then a drummer, takes to the sea and ends up as a naval commander. His riches to rags to riches story is, like Fanny's, made more vivid through his change of clothes. But Henry's tale is one of bravery and bravado, of a boy seizing the unexpected opportunities of wider horizons. While Fanny is punished for straying from the confines of home and has to acquiesce to domestic docility, Henry, donning ever more splendid outfits, is lauded and rewarded for his fortitude. These books set the trend for the popular appeal of paper-doll books. Rather than merely being playful diversions, they reflected, sometimes promoted, the social values of their time, and never more germanely than when they captured the changing lives of women.

The paper doll Betty Bonnet, who featured between 1915 and 1917 in issues of the American magazine *Ladies' Home Journal,* accumulated family, friends and servants, and their outfits for a variety of occasions. This visual representation of family life and social change was amplified by stories in the magazine itself. Betty's married sister comes dressed not just for soirées but for golf, as does her college sister, who favours plain clothes and sensible shoes and wears her academic gown with aplomb. The same year that Betty made her appearance, another American publisher included in its parade of dress-up doll mannequins a manifesto-carrying suffragette wearing a sash emblazoned with the battle cry 'Votes for Women'.

The Second World War witnessed a rush of paper dolls that saluted women's involvement in the war. They included Rosie the Riveter, Girls in Uniform, Mary of the WACS, Girl Pilots and Army Nurses. The post-war 1940s saw a new emphasis on working women, who made their entrance onto the paper-doll scene in neat and serviceable clothes. Career Girls Cut-Outs and Career Girls Paper Dolls jostled for attention beside Medical Nurse, Lois, Airline Hostess, and Miss Lang, Secretary. But peacetime also brought pressure for women to return to their role as wife and mother, a societal shift that was reflected in paper dolls. There was a surge in the production and popularity of those that promoted images of the ideal woman, dolls bedecked in bridal gowns, glamorous hostess frocks and delectable lingerie. But, despite such attempts to corral women into social conformity, some paper dolls continued to betray a more radical streak. With the onset of the civil rights movement in America, the comic *Heartbeats* not only ran storylines that confronted racism and social injustice, but introduced Torchy Brown, a black paper doll, created by the cartoonist, journalist and political activist Jackie 'Zelda' Ormes. Torchy was a stylish, sophisticated and adventurous black heroine who was a defiant departure from the hitherto stereotypical black paper dolls that depicted black women as domestic 'mammies' and black children as paupers dressed in rags.

While paper dolls were available to buy already printed, many people also made their own. As early as 1856, *Paper Dolls and How to Make Them: A Book for Little Girls*, was published in America. Its anonymous author was at pains to reassure its small owners that a skill in drawing was not a prerequisite to enjoyment, advising them that although their home-made dolls may: 'be cross-eyed, . . . their heads may grow out of their shoulders, and their fat arms may stand out straight, and end in little knobs, it is all the same, they are all "little darlings".'

But the making of dress-up dolls was not solely the preserve of little girls, as I discovered when I was invited to Paris to give a presentation on the significance of textiles to the creative team of Dior in 2024. My presentation over, I was taken for lunch and we were joined by Olivier Flaviano, head of the Galerie Dior, who had previously been director of the Yves Saint Laurent Museum in Paris. Olivier began to recount how, when Yves Saint Laurent was young, he used to cut out figures of fashion models from magazines such as *Vogue* and *Harper's Bazaar*, paste them onto card, and design paper haute-couture collections for them.

'Like dress-up dolls?' I asked, feeling a shiver of serendipity.

'Exactly,' said Olivier.

The dolls, Olivier told me, were a chance find. They were piled up in one of the many boxes that had been collected from Yves Saint Laurent's apartment after his death in 2008. This unique collection has now been digitalised and Olivier promised to send me the link. He was true to his word and, a few days after I returned home, I was able to scroll through page after page of Yves Saint Laurent's early fashion creations. Even at the age of seventeen, when he began to make them, his attention to detail was impressive. This despite never having been to Paris, having been born and raised in Oran in Algeria. Everything he created as a teenager was based on the knowledge he had gleaned from French magazines. Yet he painstakingly delineated in black ink the way a dress should be pleated or ruffled and the exact placement of the seam lines on a fitted jacket. He used coloured pencils to capture the texture and flow of fabric, carefully shading the soft folds of chiffon, employing bold colour to suggest the crispness of a patterned cotton and emphasising the flare of a skirt or the fall of a frill with gouache paint and watercolour. This was a labour not only of love but of ambition.

Of the nineteen paper dolls it is believed he created between 1953 and 1954, eleven have survived. They are over 31cm tall and some are named after the celebrated models of the day: Ivy, Suzy, Bettina, Florence. Of the clothes he made for them, 443 hand-drawn designs remain, each created with a specific model in mind, their paper tabs spaced to fit the stance of each individual's silhouette. Ivy has thirty-two outfits for daywear, cocktails and evening glamour. Her wardrobe boasts a cream coat embroidered with full-blown roses, a body-skimming tailored suit with a wide luxurious fur collar and a sumptuous evening gown overlaid in a delicate filigree of black lace. This is attire that is elegant, meticulously conceived and beautifully drawn.[1]

For the teenage Yves Saint Laurent these paper creations served as an apprenticeship for the Parisian haute-couture world he yearned to join. He invented a name and address for his imagined future fashion house – 'Yves Mathieu Saint Laurent Haute Couture, Place Vendôme, Paris' – and he organised his designs for Fall–Winter 1953 and Fall–Winter 1954 into separate collections with evocative and poetic names: Nightingale, Scotland Yard, Madison Square, Ciel de Paris. He noted his preferred suppliers of perfume (Elizabeth Arden), furs (Revillon and Bianchini) and fabric (Abraham) and provided information on accessories: the umbrellas, bags and hats that were to accompany his outfits. A photograph taken of Yves Saint Laurent in 1957 shows the young, bespectacled designer sitting, holding a paper bodice with small tabs attached, his scissors by his side. The table in front of him is strewn with scraps of paper, some already shaped as garments, the rest heaped alongside the remnants of the paper they have been cut from. Behind him, on a large velvet sofa, stands a parade of completed dolls and more lie on its cushions. When the photograph was taken, Yves Saint Laurent was heir presumptive of Dior. Later that year, at twenty-one years of age, he would become its head designer.

Despite his accelerated rise, it seems that Yves Saint Laurent stayed wedded to his paper dolls. These were not just designed diversions but visualisations of his future potential. They were the stuff of dreams. Tellingly, Yves Saint Laurent kept his paper dolls for his whole life. They were touchstones to his younger self when his imagination and creative curiosity were in free flow. Later in his career he would say: 'Every time I design a collection, I rediscover my childhood, I commune with it,'[2] and, in this, his paper dolls undoubtedly played a part. Yves Saint Laurent realised his dreams and was acclaimed as one of the most influential and visionary designers of his day, dressing the most famous of its celebrities including Catherine Deneuve, Paloma Picasso, Elizabeth Taylor and Lauren Bacall.

And the cult of celebrity pervaded the world of paper dolls where, commercially, the largest share of the paper-doll market became reserved for paper avatars of the famous from the mid-nineteenth century onwards. It is a trend that continues today. There were precedents. Dress-up dolls of Queen Victoria first appeared in the 1840s, followed by those of the actresses Ellen Terry and Lily Langtry, to offer a cavalcade of royal and stage fashion to savour at home. When cinema created the stars of the silver screen, a galaxy of paper dolls appeared in their honour, including those of Mary Pickford, Rudolph Valentino, Marilyn Monroe, Mickey Mouse and Tintin. Some paper dolls became famous in their own right, the majority christened – like Betty Burke – in cheery alliteration: Lettie Lane, Polly Pratt, Dolly Dingle and Winsome Winnie, to mention but a few. Paper dolls were also given away free in magazines and newspapers and used to promote a plethora of goods, including chocolate, pancake flour, soap and motor cars. McCall's, the sewing pattern company, included paper dolls from 1904 in its monthly magazine, dressed in fashions its readers could sew at home by purchasing a McCall's pattern. In 1951, it introduced its own namesake paper doll, Betsy McCall, who, with her family and friends, reigned over the paper-doll universe for forty years until the 1990s.

By the 1960s, however, paper dolls were facing serious competition from actual dolls like Barbie and Sindy, who were promoted not simply as dolls but dolls for whom you could buy an ever-changing assortment of clothes to suit every occasion, their wardrobes updated season by season. It was these dolls' outfits that encouraged customer loyalty and secured repeat business. Not to be outdone, Betsy McCall entered the fray as a three-dimensional doll, with her owners able to choose from a wide range of McCall's dolls' clothes patterns to ensure that Betsy remained a fashionable icon in the doll world.

Paper dolls might have become extinct had it not been for the unexpected arrival of a self-appointed champion. It was the American fashion illustrator, army veteran and designer Tom Tierney who, as the *New York Times* attested, 'almost single-handedly, revived the lost art of paper doll making'.[3] From the 1970s until his death in 2014, Tierney was tireless in his mission to secure their survival, illustrating nearly 400 paper-doll books, the majority published by Dover Publications. Meticulously researched, his books provide an invaluable and extensive archive of the history of fashion and costume design. Some reproduced iconic showpieces from the great houses of haute couture, including designs by Erté, Worth, Dior, Chanel and Alexander McQueen. Others tracked the trajectory of historical costume from ancient Egypt to the American family of the 1990s. Still more featured stars of stage and screen or presented paper versions of celebrated public figures such as the Dalai Lama and Pope John Paul II. Not content to simply register the fashions of the famous, Tom Tierney also used his paper dolls to create a social entrée for the marginalised. His pioneering book *Attitude, an Adult Paperdoll Book*, published in 1979, showcased the image-conscious underworld of New York's gay scene with dress-up drag queens, leather-clad bikers and men in bondage gear. By insisting they had a presence amongst their paper-doll peers, Tom Tierney deliberately brought his tribe into the spotlight to broker their social inclusion.

And the appeal of paper dolls continues. In America, the Original Paper Doll Artists Guild helps to perpetuate their allure by encouraging new artistry in paper-doll design. Every year, for its annual convention, it throws out a challenge for professional and amateur artists to submit hand-made paper dolls on specific themes. It conserves their history, supports would-be makers with templates and advice, and provides novice collectors with useful information.

There will be many who dismiss paper dolls and deem them of scant creative or cultural value. And it is true that the artistic work, that of designing paper dolls and their wardrobes, is generally undertaken by professional illustrators. But many dress-up-doll books are produced with black-and-white images for their purchasers to colour at home and, even when reproduced in colour, the dolls and their outfits still require the fiddle of cutting out and mounting onto card. It is only then that the fashion can be styled, the most pleasing permutations of garments and accessories selected and showcased. This is when imagination comes into play as the doll becomes part of a narrative invented by its dresser. The considered creativity of choosing and changing a paper doll's outfit is an act of connection. Being in charge of its alteration elicits a sense of intimacy. While children might enjoy the construction, the company, the tactility of playing with paper dolls, for adults these paper personifications amplify allegiance, evoke their heart-held loyalties to a pop star, an era or a cause. They reinforce the spirit of cultural – even at times political – identification.

Whie the making of dress-up dolls might be regarded as simplistic, the creative challenges posed by the craft of paper engineering is beyond debate. It necessitates the folding, scoring, pleating, cutting, bending and creasing of paper to fashion three-dimensional artefacts. Its methods have always intrigued me and, some years ago, I signed up for a course in paper engineering at the Edinburgh College of Art. In the first few sessions we tussled with folds, scoring the paper in different directions to create myriad shapes – crescents, cones, domes and diamonds – all achieved without a single cut. It was riveting to watch paper turn sculptural when the only tool involved was a hard pencil or a dulled knife. We practised indenting and embossing paper, experimented with its different weights, layered and curled it, twisted and tore it. We discovered its malleability by sensing how it shifted and was shaped with unexpected ease beneath our hesitant hands.

Paper-cuts and Pop-ups

Next, we moved on to cutting, to explore how paper's form and texture could be radically altered and, with just a few folds and incisions, a flat piece of paper could be transformed into a lattice, a Chinese lantern or a net when it was opened out. We worked on altering the paper's surface, notching and slitting, punching holes and bending flaps.

I found that paper was conspiratorial. It yielded to a fold, surrendered to a crease more willingly than I could imagine, allowing itself to fall, languorously, into a twirling spiral when loosed from a tight wad of cut folds. Paper seems ever-willing to become more than it is, as if relieved to be set free of its straight, squared-off boundaries and relinquish its flatness and one-dimensionality. Cutting into paper demands the lightest pressure and, while the precision of paper-cutting requires concentration – a momentary slip of the knife can bring disaster, each cut unable to be reversed or edited – such attention generates a repetitive, mesmeric rhythm. You fold and fold again, you cut and cut again, in a rhythm that settles. If you go with its flow, a serenity ensues. This is an uncluttered, silent art. Just you, the paper and a knife working together – hand, tool, mind and material – connected in suspended time until the work is done.

For our first assignment, we were asked to produce a portfolio inspired by something we could encounter five minutes from where we were sitting, I took myself out onto the street and photographed its ambient surfaces – pavement cracks, railings, brickwork, window blinds – and set about replicating their textured patterns in paper. The effectiveness of my emulations of those hard, rough surfaces in paper's smoothness surprised me: paper ridges evoked iron grids, pleated paper mimicked air vents, appliquéd paper dots simulated decorative slabs.

Our final project was more taxing. We were to produce a portfolio on a specific theme that tracked the progression of our ideas and culminated in a final artwork. I decided to concentrate on trees. I was curious to see what I could make of them in paper, how I might explore the ways that light and shadow played on them. My first experiment was paper engineering at its simplest. I took a sheet of printer paper, cut out a tiny tree from its centre, excised minuscule leaves from its crown and left the tree attached at its base. Then I pressed the tree upwards so that it stood proud of the page and cast its shadow on the remaining white surface. For my second attempt I drew the outline of a tree on a multi-folded concertina of paper and cut around all but a part of the tree's crown at the fold so that it opened out into a leafed avenue of connected trees.

Flushed with the success of these early trials, I became more experimental, working with multiple sheets of paper and cutting away the negative space to leave a tangle of branches. When the light passed through them, each shadowed the next, creating depth and shade. This idea was developed with a picture book based on the story of Hansel and Gretel, the children who became lost in a wood. I designed a book that could be 'read' in single images or – with the cut-outs from one page allowing a glimpse of the next – viewed as an accumulating visual narrative, with the story gathering texture and meaning as its pages merged. For my final work I fashioned a long, narrow book of trees, each page wider than the next. On the fore-edge of each page I cut out a different species of tree – pine, beech, rowan, eight in all – their different shapes and structures gleaned on local walks, a camera in hand. As I had hoped, when it was fanned out, each tree cast its shadow on the next to conjure a ghostly, fragile forest. This was drawing with a knife, replicating branches dappled in the last rays of the afternoon sun through the simple act of cutting away between imagined leaves to delineate their patterning more distinctly.

Through my course at Edinburgh College of Art I learned that paper, seemingly plain and pedestrian, was enticingly expressive. That with just a piece of paper and a knife it is possible to evoke mood, tell stories and mark a sense of place. Paper craft can be done at home with materials that are ready to hand, to make a special greeting card, a Christmas decoration, an unexpected gift. And it can be designed to carry meaning not just because the paper-made object is hand-crafted, nor because it is personalised, but because paper, in all its diverse manifestations, is expressive in its own right. Its provenance, the text or images it features can be chosen to amplify the message of the object that it services. In March 2011 at the Scottish Poetry Library, the librarian arrived one morning and was astonished to find a truant open book lying on the desk. Not so extraordinary in a library, one might think, but this book was unique. From its open pages grew a paper tree, made from spirals of excised text. Below it was a scatter of leaves and a broken gilded egg, also fashioned from paper. Attached to the small sculpture was a tag on which was hand-written, 'This is for you in support of libraries, books, words, ideas . . .'

It was the first of what were to become a series of unexpected gifts, made and donated by an anonymous paper artist, left covertly in places where books mattered: the

National Library of Scotland, the Scottish Storytelling Centre, Edinburgh's Central Lending Library, the Edinburgh Book Festival. It was a private campaign, to draw attention – and publicity – to the predicted closures and cutbacks to public libraries that threatened people's access to books. The artist did not make the sculptures from random pieces of paper. Rather, the books on which they were staged, the text used to craft them and the design of the sculpted works were all carefully chosen to amplify their message. This was paper engineering layered in visual and textual meaning. A paper-crafted gramophone referenced Ian Rankin's tartan noir, *Exit Music*, made from its excised pages; the gilded egg left in the Scottish Poetry Library held scraps of paper which, when pieced together, formed a quotation from Edwin Morgan's poem 'A Trace of Wings'; and from an open copy of Arthur Conan Doyle's science-fiction novel *The Lost World* emerged a paper dinosaur constructed from its tattered text. These were demonstrations not just of how paper could be manipulated creatively, but of the creative potential of the paper itself, that what is written or illustrated on it has its own visual vernacular: that paper carries its own intrinsic expressiveness.[4]

Paper, while it might be expressive, is also lamentably fragile. It does not respond well to the ravages of time. Colours fade, edges curl, the paper itself disintegrates. However, in exceptional circumstances, in the right environment, paper can persist against the odds. The earliest known surviving paper-cuts are over 1,500 years old. They were discovered during an archaeological dig in the underground tombs of Turpan, in the region of Xinjiang in China. They are circular and symmetrical, rimmed with an outer series of triangles. The triangle is a symbol that is present in myriad material cultures throughout the world. It can signify the teeth of a dragon or a saw. It also simulates the barrier of a mountain range and the female pubic zone, the site of fertility. It is conjectured that the paper-cuts of Turpan played some part in ancient funereal rites as protective talismans to ward off evil spirits and dissuade tomb raiders from desecrating the graves. The stylised images of birds, animals, flowers and stars they depict reappear as patterns on the fragments of burial attire that were also unearthed.

In China, the connection between paper-cuts and other decorative crafts persists. Embroiderers use them as stencils, pasting them onto cloth and stitching over them in bright silk thread. Potters use them as embellishments, gluing them down before applying a slip. They appear on lanterns, on fans, as adornments for windows and doorways. Over the centuries, the vocabulary of paper-cuts in China has expanded into a highly eloquent form of symbolic communication.

In contemporary China, nostalgic for practices and imagery that evoke its ancient culture, the appeal of paper-cuts is increasing. Not only is there a growing impetus by curators to safeguard a cultural heritage rooted in ritualistic folk traditions, but also a desire to exploit traditional artefacts as tourist mementos to present, however inauthentically, an idealised past age of rural simplicity and contentment. While much of their original significance is now lost, even to those who make them, the symbolism of paper-cuts, as with other traditional crafts, embodies a sense of cultural continuity as an expression of national heritage and identity. They capture China's soul. There is emotional reassurance in maintaining a belief in the efficacy of ancient auspicious symbols: pomegranates for fertility; dragons for luck; peonies for prosperity; peaches for longevity. Paper-cuts bearing such symbolic messages are bestowed as blessings on newlyweds, given to family members to promote harmony and used as shields to protect family homes from danger.

In 1995, when I travelled to China, I ended my trip with a visit to Kunming, the City of Eternal Spring. I was met there by the botanical artist Yitao Liu, a more than generous host, who I had been introduced to when he was exhibiting his exquisite paintings in Glasgow the previous year. Knowing of my interest in Chinese crafts, he took me to meet an 86-year-old woman whose family had been renowned paper-cutters and embroiderers for centuries. She was a small, spry woman, her sleeves rolled up, dressed for business in an indigo apron. In preparation for our visit, she had heaped her kitchen table with piles of paper-cuts slipped between protective sheets of tissue paper. We pored over them as she peeled them off one by one, explaining their meaning as she did so. The paper-cuts were as flimsy as air. I had never seen, never run my hand over, paper as delicate as this and, with Yitao Liu translating, she described how she cut a number at a time from layers of paper, fastening the separate sheets tightly so they would not move, working quickly and deftly with the entire design held in her mind's eye. She said that she could almost cut without seeing, guiding her scissors or knife around curves as if taking a well-worn route back home. These were designs she had known all her life, had memorised not just as visual images and patterns but as movement. In making them she followed the tactile, physical paths she had known since her childhood, memorising the motions made by her grandmother and mother as they traced them out and cut around them, time and time again. She had not only tracked the contours they made with her child's hand, but absorbed the choreography of their incisions.

Listening to her talk, viewing paper-cut after paper-cut being laid out before us, it was not only their delicacy that was so admirable but the complexity of their imagery. Here were fish scales executed in a gossamer mesh; the flare of a flower's petals and the veins of its leaves demarcated in outlines as fine as thread. Some of the paper-cuts, she told us, illustrated favourite Chinese myths: myths conserved in shadow-puppet plays and operas, in songs and poetry, but also in paper pictures. Those she had made, she told me, carried the mark, the artistry of her ancestors. Their designs had been replicated from one generation to the next, until they had come to her. She had become their guardian, responsible for keeping alive the creativity of those who had gone before, for rekindling their talent and their spirit. In her grandmother's day, she said, when the art of paper-cutting was truly revered, such paper creations were jealously guarded as expressions of distinct family heritage and there was fierce rivalry between those who practised the craft. One of her relatives, a talented artisan, had even been murdered for his paper-cuts, assassins killing him so they could procure his unique designs for themselves.

Thoughtfully, she rummaged through the pile of paper on her table and carefully pulled out a sheaf. 'These,' she told us, 'are irreplaceable, they come from my family.' And she placed them down in front of us. They were, Yitao Liu explained, a set of illustrations of one of China's four great folk tales, *The Legend of the White Snake*. As she lifted each one, she told us its tale. A magical snake, curious to know what it was like to be human, transformed itself into a beautiful young girl, who then meets and falls in love with a scholar. Appalled at the idea of intimacy between a spirit and a human, a powerful monk tried to foil their union. The couple were separated but the girl bore a son. Poison, death, resurrection, captivity and battle followed in quick succession until, finally, the now-grown son was reunited with his mother.

The story told, the paper-cutter pressed on me one of its scenes as a gift. I was taken aback. It seemed far too precious, far too generous. 'I have others,' she reassured me. 'Take this one back home.'

Often dismissed as a domestic peasant craft, paper-cutting has long been practised in different cultures, with each developing its own signature style and distinct objective. In the Jewish faith, paper-cuts serve a ritualistic purpose. They include the *ketubah*, a form of marriage contract that sets out the rights and responsibilities of a husband, to be signed by the bride and groom. Others are hung up in the home to indicate the direction of prayer, still more act as commemorations for the dead, or are made to mark a boy's bar mitzvah. While the design of paper-cuts once differed from region to region and their origin could be determined through their particularities, the Holocaust saw much of Jewish material culture destroyed and, with it, many of the nuances of traditional regional and familial design. The oldest surviving examples of Jewish paper-cuts, however, bear witness to the rich ornamentation of its historical ceremonial culture. Crammed around borders and illustrating the text itself is sacred and symbolic imagery: the Star of David, the menorah, the synagogue, the tree of life, the signs of the zodiac, the signs of the twelve tribes. These are paper-cuts that played a part in the beautification of ritual, a fundamental aspect of Jewish devotion. Throughout the world, wherever the Jewish diaspora have settled, paper-cuts provide a soundless assertion of identity and faith. Behind closed doors, in the privacy of home or in the sanctity of the synagogue, they continue to mark the stepping stones in Jewish life.

In Mexico, the *papel picado*, a cut-paper banner or flag, is a descendant of pre-Hispanic ancient rituals. While the effect is delicate, the tools used to fashion them are not. Rather, a hammer and a variety of chisels are employed to punch through up to fifty layers of thin, variously coloured tissue paper at a time: spaces chipped away to leave a cobweb of motifs and text. The colours used are significant, most meaningfully for the Dia de los Muertos (Day of the Dead), a festival that celebrates life and death. Green signifies the death of an elderly person, yellow that of a child, blue someone who has died by drowning, and red a victim of war, while orange and purple are the generic hues of mourning. The word *muertos* (the dead) is often incorporated into the design below images of dancing skeletons, praying angels or flying birds. Some families devise their own specific designs to pass on to future generations to further connect the living with the dead. The flimsiness of the paper itself symbolises the fragility of life and, strung together, the *papel picado* banners that are looped around city streets, canopy public venues and decorate shrines flutter in the wind like the whispering of ghosts, as reminders that death comes to us all in time.

In many cultures, the folk craft of paper-cutting was undertaken by rural peasants to decorate their homes at times of festivals and family celebrations. Ukrainian agricultural workers made scenes of village life and created paper hangings for windows and doorways and to place above a baby's cradle, with their symbolic motifs acting as protective amulets to ward off evil. Polish shepherds cut their *wycinanki* with sheep shears, snipping birds and trees of life as symbolic blessings for their homes. In time, some rural forms of festive paper-cutting spread into popular culture, adopted and marketed as indicators of a distinct national identity. In Poland you can now buy ceramics, textiles, wrapping paper and a plethora of souvenirs all featuring traditional Polish paper-cut designs, and they were also the inspiration for the Polish Pavilion at the 2010 World Expo in Shanghai.

Yet, despite their widespread popularity, paper-cutting has rarely been recognised as an art until more recent times. There have, however, been some rare exceptions.

In seventeenth-century Holland, the paper-cutter Joanna Koerten was accepted as an artist, and admired as much as Rembrandt or Vermeer. Celebrated as 'Scissors Minerva', after the Roman goddess of handicrafts and art, Koerten fabricated portraits and landscapes with such attention to depth and shade that they belied the simplicity of her medium. In her hands, texture and mood, atmosphere and personality were captured with astonishing nuance. Sadly only fifteen of her works have survived and she, like so many women artists of her time, has been largely erased from the annals of art history.

While people in Germany enthusiastically embraced *scherenschnitte*, or scissor cuts, to create profile portraits of family members and celebrities and produce romantic, delicately fashioned love letters, it was the work of the late eighteenth-century artist Philipp Otto Runge who, through masterfully capturing the botanical diversity and vitality of living plants in paper, won artistic credibility and increased public appreciation for the craft of paper-cutting. Germany's fascination with paper art was still in evidence two centuries later in the work of Lotte Reiniger, a pioneer of silhouette animation, who from the 1920s until her death in 1981 created mesmerising and enchanting films, mostly based on traditional fairy tales.

The virtuosity of Swiss paper-cutters only became recognised in the mid-nineteenth century. It was then that the artistry of a woodsman, Johann-Jakob Hauswirth, attracted attention. His gently hued vistas of alpine life brimmed with documentary detail – farmers leading their cattle from lowland pastures to fertile uplands, women fetching water, roofers hard at work. His hands were so large that he had to fit his scissors to them with wire hoops in order to manipulate them and yet, despite this limitation, he created work of exquisite dreamlike delicacy. Hauswirth's paper masterpieces later inspired the imagination of a village postman, Louis-David Saugy, who at the start of the twentieth century began to attract attention for the expressiveness of his paper montages depicting the seasonal shifts in everyday country life. The work of these two men awakened in Switzerland a respect for and emulation of a craft that, until then, had been viewed as amateur and naive. It bred an enthusiasm for paper-cutting that quickly spread throughout the country to be fostered as a unique articulation of Swiss identity.

Over time, paper-cutting became embraced by established artists, the most celebrated being the French fauvist artist Henri Matisse who, in his later years with his mobility compromised, turned to paper-cuts to continue his experimentation in the fluid use of colour and form. His vast, boldly coloured cut-outs of stylised, simplified natural phenomena and people have become acclaimed as art masterpieces. And, at the Bauhaus, Josef Albers engaged his students in exploring the textural, spatial and flexible potential of paper. Today, paper art is an accepted genre within the fine-art world and a new generation of paper artists are demonstrating that paper is a material that is economical, ecologically sustainable and expressive, and that paper art has a rich, if neglected, heritage. They are embracing its versatility to fashion extraordinary creations, from large-scale installations to small poetic sculptures, repurposing paper as a transcendent medium that can astound our everyday expectation of it.

In Ukraine, it is the artist Dariya Alyoshkina who has won an international reputation for her mastery of paper-cutting, which she renders on a monumental scale. Having had to leave the country to escape the war, she has retreated to Poland with her family. In her work she often references the Ukrainian goddess Berehynia, the protector of small children and defender of the home, an inclusion that in more recent times has become more pertinent than ever. Now that she is in exile, Alyoshkina's paper-cuts have become a way not only to conserve a fragile tradition but to assert a threatened national identity. She and other exiled Ukrainian paper artists are using their artworks to raise funding to support the Ukrainian war effort through online commissions.

Paper-cutting is not just an artisanal craft, it is also a performative art. Hans Christian Andersen, the writer of fairy tales, would never travel without his scissors, ever ready to stop and tell a story while cutting out a palace, swan or fairy to reveal at its end. Some of his paper-cuts have been conserved and can be seen in the Museum Odense in Denmark. In Japan, the performance of paper-cutting encourages audience participation. For *kamikiri*, a storyteller illustrates their tales by cutting paper images as they talk. They respond to audience requests, creating live visual commentaries, sometimes even caricatures of audience members. Such stage performances emanate from older Shinto purification rituals when small paper effigies of humans or animals were made by shaman as spiritual envoys, to be cast into moving waters and journey on to complete a specific task.

Paper is so familiar in our lives that its transformation from a plain, flat and nondescript object into something decorative, three-dimensional and surprising feels like an act of alchemy. And nowhere is the art of paper folding and paper mechanics more ingenious than in the design of moveable or pop-up books. Their earliest manifestations were as volvelles, paper instruments with moving parts, that were introduced in books of the sixteenth century as aids to astronomical, cosmological and navigational exploration. Petrus Apianus is celebrated as their pioneer. His *Astronomicum Caesareum* (Astronomy of the Caesars), published in 1540, included four paper instruments that were constructed with revolving discs, compass pointers and plumb lines. His was a revolutionary innovation in what print could disseminate, not only imparting current knowledge but allowing readers – both established scholars and the curious amateur – to undertake their own calculations and participate in discovery.[5]

It took another three hundred years for moveable books – books with rotating wheels, pull tabs and other ingenious mechanisms – to become popular novelties. At first these were simple flap books aimed at the young that, when flipped vertically in two or more sections, changed characters or their clothes to create an outlandish gallery of eccentric personalities dressed inappropriately. In the late nineteenth century, the London publisher Dean & Sons introduced what it called 'the living picture book', which changed a picture on the pull of a ribbon. Other revolving or dissolving picture books followed where the turn of a wheel or the pull of a tab changed a landscape's season from summer to winter or transformed an interior scene to an exterior vista.

But it was the German illustrator Lothar Meggendorfer who, in the late nineteenth century, with Germany leading the way in quality printing, grasped the sensory potential of books and paved the way for ever more inventive paper pop-ups. While paper theatres and paper peepshows already existed, he was the first to invent a book that offered visual, tactile and – seemingly – audio discovery. His *International Circus*, published in 1887, was unique in its time. It was a paper marvel. In six pull-down sections, Meggendorfer re-created the thrill of daredevil circus acts in ebullient three-dimensional pop-up drawings. The personalities of his fourteen circus performers – the intrepid bareback rider urging his horse to vault over a wall of flames, the uneasy ballerina precariously perched on the palm of her strongman partner, the bemused antics of a Pierrot clown and the bold bravado of Japanese acrobats – were brought to life with exuberant flair. The musical zest of his orchestra was captured in the puffed cheeks of its trombone player, the furious playing of its flautist and the sawing enthusiasm of its cellist, and his big-top audience was particularised in 450 individual portraits. As well as being an illustrator, Meggendorfer was a puppeteer, and the theatricality of his creations marries visual fun with the suggestion of accompanying sound effects. In his *Always Jolly* (1890), when a lion's jaw opens on the pull of a tab you can almost hear its roar, and when a pianist runs his fingers along the piano keys you think you hear his arpeggio. And, despite their high price, his books sold in their millions.

Since Meggendorfer's day pop-up books have continued in popularity. Not only that but their creators, like Meggendorfer himself, have sought to defy the laws of physics and bring us books that confound us by folding within their pages ever more complex pictorial surprises that jump out to test our incredulity. In 1979 *Haunted House*, devised by the Polish refugee artist Jan Pieńkowski, was published. Its cover features a lurid green door with a scrap of paper attached to its doorknob on which is written, 'Let yourself in'. What lies within is a treat of unexpected and spine-chilling horrors. With the aid of pull tabs, a giant octopus emerges with tentacles flailing from a soap-sudded sink; a teeth-bared gorilla suddenly appears from the depths of a floral-upholstered armchair in a cosy parlour; and a grimacing ghost materialises floating behind the bed. Just when you think things cannot get any spookier, you turn the final page to find a wooden crate stamped with its place of origin: 'Transylvania'. The crate is being sawed open from within by an unseen hand. Here Pieńkowski's genius is irrefutable for, as you pull the accompanying tab backwards and forwards, the saw moves and you actually hear its rasp.

Today, the master of pop-up books is the American artist Robert Sabuda. He has brought feats of paper engineering to new heights. Each page in his books explodes with a paper marvel that is incomprehensibly constructed and exhilarating to experience. Moreover, mounted on the margins of his books are other tiny booklets that contain the text of the story, their pages also secreted with additional surprise pop-up cameos of characters, creatures and objects that are mentioned in that part of the narrative. On different pages, his *Peter Pan* opens to an aerial view of nighttime London, then a jungle island, and finally a fully rigged pirate ship. In his *Alice's Adventures in Wonderland*, the tranquil scene of Alice and her companion peaceably reading in a sunny field abruptly changes on the turn of a page to an explosive depiction of Alice's expanding limbs as she gets larger and outgrows the parameters of a house. By its end, we see Alice beset by an enormous arch of swirling playing cards that rise 20cm above the page itself. This is glorious paper engineering, a riot of emergent images that beggars belief, that elicits not only surprise but stupefaction.

Compared to these extraordinary marvels of paper engineering the apparent simplicity of origami, the origin of paper creativity, might be thought lacklustre, requiring just a sheet of paper and some folds. But the ingenuity and precision of origami is breathtaking, able to conjure a menagerie of animals, a flock of birds, a horticultural paradise or an armada of sailing ships. This is no idler's pastime. Origami is a sophisticated art that demands meticulous precision and an engineer's exactitude. It is a contemplative craft and an evocative art. While birds and jumping frogs are still popular challenges there are, as with the many other forms of paper manipulation, new approaches. The American physicist and engineer Robert Lang has become renowned for his tireless and talented exploration of origami possibilities. Using computers, laser technology and mathematical principles he has elevated the art of origami still further. One of his masterpieces is a working cuckoo clock made from a single sheet of paper. It has leaves encrusted on its surface, a pendulum swinging at its base, a stag's head at its top and a tiny cuckoo peeping out of its small door. This is the simplicity of paper turned into an extravagant spectacle. As with many forms of paper engineering, what Robert Lang creates is visual, theatrical drama.

3
Paper Theatres

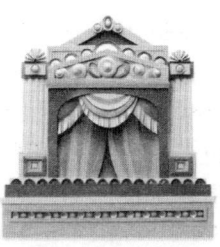

A person's a person, no matter how small
Horton Hears a Who, Dr. Seuss

Paper toy theatres are designed to be captivating. From the early nineteenth century and into the twentieth, their popularity was widespread. Created as small-scale versions of actual theatres and opera houses, they were made in cardboard with a proscenium, approximately 45cm high, crammed with colour and adornment. In eclectic albeit Lilliputian magnificence, Corinthian columns and Grecian urns, golden harps and heraldic shields, cavorting nymphs and victorious gods all claimed attention. Busts of Shakespeare jostled for position alongside angels and satyrs. The scenery was equally lavish, 'complete with a full complement of top drops, sky pieces, ground rows, curtain wings, cut woods, practical drawbridges and panoramas to be drawn across the stage' to mimic the fanciful set designs of the day.[1] Cardboard stage curtains, decorated with gold fringes and tassels, emulated luxurious velvet drapes, and powerful and wealthy patrons were painted lolling on velvet chairs in stage boxes just as they did in the grandest theatres. And there was an orchestra pit where a motley group of moustachioed musicians tuned up as their conductor stood, his baton poised, ready to strike up an overture before the curtain rose. And, when it did, when the lamps were extinguished and the room fell to dark, when all that was illuminated was the tiny theatre, its colours vibrant in the glow of colza oil lamps, it was revealed as a jewel shining in the gloom, its smallness and bright isolation intensifying its presence.

In the intimacy of their own homes, audiences were beguiled, transported to magical and exotic worlds on a miniature stage that lay but an arm's length away. A print from a Victorian playbook captures the scene. A toy theatre sits on the dining room table and a young boy stands behind it, directing and stage-managing the production. On either side of him are his subordinate siblings tasked with moving characters and pieces of scenery on and off stage when he cues them to do so. His mother, sitting beside the theatre, holds an open book in her hands from which she is reading the script or narrating the story while, close by, other family members are clustered, their heads thrust forward in rapt attention, their eyes fixed on the drama unfolding before them.

This is the thrill of the theatre transposed from the vast, noisy auditoriums of the day to the quietude of home. An entertainment in which the whole family can participate. For their spectators these tiny characters and scaled-down scenery epitomised glamour, sophistication and sentiment, caught and pinned like an exotic butterfly to be studied, exclaimed over and relished. They were useful to theatre impresarios as a novel way to promote their current plays and their theatrical stars, sold as souvenirs for theatre-goers to be displayed as conversation pieces and as visible evidence of their cultured sensibilities. While, for those unable to attend, paper theatres were vicarious purchases that captured the frisson of theatrical extravagance.

Paper theatres not only entranced the general populace throughout Europe but won the hearts of celebrated writers. The novelist Charles Dickens was enraptured by these scaled-down dramas, a fascination he captured in his 1850 tale *A Christmas Tree*:

> And now, I see a wonderful row of little lights rise smoothly out of the ground, before a vast green curtain. Now, a bell rings – a magic bell, which sounds in my ear unlike all other bells – and music plays . . . Out of this delight springs the toy-theatre . . . with paste and glue, and gum, and water colours . . . a teeming world of fancies . . .[2]

And that master of dramatic adventure Robert Louis Stevenson penned his own eulogistic essay, 'A Penny Plain, Tuppence Coloured', in honour of paper theatres. The essay's title referred to the way in which paper theatres were sold: a 'penny plain' would buy you sheets of card printed in black ink depicting the various components of the stage and its proscenium for you to paint and assemble at home. More sheets with the characters and scenery of specific productions could be bought separately. For those with less time and artistic inclination, 'tuppence' would buy you a similar version already coloured in bright, bold hues. In the same essay Stevenson cajoles his readers to avail themselves of a paper theatre from one of the most popular toy theatre purveyors of the day, declaring: 'if you love art, folly, or the bright eyes of children, speed to Pollock's'.[3] And it was to Pollock's that the writer Sacheverell Sitwell took the ballet impresario Sergei Diaghilev in search of inspiration for his British themed ballet *The Triumph of Neptune*, and to Pollock's that Charlie Chaplin, the great silent-movie star, appealed when trying to locate a copy of *The Miller and His Men*, a popular toy theatre play.

So it was to Pollock's toyshop that I too went in 2023, to revisit its antiquated labyrinth of enchantment. It is a place I have often frequented through my life and my house bears witness to its temptations, harbouring a variety of theatrical mementos I have bought there over the years. They include a splendid, small-scale reproduction of the nineteenth-century Victoria Theatre, published by John Redington, father-in-law of Benjamin Pollock, from whom the shop takes its name. The original Pollock's print shop had been expanded over time to include a toy museum filled with a tantalising array of nostalgic childhood diversions: dolls' houses, articulated toys, paper scraps and a unique collection of toy theatres. I climb its rickety wooden stairs upwards and onwards to floor upon floor of memorabilia that preserves a playful past. Pollock's traps merriment within its walls. Anticipation and amusement linger in the air like an emotive aroma. But Pollock's has never felt to me like a sentimental guardian. Whenever I visit, I feel as if I have recovered and reconnected with a past self, not as a memory but as a reawakened joy: each experience as fresh as the first, each one proffering the same enticing promise of discovery.

This latest visit to Pollock's museum and gift shop finds me buying one of its 'penny plain' paper theatres, a reimagining of a court performance of extracts from

Shakespeare's *Twelfth Night* staged in the presence of Queen Elizabeth I and her courtiers. With all the optimism of a 'penny plain' novice, I think that its painting and assembly will make a pleasant diversion for a wet autumn afternoon. I take it home, settle myself at the table, select my smallest brushes, arrange my inks and, filling a tumbler with water, set to work. But the afternoon turns all too quickly to evening with barely the proscenium finished.

The next day, determined to speed up the process, I organise a production line: one colour applied to all the relevant sections, before another is employed. Again, the day and evening speed on with no end in sight, as does the next. It takes me nearly a week to paint and cut out the forty-four diminutive figures, to dab flesh tones onto their tiny faces and eighty-eight tiny hands, to pick out the embroidered detail of their costumes in contrasting colours and embellish them with sprinklings of gold. And then there are the accessories: the ruffs, gauntlets, stockings and feathered bonnets. It is their scale that slows down my progress. Each tiny element requires such close attention. The scenery – a daunting plethora of latticed windows and ornate columns, heraldic adornments and sculpted embellishments – is equally demanding. On and on I go. And I realise, as I toil, that while the card figures might be flat, in performance they have to infer a greater dimensionality. It is the contrast of their colours that will emphasise their individual presence on stage. Neither should the scenery dominate. I have to keep scale in mind and must constantly consider the overall visual effect that reduction engenders.

With everything inked I consider my progress. Despite my best efforts and the time taken, I am dissatisfied. The colours seem blotchy, their tones drab. It is harder than I thought to effect the crisp contours of costumes when working in miniature. Determined on artistic success, I invest in a range of high-quality felt-tip brushes and pens and set to work again, touching up each and every figure. This is no longer a fleeting diversion. It has become a challenge, a compulsion or – as my husband wearily ventures as he yet again moves my endeavour, now spread all over the kitchen table, to one side to make room for tea – an obsession. That is the snare of making. It is a needy occupation. Its allure catches you unawares and makes you unconsciously ambitious. Colouring in is rarely judged to be one of the highest echelons of creative labour. It is supposedly simple. But it still requires thought and care, discernment and flair. It takes time. Moreover, in its repetition it is addictive, mindful and meditative, lulling you into a cocoon of calm.

It is soothing to spend hour upon hour in an immersive activity, to pay attention to small things. I find I have become totally focused on seeking, if not perfection, then, at the very least, satisfaction. And such concentration cuts me adrift from the everyday and time becomes suspended. I recall once hearing on the radio two boffins discussing the nature of time. How it is elastic not linear, and that if you become wholly absorbed in something, whether that be an activity, an event or an experience, time stretches in your mind not just then but later, and that when your attention is engaged so intensely you assimilate the detail of your experience more precisely and it remains clearly in your memory for longer.

I realise that making a paper theatre does not just involve colouring in and cutting out but that there are particular conventions inherent in its use that affect its creation. As the main characters are card cut-outs, only able to shuffle backwards and forwards in a straight line, it is the grouped figures around them which provide the illusion of energy, and most paper theatres are designed with crowds of walk-on characters caught mid-action. These are grouped together on the same length of card to enable an operator to quickly fill the stage with a larger cast. An 1855 paper-theatre dramatisation of Walter Scott's novel *Rob Roy* comprises 130 different figures and has phalanxes of musket-grasping, red-coated soldiers; a knot of twirling kilted dancers; a huddle of lamenting Highlanders and a gang of protesting villagers. Some figures feature the same character in a variety of roles. The minuscule Rob Roy comes with a range of personas – nobleman, captive, fighter and fugitive – each one dressed in a different costume and posed in a different stance. And the scenic worlds these characters inhabit must offer ever-changing locales to animate the action and keep an audience enthralled. *Rob Roy* includes a dozen backdrops illustrating diverse settings, from a mountainous glen to a book-lined library, from a city street to a village idyll.

For my *Twelfth Night*, I only have two acts and, although there is only one figure per character, I have the addition of the many courtiers and the queen herself to prepare. And as I paint them I realise that all this handling of the small figures is useful in a way that I had not envisioned. When, and if, the play is ever performed, I, as its operator, will only ever see the back of my players as I push them on and off the stage. But by constantly picking them up and putting them down, scrutinising every piece for omissions – an uncoloured stocking or an overlooked ruff – not to mention cutting them out, I am instilling a familiarity. As I feel out their different physical stances – the crook of an elbow, the bend of a knee, the flutter of fingers on an outstretched hand – I am getting the measure of them. And this is expedient tactile knowledge. It will enable me to identify them quickly and speed up their entrances and exits while working in low light. Moreover, as they are essentially stiff and mostly front-facing, their personalities and relationships can only be inferred by how they are moved, the pace at which they traverse the stage, their spatial proximity to or distance from each other. By getting to know my cast through touch I will have a better grasp of their dramatic potential and limitations.

Making always leads to discoveries that are unpredictable. That is one of its charms. Whether it be learning how something works or what materials afford the best results or, as with my paper theatre, insight into specific challenges, it takes you down unexpected rabbit holes that, each in their own way, prove interesting (if, at times, frustrating). It is overcoming difficulties that brings the greatest sense of achievement. Eventually, my theatre is done. All its disparate parts have been coloured in and cut out, all its characters are standing proud on their cardboard strips, and the stage and the proscenium arch have been assembled. I dragoon my husband Charlie and the dog as my audience and, with the lights off and a torch as illumination, I bring my theatre to life. And, as Viola laments – 'O you should not rest /Between the elements of air and earth/ But you should pity me' – I feel a pang of pleasure at having persisted. This is indeed a theatre: tiny but triumphant.

My paper theatre is based on one in a Tudor court, elegant but not flamboyant. But the majority of paper theatres published from the nineteenth century onwards were inspired by grand contemporary theatres. Groups of artists were despatched to actual performances, one to hastily sketch the changing scenery, another to draw the costumes, a third to illustrate the dramatic postures of theatrical luminaries such as Edmund Kean, Sarah Siddons, Ellen Terry and Charles Kemble. Publishers printed characters and stage sets from the most thrilling current productions at Covent Garden, Drury Lane and Sadler's Wells, and authenticity was key to consumer appeal. These artists had to work – much like courtroom artists of today – at speed, capturing not just the stage décor but its dramatic mood. And their sketches left an unexpected legacy, a rare visual record of early nineteenth-century theatre. Moreover, it was their depictions that remained in circulation, reprinted over and over again in the decades that followed to continue to delight paper-theatre enthusiasts. Some of their designs are even still available online to purchase as vintage ephemera or as digital downloads.

It was boys who traditionally made paper theatres. Boys who cut out and constructed the different segments of their staging, who mounted the printed sheets of scenery and characters onto card, painted the detail of both, devised the sound effects and chose the musical accompaniment. It was also boys who usually performed the plays. Their sisters might have been allowed to help with the painting if a performance was imminent but paper theatres were predominantly a boy's domain. *The Times* theatre critic John Oxenford, writing in 1871, observed that:

> The boy with his bare stage yet unprovided with proscenium and curtains, with his sheets of scenery and characters yet uncoloured, was supplied with ample employment for all the spare hours of the winter holidays ... I am speaking of a most valued treasure a boy in his early teens could possess. The little stage was regarded as something above a mere toy and its management was deemed neither a childish nor [an] effeminate pursuit.[4]

For some famed literary and artistic notables, having a toy theatre, and being its designer and director, was a prelude to a creative career. The Swedish film director Ingmar Bergman chose to open his semi-autobiographical film *Fanny and Alexander* (1982) with footage of a boy playing with his toy theatre. The French cinematographer Jean Cocteau said that he caught what he called 'the red and gold disease of the theatre' when as a child he created designs for his toy theatre.[5] Peter Brook, the visionary British theatre director, stated in his autobiography that seeing a performance in a Victorian toy theatre remained 'the most vivid and most real' of his childhood experiences.[6] To them can be added Lewis Carroll, Oscar Wilde, George Bernard Shaw, Aubrey Beardsley, Edward Gordon Craig, G.K. Chesterton, John Gielgud, Pablo Picasso, Noel Coward, Orson Welles, Dario Fo and Andrew Lloyd Webber, who all retained fond memories of their toy theatres and who asserted that it was their early encounter with them that fanned their later creativity.

A boy's enthusiasm for his home-crafted theatrical dramas was kept alight by the paper-theatre publishers and they were constantly devising new ways to keep their young customers' interest. Cunning contraptions were on sale that could articulate the characters' limbs by means of simple levers or pulleys. A character could also have another version of themselves secreted along their length, able to be switched in an instance with the pull of a string. By such means a ragged Cinderella could metamorphose, as if by magic, into a dazzling princess and the wizened grandmother of Red Riding Hood could be transformed into a predatory wolf. With the use of a gauze backdrop and clever lighting, the scene of a rural idyll could dissolve into that of an eerie forest, and there were other purchasable devices that would operate a trap door to despatch Aladdin to Abanazer's cave or make clouds part to reveal a heavenly angel. But it was the special fire effects that won the hearts of boys: powders that allowed red and blue fire to spurt from a dragon's breath or billows of smoke to accentuate the magic of a fairy wand. Firecrackers ensured a startling and exciting end to an evening's melodramatic entertainment. They were not without their hazards, as the schoolboy Charles Dickens found to his cost. For a production of *The Miller and His Men* he mounted for his classmates, he conjured a fire-cracking inferno for its final dramatic scene when the mill is demolished. His zeal for such a splendid finale brought the police to the school door.[7]

A boy was also tempted to part with his pocket money with the lure of tinsel ornaments: embossed decorations in different colours of copper foil or scraps of fabric – silk, velvet, satin – to be glued onto existing costumes and sets. Now the armour of a medieval knight could blaze in silvered glory, a fairy's skirt gleam in silk and twinkle in glitter. Tinsel heightened the theatrical impact of these truncated dramas. Under the glow of the lamps that ran along the front of their small stages, the cut and parry of a battle could be made more gripping with the glinting thrust of swords, the magnificence of a palace magnified in gilded adornments, and the narrative of fairy tales be made more magical with iridescent flowers set in lustrous gardens. So ubiquitous did 'tinselling' become that the 1869 publication *Every Boy's Book: A Complete Encyclopaedia of Sports and Amusements* accorded tinselling its own section with the following advice:

> The artist may now proceed to the work of tinselling, which consists in gumming little spangles and embossed ornaments over certain parts . . . Every piece of armour, every button, every jewel, and every weapon, should be represented in embossed work. All the pieces required for tinselling a figure may be purchased at the proper shops.[8]

One such 'proper shop' belonged to Mr H.J. Webb, one of the earliest publishers of paper theatres. His extensive compendium of tinsel ornaments – 13,000 and more – offered golden swords and silver helmets, velvet cloaks and satin shoes. And boys found their own ways to visually enhance their productions, adding sugar to paint pigments to create a sheen on costumes and make them appear more luxurious under the flare of candlelight.

It is surely no coincidence that many of the celebrated men for whom paper theatres played a significant part in their childhoods had experienced early trauma: the death of siblings, incipient poverty, alcoholic fathers, broken homes or boarding school bullying. For those sent away, deprived of the sensory comforts of home and cast into a harsh, and sometimes abusive, regime, holidays offered a temporary respite. Small wonder then that they embraced the escape, the visual and tactile make-believe of toy theatres, seizing the opportunity to lose themselves in the safer world of theatrical fiction. It was also a way for them to seize control, directing the action, mobilising their paper actors; a way to feel in charge, albeit in a fantasy world.

It was a world that the fashion designer Yves Saint Laurent savoured as a boy. In the years before he commenced his dress-up doll collections it was his toy theatre that gave him succour. It offered him a creative reprieve from the bullying he experienced at school, retreating to the haven of his bedroom to become preoccupied in what he called 'the silence of the imagination . . . a world of illusions'.[9] The theatre director and playwright Patrick Sandford tells a similar story. In a videoed interview he talks of being sexually abused at his primary school and how he found emotional salve in his paper theatre. It became, in his own words, his 'safety net', a tangible reprieve from distress into a world of pretence. He would spend, as he relates, 'hours and hours and hours and hours' absorbed in the quiet creativity it offered him. It was, he believes, his paper theatre that saved him and propelled him towards a theatrical career. It acted as a signpost to a safe path to follow.

The desire to escape into a world of make-believe was not limited to boys. The social upheavals of the nineteenth century fanned an avid and widespread embrace of diverting and spectacular entertainment by the population as a whole. With the Industrial Revolution luring the rural poor in their thousands to the city to seek an urban utopia, taking advantage of accelerated travel and expanding employment opportunities, the hitherto settled way of life was becoming unmoored. People were crowding into Britan's burgeoning cities and London's population grew exponentially over the century – from one to six million – to make it the largest city in the world.

The hopes and aspirations that lay in the hearts of those seeking a better life were exploited by impresarios. While the century had begun with only three licensed theatres in London, by its end the city could boast over sixty theatres that showcased ever more magnificently extravagant productions, staging a diverse programme of plays, musicals, operas and light entertainment. Pantomimes and melodramas were popular panaceas to social disruption, feeding the prevailing hunger for rags-to-riches stories: Cinderella and Aladdin, Jack and the Beanstalk, Dick Whittington and others. The stage was awash with pirates and princesses, brigands and buccaneers and the heroics of Jack Sheppard, Dick Turpin and Joan of Arc. Such thrilling adventures, with their stories of adversity overcome and courage rewarded, presented the fantasy of success to audiences eager for a temporary lull from the anxiety generated by the intense societal changes they were experiencing.

Such popular dramas became fodder for paper-theatre publishers, who milked the public appetite for spectacle and escapism. And paper theatres held particular allure. Through them, their spectators could encompass a whole universe in their mind's eye. They offered the impression of a manageable world, one that could be contained and controlled. One celebrated publisher, William West, when interviewed later in life, recollected the rise in paper-theatre popularity with nostalgia, saying that he used to sell 2,500 a year. His advertisement in those halcyon days was fulsome in its description of what he proffered, temptations that were guaranteed to whet the appetites of his customers:

> West's Catalogue of Original, Tragic, Fancy, and Comic Characters. As performed at the Theatres Royal, Covent Garden, Drury Lane, Lyceum, Surrey, Astley's, Sadler's Wells etc., etc. New plates of pantomime tricks, ditto miniature equestrian combats, plates of theatrical robbers, ditto small theatrical combats, ground pieces, horizons, plates of small seawaters and boats, ditto fairy cars, ditto magic characters, new plates of good and evil geniuses, and all theatrical representations that will be reproduced...[10]

Once publishers had secured a market for their paper theatres, they began to augment their catalogues with abbreviated scripts, mostly drawn from theatrical classics and contemporary plays and pantomimes: productions to reprise at home. Sometimes they issued a shortened edition of a current show before the curtain had even fallen on the first night. They also ransacked plays drawn from the literary canon, printing truncated versions of those that had already been adapted for the stage. These included Charles Dickens's *Oliver Twist*, Harriet Beecher Stowe's *Uncle Tom's Cabin* and ten of Walter Scott's novels. West, ever keen to find a new marketing ploy, began to augment his paper-theatre scripts with stage directions. By the mid-nineteenth century, competition was stiff. There were over fifty paper-theatre publishers in London alone, offering between them a repertoire of over 300 plays. None were devised specifically for children. Rather they represented adult fare in miniature.

Publishers in other countries had also become alert to the commercial and creative appeal of paper theatres. They began to appear in Italy, the Netherlands and central Europe, in Norway, Sweden and Denmark. But it was in France and Germany that fascination really took hold, each country evolving its own style of paper theatre and a selective repertoire of plays. In France, Jean-Charles Pellerin, the son of a French illustrator and printer based in the north-eastern town of Épinal, expanded the business with the production of exquisite paper theatres. His intricate scenery, tinted in delicate shades of pale blues and greens, soft greys and browns, made a striking contrast to the bolder, more garish colours of its British alternatives. The engraved sheets he supplied were of stock characters – soldiers, courtiers, dancers, musicians – with individual characters from well-known fiction and famous dramas available as separate purchases. With these, people could create their own miniature revivals of productions performed at the Comédie Francais or the Opéra Comique, or, if they preferred, they could invent their own. Pellerin did not sell scripts but relied on the splendour of his stage sets and prosceniums, sumptuously gilded in gold, to win custom.

Spain was more nationalistic, favouring paper reproductions of plays that dramatised its history, or Spanish fairy stories and classic tales. Its paper theatres were also more inventive than their British counterparts, with more modern, often surrealist designs, and there was more emphasis on atmospheric theatricality, with semi-transparent backdrops and ingenious lighting able to create vistas of bewitching beauty. Interest soon spread to America, fanned initially by imports from Britain and Europe. But in the 1870s, American publishers began to design their theatres with gas footlights installed along the stage, an exciting technical advance unavailable in Britain. They also started to produce their own home-grown dramas with Seltz's American Boy's Theatre, published by Scott & Co in New York, offering such plays as *The Pirates of the Florida Keys*, *The Fiend of the Rocky Mountain*, *Pocahontas* and *The Battle of Bunker Hill*. In Denmark, the publisher Alfred Jacobsen also introduced greater technical sophistication with rotating lighting and flown-in scenery.

But it was Germany that became Britain's keenest rival in paper-theatre popularity. Not only were their theatres larger than those available in Britain but the scope of their theatrical repertoire was broader. As well as whimsical nursery stories and dramatisations of traditional folk tales there was grander fare: Mozart's *The Magic Flute* and *The Marriage of Figaro*, Rossini's *Barber of Seville* and, in later years, Wagner's *Ring Cycle*. Keen to secure international sales, some German publishers printed their scripts and stage directions not only in German but also in French and English, and they were successful in securing a flourishing export trade. To the dismay of other paper-theatre publishers, the stylised elegance, improved scenic perspectives, greater articulation of paper figures and the dramatic ambitions of German paper theatre was met with international enthusiasm, particularly in Britain, where the continual churning out of old favourites was beginning to lose its charm.

By the end of the nineteenth century, although it still had loyal devotees, British interest in paper theatres was waning. After the 1880s very few new works customised for paper theatres were being published. And theatre itself was changing. Dramas that focused on personal and social relationships, and that debated current issues under the cover of wit and irony, had come into vogue. The theatre-going public became more interested in social comment than in spectacle. Of the fifty paper-theatre publishers that had existed half a century before, only a handful now remained and even their output was desultory, largely confined to printing old favourites. Unwanted stock began to pile up on dusty shelves in run-down shops that had once been Aladdin-like caves of wonder. The fate of many of the most famed purveyors of enthrallment, the suppliers of the stuff of dreams, was tragic: the lack of trade reduced them to poverty, to the workhouse and, for some, a drinker's death. Of William West, who had been a pioneer of paper theatres, the producer of over 140 plays, it was reported:

> ... poor Willie West ... finally closed his little dark shop, whence had emanated so much salutary amusement to the boys of a former age. A short time before his death, he commenced selling off his stock at ridiculously low prices. The poor man could be heard gasping behind the simple screen which divided his death bed from the public portion of the shop.[11]

There were a variety of reasons why paper theatre fell out of fashion. It was not only a matter of a shift in public taste. The publishers of paper theatres faced competition from publications such as *The Boy's Own Treasury* of *Sports and Pastimes*, *The Boy's Budget* and *The Boy's Halfpenny Weekly Budget of Plays, Stories, Characters and Scenes*, which provided instructions on how to make your own theatre or included paper theatres as free give-aways. But the quality was poor, printed on inferior paper in inferior colour, the illustrations cruder. Lacking the seductive brilliance of the earlier paper theatres produced by Webb and Pollock's, people's delight in them faltered. Moreover, an enticing variety of new optical inventions were now on sale, competing for recreational attention. Webb pointed his finger in a different direction, lamenting that: 'Education has ruined the business . . . Our children in these days neither have the patience nor the time necessary to colour and ornament the sheets.'[12]

But, despite its fade from parlour room popularity, a love of paper theatre persisted, preserved by diehard devotees and others who continued to find solace in its home-made dramas. Pollock's became their main supplier, keeping interest afloat by extending and modernising its range with spotlights, floodlights and colour filters specifically designed for a miniature stage. While interest was declining in Europe, in 1930s Japan a new form of paper theatre was emerging: *kamishibai* presented paper-theatre plays that were performed by itinerant storytellers who rode around the cities on bicycles. Unfolding a small wooden proscenium, they slotted dramatic scenes, painted with bold brushstrokes on heavy varnished boards, into place sequentially as they narrated thrilling tales of superheroes, aliens, child detectives and supernatural spirits. In the gloom of the Great Depression of the 1930s it was these small street-corner shows – with a reputed 2,500 operators in Tokyo alone, entertaining over a million children a day – that brought cheer. Later, during World War II and the American occupation, their storyboards had a more serious intent, to keep adults informed on current affairs through pictorial news. The boom of *kamishibai* only ended in 1952 with the advent of television but, by that time, it had given rise to a new genre of popular Japanese fiction. It had given birth to manga.

Although from the 1880s new paper theatres and paper-theatre plays were rarely published, special promotional editions were sometimes still produced over the ensuing decades, In 1948 J. Arthur Rank, for example, distributed a paper-theatre version of Laurence Olivier's *Hamlet*, featuring the impressionistic original sets designed by Roger Furse to coincide with the release of its film of Olivier's production. The late 1960s witnessed a revival of interest in paper theatre with the reprint of George Speaight's seminal work *The History of the English Toy Theatre*, first published in 1946. Victorian paper-theatre productions began to be reprised and new shows devised, mounted by those keen to present a more intimate alternative to establishment theatre. And in contemporary culture, with the onset of social media, disparate collectors, producers and designers of paper theatres are emerging, having found a new channel through which they can share and promote their passion on a wider international stage.

In October 2023 I took myself off to the town of Preetz in northern Germany for *Preetzer Papiertheatertreffen*, its thirty-sixth annual gathering of paper-theatre enthusiasts. Over sixty productions were programmed to take place between Friday night and Sunday afternoon, with a variety of companies, mainly from Europe, presenting their short (usually half-hour) shows two or three times across the weekend. I booked to see eleven shows but, in truth, my curiosity lay not so much in the dramas but in the participants. Who were these people who had travelled across Europe to immerse themselves in tiny theatrics? Were they guardians of past memories nostalgically revisiting an amusement of childhood, or collectors hoping to discover rare remnants of nineteenth-century ephemera? Or were they young creatives keen to explore the visual potential of miniature theatre as a medium that could offer a more immersive and emotive theatrical experience to audiences jaded by large auditoriums, lacklustre repeats of well-worn plays, and the exorbitant expense of a night at the theatre?

What strikes me immediately when I enter the school in Preetz, where the festival is based, is the soft burr of camaraderie. These might be people with diverse reasons for attending but they patently share a joy in being reunited with each other and their love of paper theatres.

The cafeteria not only serves refreshments but is set out with tables heaped with paper-theatre memorabilia to pore over, discuss, buy and exchange. Here are scenic backdrops for countless dramas, the small-scale stage façades of some of Europe's grandest theatres, and boxes piled high with characters who once graced the cardboard stages of America, Spain, Germany, France and other countries. Now they lie jumbled together in a timeless democracy. Medieval knights jostle with pantomime dames, mythological goddesses rub shoulders with street urchins, Aladdin has his head on Bluebeard's shoulder. I pick up one figure, a young American Civil War hero, his arms raised high in triumph. When I turn him over I discover that 'Tom Hunter' is scrawled on his back and so, for 10 cents, claim him out of familial respect. There are books and magazines, cards and posters – the still alluring materiality of paper-theatre accoutrements – all begging for attention, for appreciation, for value.

Over the next two days I go from classroom to classroom, sitting on chairs that are crammed together to accommodate the squeeze of the shows' eager audiences, all of us leaning forward to peer into make-believe miniature worlds. This, I come to realise, is unhurried theatre: a curtain slowly rises, operators' hands carefully place each character on stage and, almost tenderly, remove them when they have played their part. Backdrops and side wings are slotted into place and substituted with considered attention. While my focus is on the stage, I find that I am also drawn to the silent movements, the presence of the black-clad operators. It is their attentiveness that sets the tone for the performance, that encourages our concentration. Moreover, the proximity of the audience – to one another, to the paper theatre itself – inculcates a communal bond, the feeling that we are sharing a unique and precious experience. For a short while we are closed off from our everyday lives, caught in a world of imagination and enthralment.

And it *is* enthralling. Each production, while different from the next, disarms me. In Preetz, tradition is intermingled with innovation. Yulya Dukhovny presents her one-woman show *Little Tree Giant* on a simple table. There is no theatre as such. Instead, she uses a large book as her theatrical backdrop. She holds its pages open towards the audience and slowly begins to turn them, each page revealing a scene from her unfolding story. It begins with the silhouette of a traveller sowing seeds along a barren trail. She turns a page and a seed become a seedling, another page and it is now a sapling, then a tree. Dukhovny inverts the book, so that it is horizontal, and we see the tree now shading a house, which is nested in its shadow. She pulls a tab and the house falls forward, becoming a three-dimensional home. We move inside the house and find a young couple keeping watch over their baby's cradle and, as she pulls another tab, the cradle begins to gently rock. The book becomes a child's picture book: 'A is for apple, C is for Cat, P is for Peace, W is for War'. We follow the child, a boy, as he grows up, explores the world around him, dreams of travelling further afield. This is a personal reflection on immigration symbolised by the story of planting trees in distant lands. In just fifteen minutes we have witnessed a landscape alter, a family emerge, a boy mature and dream of building his own home. We have been told the story of a land, a family, of hope and expectation, a story of love captured in the simplicity of paper.

Dukhovny is a multidisciplinary artist who has worked as a stage director and teacher and who trained as a classical pianist. In *Little Tree Giant*, her musicality lingers. It is there in the pace of her turning pages, in how she modulates the rhythm of her drama. It is there when she pauses, holding one image a little longer than another to let its poignancy persist. It is there in the small crescendos of animated surprise that counterpoint the stillness of the book, and it is there in the slow fade of light she manipulates by simply shifting the beam of her handheld torch. This is the tone of a soundscape made visual. It is as if each page is a note and each note joins to the next in a visual melody that catches at loss and yearning, hope and promise: feelings that stay with you long after the book is closed.

In contrast to Dukhovny's innovative modern interpretation of paper theatre, *Sarah's Paper Theatre* goes back in time to recreate the delights of a Victorian toy theatre. Sarah Peasgood, whose parents Peter and Sylvia Peasgood were celebrated conservators of paper theatre, has revived their production of the pantomime *Jack and the Beanstalk*. The pantomime was published by Webb in 1820 and Sarah presents it in an original 1857 Redington paper theatre now illuminated with LED lighting. Fairies sparkle in tinsel, Jack's magic bean grows into a gigantic tree with the help of unseen pulleys, growing on and up, until its branched leaves fill the stage. We experience the glorious escape such paper theatres proffered to their contemporary audience. And, in true pantomime style, we are encouraged to participate, to shout out to Jack not to barter his cow for a bag of beans and to cheer when his minuscule silver sword fells the giant in a single, improbable blow. The adults, as well as the children present, are transfixed by the magic of the drama and when the curtain falls it is to rapturous applause.

After the performance, Sarah invites us all to come and see the theatre's backstage workings. She shows us the devices invented by her parents to better animate the characters: the clever jointing of the giant to effect his more dramatic collapse, the mechanisms that allow Jack to wave his sword-wielding arm and climb the tree to the giant's lair. On the tables that flank the stage are scenic sets and figures arranged in serried ranks, each one numbered on the back, a necessary precaution for a production where swift changes are necessary. Sarah's invitation to see backstage is repeated by other operators at other shows. And being able to examine the workings of different productions is one of the unexpected pleasures of this festival. Before each performance, the conventions of theatre are preserved – our tickets are scanned, the curtain is down, the characters and scenery are kept out of sight – but after the show this community of paper-theatre practitioners are eager to share traditions, differences and innovations: how tiny discs wound with elastic can be attached to the strips of card on which the figures stand to enable their rotation; how transparent cut-outs on a backdrop can, when lit, be revealed as glittering stars or the coloured curve of a rainbow.

What surprises me is just how varied the festival programme is and how much paper theatre has changed since its Victorian heyday. The festival's surprisingly eclectic range of plays includes a haunting adaptation of Ernest Hemingway's *The Old Man and the Sea* told with poetic charm and paper motifs that somehow capture the essence of the original; a history of bridges that through visually witty and laugh-out-loud historical re-enactments traces how man managed to straddle his world; and a fast-moving horror show of a robotic rebellion by Robert Poulter based on Karel Čapek's 1920 dystopian play, *R.U.R.* And in that convivial atmosphere, when all around me feels joyful, interested and engaged, I realise that paper theatre captivates because it distils human stories simply, with just paper and card, in a way that is not just bewitching but inventive.

*

In 'Toy Theatre Thrives Online during Quarantine', an article published in *The Theatre Times* in 2020, the Franco-American scholar, artist and curator Marisa C. Hayes writes of the revival of paper theatre during the Covid lockdown in America. She writes about the New York collective Great Small Works, which organised a virtual paper-theatre festival during the pandemic as an alternative to their biennial Toy Theater Festival: a platform for innovative exponents of the paper theatre.[13] Great Small Works had already gained a reputation for championing paper theatre as a medium that, because of its reduced scale, they felt offered a more impactful exploration of current issues. In 1991 they devised the *Toy Theater of Terror as Usual*, which they described as a 'surreal news serial', and in which cuttings from newspapers, photographic images and extracts from philosophical works were combined with paper actors to stage debates on the prevailing public attitudes to the Gulf War, American gun culture and the 1992 Los Angeles riots, as well as other pressing topics. For its virtual festival, screened via Zoom and Facebook, productions were live-streamed around the world, with contributions from countries including China, Mexico, Canada, Germany and Chile. The repertoire was aimed at an adult audience, incorporating themes of war, ecological disaster and human frailty. Each show began with the buzz of voices in an auditorium and intermission bells rang to suggest a real theatre-going experience.

Paper theatre is also being nurtured by the American universities of Connecticut and California, which harbour extensive puppetry archives and which programme live and online events and exhibitions to keep the flame of toy theatre alight. The Rencontres Internationales de Théâtre de Papier in France, the Hanauer Papiertheatermuseum and forum in Germany, as well as the British Puppet and Model Theatre Guild, are all dedicated to ensuring that paper theatre remains, if not mainstream, then at least safeguarded by those who recognise its dramatic value. The workshops, symposiums, online tutorials and blogs that these organisations promote signal that there is still an active community of practitioners and enthusiasts who are resolute in securing its continuance.

Surviving vintage editions have become treasure troves for interested collectors, with character sheets, scenic sets and the theatres themselves reaching high prices at auction. Sadly, Pollock's in London closed its doors in January 2023, after over 170 years. There is a hope that it might one day be resurrected somewhere else. Happily, Benjamin Pollock's Toyshop – a later and separate emporium from the original Pollock's shop and subsequent museum, spawned from it but now unconnected – continues to ply its trade in Covent Garden in London. There you can still purchase reproductions of early paper theatres as well as modern versions designed by contemporary artists and designers. Amongst them is Clive Hicks-Jenkins who, in 2016, created a paper-theatre version of *Hansel and Gretel* with a script by the future Poet Laureate Simon Armitage. He also collaborated with the painter David W. Slack and the writer Olivia McCannon to produce a paper-theatre adaptation of the French fairy tale 'La Belle et la Bête'. *Beauty & the Beast* was produced as a limited edition in a *Design for Today* publication in 2022 and carries the strapline, 'The limit of a toy theatre is your imagination'.

It is a paper theatre far removed from the gilded glory of its predecessors. With a black stage flanked by a proscenium from which juts columned stags and prowling wolves in ruby red and grey, with a backdrop featuring the glowering, gleaming eyes and open jaws of a wolf, it encapsulates a world of mystery and threat. Its tiny figures are painted with flowing brushstrokes to suggest movement, while the interior of the beast's castle is rendered in icy blue. This is paper drama caught in emotional shades – red for danger, blue for detachment – a visually stylised evocation of the story itself.

On his website, Clive Hicks-Jenkins shared his thoughts on paper theatres:

> By some alchemy when the stage shrinks, then new rules apply, and new ways of creating and seeing have to be devised . . . I've been tumbling down the rabbit-hole of toy theatres all my life, and I'm tumbling still.[14]

4
Snow and Sand

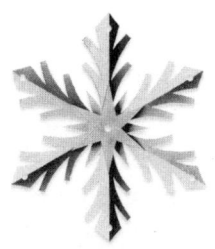

Nature always wears the colors of the spirit
Nature, Ralph Waldo Emerson

It is not water that makes snow but vapour. Trapped in clouds and released when temperatures drop below zero degrees Celsius, the vapour transmutes to ice crystals that muster into snowflakes of individual beauty, weighty enough to fall from the sky. They fall over hills, linger along the branches of trees, cluster in hedgerows and blanket the earth to envelop us in a transformed world. When snowflakes muster to become snow, familiar landscapes undergo a sensory change. Snow hushes all around us and alters the texture of our lives. It is seductive.

A snowflake is ephemeral. It drifts, settles and evaporates. Each one is unique. Some are formed star-shaped, others as hexagons or columns. It was an American, Wilson A. Bentley from Vermont, who first recorded their diversity. In the latter half of the nineteenth century, 'Snowflake Man', as Bentley became nicknamed, peered at snowflakes for hours through his microscope, trying to sketch them in detail. It was a frustrating task. The snowflakes melted too quickly, making precision challenging. The gift of a camera and its capacity to photograph them enabled him to capture over 5,000 images of different snow crystals. For the first time, the astonishing range of their delicate beauty was revealed.

In his book *Landmarks,* the writer Robert Macfarlane traces the lost vocabulary of landscape, unearthing and rediscovering local lost words for the weather and the natural world, words that were once in common usage but now are all but forgotten. His glossaries, compiled chapter by chapter, rekindle the attentiveness communities once paid to the small changes in their environment and reveal their sensitivity to any nuanced shift of temperature, wind or water flow that affected the livelihoods of those in rural Britain. In Chapter 3, 'The Living Mountain', Macfarlane garners words related to winter: *billow*, an East Anglian snowdrift; *clinkerbell*, an icicle in Dorset; *flaught*, a Scottish snowflake; *shockle*, the word for a lump of ice in Scotland and northern England.[1] This vocabulary, now largely extinct, describes the detailed variances of snow: the weight of its fall, the extent of its drift, the depth of its cover and the length of its persistence. For snow is transient. Its presence is temporary and, as such, presents not just a change of atmosphere but of opportunity.

In 2003, one of my then colleagues, Lizzy, arrived at the office where I was working in a fluster. 'You will never guess what that Peter McCaughey has gone and done,' she exclaimed. 'He's only just gone and brought me back a bag of snow from Helsinki.' She flopped down and told us the story. Peter, her husband, is an Irish artist who has gained a reputation for devising imaginative, heart-touching art installations – some permanent, others more temporary – all inspired by a community vision. His gift of a bag of snow, however, had surpassed even Lizzy's expectations of his dare-and-do creative exploits.

Peter had gone to Helsinki to run a week-long workshop with students at the Academy of Fine Arts who were studying under Mika Hannula, the author of *The Politics of Small Gestures*.[2] Peter had been hesitant about accepting the invitation as Lizzy's much-longed-for pregnancy had just been confirmed. But with her stoical encouragement, and with a somewhat anxious heart, Peter flew to Helsinki.

When the cases rolled out from the carousel at Helsinki Airport, Peter's bag was not among them. It remained undelivered for the first three days of his trip and when it finally arrived on day four, the day before he was due to fly home, Peter found that he had become accustomed to its loss. He had managed so well without the bag's contents that he reckoned there was little need of them for his last twenty-four hours. Instead he decided to give them all away, gift them to the friends he had made during his short stay. He made an inventory of his packed possessions, forty-eight items in all – books, socks, toiletries, clothing, and a treasured Swiss Army knife – and distributed them amongst the people he had met: students at the academy, a couple who had befriended him in a bar, Mika Hannula and other staff. He emailed Lizzie to tell her what he had done: that he was coming home with an empty bag. Her curt reply signalled her exasperation at his generosity.

On the day Peter left Helsinki, the snow lay thick on the ground. On his way to the airport in a taxi, the empty bag beside him, Peter had an epiphany. He asked the driver to stop, got out of the cab, and hurriedly scooped up handful after handful of snow, packing his bag to the brim with it. At the airport he checked it in and was amazed to watch his bag of snow go through with no questions asked. It was only when he had settled into his seat, after the safety announcements had been made, the arm rests and seatbelts checked, that he began to have misgivings. Was it illegal to import snow? What was the required temperature in the baggage hold for aircraft safety? Would it melt? While he was changing planes at Heathrow Airport in London, his bag was going directly to Scotland, and Peter had no idea what might happen to its contents during its five-hour journey. What if he found himself interrogated on his arrival back in Glasgow, questioned on why he was attempting to import a bag of sodden Helsinki snow? He knew he had no reply. He had no idea why. It just seemed the right thing to do at the time.

It was, therefore, with a sinking heart that Peter disembarked at Glasgow Airport. He stood nervously at baggage reclaim waiting for his bag to materialise. And down it came, tumbling off the rollers, looking exactly as it had done when he had checked it in at Helsinki: the same shape, the same size. There was no sign of seepage or melting. It was just as sturdy as it had been when he had packed it with snow. Peter was so jubilant that he shared his euphoria with disconcerted fellow passengers, telling them of his triumph, unzipping the bag to show them its cold contents. He even cajoled one of the baggage scanner staff to take his photograph as he put the bag through the X-ray machine. Then, with his loot of snow swinging from his shoulder, Peter went home to Lizzy.

Lizzy had a fire burning to welcome him and, as they sat, the bag lying between them, they debated what to do with the snow. Peter suggested that he could make a cast of it and preserve its physical shape, or he could sculpt something from it, create some kind of meaningful visual metaphor. Or maybe he could put some in the freezer and they could keep it forever. But he concluded all these ideas would change the value of it. They went against the spirit of spontaneity in which the snow had been collected. His snow, this snow, had been impulsively harvested without any permanence in mind – it represented an active not a passive joy.

So, over the next week, Peter visited friends and neighbours, bringing the bag with him. He asked them to take some snow from the bag, put it on the ground, stand on it in their bare feet and be photographed on a little bit of Helsinki. As the bag emptied, an archive of camaraderie and shared silliness accumulated.

Peter still has the bag. He has kept his inventory of its original contents and the list he made of their recipients that detailed what they were gifted. He still has an album of the photographs he took. They are keepsakes of a precious time, when he and Lizzy were on the brink of parenthood, when he believes he was particularly susceptible to joy, to recklessly testing hope and fortune in a bag of snow.

Why does something that cannot last have so much appeal? Perhaps, Peter suggested when I asked him twenty years later, it is not the thing itself that is significant but its story, the memory of a singular experience, our emotions at a specific time and moment of change. Something that is fleeting becomes more valued because we anticipate and almost savour its loss at the very moment we possess it, knowing we can only enjoy it for a short while before it disappears. Peter's snow could not sit on a sideboard for years collecting dust. It could neither become familiar nor overlooked. Its impermanence intensified his and Lizzy's experience of it, sharpened their recollection of it and kindled a greater treasuring.

To those beleaguered each year by heavy snow, its arrival is simultaneously a blight and a blessing. While its presence closes schools, hampers traffic and cuts off rural communities, it also heralds a seasonal opportunity; the chance to build a snowman. This iconic figure is a plump effigy of genial humanity personified by a bulbous carrot nose, coal-black button eyes, twigged arms and a knitted muffler. Throughout snow-clad countries, sentinel snowmen preside over front lawns, back gardens and village greens for as long as the cold weather persists.

Not everyone, however, has access to the seduction of snow. My sister tells of visiting friends in Hong Kong where their children, who were born there, plagued her with questions about what snow looked like, felt like, what you did with it. Eventually, worn out by her interrogators, she decided on a demonstration. She scraped some frosted water from the inside of the freezer and fashioned a minuscule snowman. The girls were fascinated and when she told them that elsewhere, in places that had a surfeit of winter snow, people built human-sized snowmen in their front gardens, they were astonished.

But who made the first snowman? When and where was the idea of a snowman first conceived? To answer these questions we need look no further than Bob Eckstein's entertaining book *The History of the Snowman*:

a surprisingly informative and laugh-out-loud read. In it, Eckstein, an American humorist and cartoonist, employs his acerbic wit to describe the various ups and downs of Frosty's public image through the centuries. It is a reverse chronology, tracing the snowman's story from the present day to medieval times when, in the marginalia of a fourteenth-century Book of Hours manuscript, the first known depiction of a snowman appears. This, however, is no jolly festive doodle. The snowman wears a hat, which according to the sartorial signals of the time infers that he is a Jew. More ominously, he has been doomed to an accelerated meltdown, shown straddled over a flame-warming brazier. This tiny sketch documents medieval antisemitism.[3]

Eckstein's unravelling of the snowman's history is thrillingly comprehensive, taking us from the inflatable snowmen of today's manicured, often snow-free, lawns to fifteenth-century Florence, where the nineteen-year-old Michelangelo was busy sculpting a statuesque snow sculpture of a snowman as a commission for the courtyard of Piero de' Medici's palace. Eckstein also reveals that snowmen have a surprisingly subversive past. He relates how, in the early sixteenth century, during what was called the 'Winter of Death', the burghers of Brussels organised a festival of snow-people in the hope of diverting the fury of its starving citizens and distracting them from rebelling at their impoverished plight. The Miracle of 1511, as the event was dubbed, saw over one hundred snow-people installed throughout the city. Some were devotional or whimsical portrayals inspired by biblical, mythological or allegorical imagery – Christ with the Woman of Samaria, the Man in the Moon, unicorns and mermaids – but others were intent on political satire, still more on pornographic voyeurism. A group of snow-people were to be found defecating outside the castle walls: a jibe poked at the castle's cowardly commander. Here was a pissing boy, there a farting prelate, elsewhere an amply endowed prostitute and some graphic scenes of copulation. But, despite their bawdiness and blatant ridicule of authority, the city magistrates insisted on protection for the snow-people, decreeing that anyone found vandalising them would be punished. Snowmen festivals were common throughout Europe at the time, but the notorious Miracle of 1511 has lived on in our memory because it is the only one to have been described in detail. Brussel's civic poet of the time, Jan Smeken, wrote about it, setting down in verse vivid descriptions of the snow-people erected to enchant, offend and titillate its hard-pressed citizens. His poem also records the aftermath of the event, the floods that followed as one hundred snow-people thawed and turned to water in the city streets.

The building of a complex snow statue, as opposed to the popular three-ball model beloved by children, is not for the faint-hearted, as I discovered when, in the winter of 1976, I started work as a community artist in Northampton, employed by the town's Development Corporation. The corporation, responsible for grafting onto an historic town a series of small newly built estates, was aware that providing decent housing stock did not magic up a contented nor integrated community. It needed to foster a social infrastructure through which links could be built between existing and new communities and between the newcomers themselves. It was decided that community arts, a recently forged approach to creative inclusion, might offer an imaginative way to achieve both.

The new Northampton residents, mainly Londoners who had been displaced from their old way of life, discovered that the new-found benefits of fitted kitchens and pristine housing came at the expense of the easy camaraderie of city living. They were detached from the hurly-burly of everyday life. While each of the estates had been assigned a small community centre and a tiny piazza, there were no busy streets to walk down, no family-run shops to pop into for a chat. After the excitement of the move and the flurry of home decorating had died down, those who lived in these neat estates were, quite simply, bored.

I was charged with organising social and creative activities and dreaming up a programme of events that could bring incomers into the heart of local community life. It was a tough job and one which, that winter, I was unsure of how to start.

I tramped through the new estates looking for inspiration, staring at freshly curtained windows and paint-bright doors, walking on clean, usually deserted, paths hoping for ideas. It all seemed so quiet, so blank. In those first days, unnervingly devoid of passing people, I became disconcerted and hesitant. As luck would have it there was another artist, the creative maverick Jamie McCullough, treading similar ground. He was known for his pioneering environmental artworks: in particular, one of the oldest skateboard parks in London, *Meanwhile Gardens*, which he created with the local community in 1976. In time he would devise and build *The Beginner's Way*, an extraordinary, sculpted landscape that mimicked the trajectory of creativity. Meanwhile, here in Northampton, he had been asked to reverse the community's aversion to Lings Wood, a wooded walkway on the edge of one of the housing estates. Recently struck by tragedy, it had become a place to avoid – a perception the corporation were keen to change. Jamie was considering connecting audio equipment to its trees to amplify the sound of their rising sap and make a mesmeric soundscape, reinventing the woods as a place of meditation.

Over a beer, one winter's night, I confessed to Jamie my burden of indecisiveness. He listened but kept his counsel. Then, early next morning, Jamie appeared at my house. It had been snowing all night and I opened my door to a Northampton draped in white. Jamie told me to come with him but remained evasive as to where we were going. 'You'll see,' was all he would say.

He parked his van in a housing estate layby, took out two shovels and walked me to its small piazza/play area. I was apprehensive. While Jamie was undoubtedly an imaginative genius, he also had a reputation for impulsiveness. I was alarmed that my 'softly, softly' approach to community engagement might be ruined by some guerilla act of artistic terrorism. Jamie began to gather up snow, rolling it into a gigantic ball. I joined in his gathering, even while I worried that local children might view us as trespassing on their own bounty. With two huge balls collected, Jamie heaved one on top of the other and I realised that he had a snowman in mind. Now voices could be heard. The clink of breakfast dishes being cleared and the hum of morning radio music signalled that people were on the move. Children began to appear, curiosity high on their agenda: 'Who are you? What are you doing? Can I help you, mister?'

Jamie had that knack of being industrious and welcoming at the same time, of offering a neutral territory that might be entered without challenge. 'We are building a snow king. You can help if you like.' Nonchalantly, he set allcomers to work, issuing requests in a quiet drawl. 'We need more snow for his arms. Can you collect two large clumps of snow for his hands? I think a crown would be good. Put snow on top of his head, yes, there, that's perfect.'

The van became emptied of tools as Jamie attracted more helpers, showed them how to sculpt fingers and toes, how to pack down the snow hard enough to take the imprint of the folds in a cloak. Our majestic snow king emerged sitting on a splendid throne, his huge hands resting on regal thighs, his crown glimmering with sweets some child had sacrificed to the greater creative cause. This was not just a snowman; this was a wondrous collective work of art.

As we worked, the adults ventured out, one by one. They surveyed the bustle of activity and reappeared with hot soup for us, juice for the children, and biscuits and cakes for all. A door was left open to let Christmas jingles float out and older residents parked themselves on nearby benches to direct operations. Conversation and chat was inevitable. In the cold crisp of that winter's day I was welcomed without any explanation, not as a council employee but as a snowman builder: a giver not a taker.

The cold of that winter ensured that our snow king persevered for a few days, surveying his realm, watching over his subjects with his coal-black eyes. As he did so, I went back to the estate to be greeted by children calling out my name, to find a cup of tea waiting at Betty's or John's. I fell into easy conversation with residents who regaled me with stories of their past lives and present worries, eager to suggest ways to make their community more convivial. With their help, I devised a programme that prioritised outdoor events – craft picnics, fire shows, summer extravaganzas – events where people could gather in large sociable numbers, where they could show off their skills in making, in performance, in being together. Sadly Jamie died well before his time, but he taught me a precious lesson: to go to where people are, to use what is around them and show them that their input is valued. He taught me that by helping people to make something memorable, unexpected and wonderful together social barriers can be dispelled and affection and trust accrued.

The intriguing thing about building a snowman is that we know, even as we roll up our first ball of snow, that what we are making will not last, that our achievement will be short-lived. Usually, we have barely finished tying a jaunty scarf around its throat before our snowman starts to subside and the small traces of its human-like character blur. But it is the opportunistic nature of snowman building that makes it irresistible.

And it is the unpredictability of snow, its inevitable thaw, that has attracted the sculptor and photographer Andy Goldsworthy to experiment with it. What began in 1977 in the hinterland of Leeds, when Goldsworthy photographed a large snowball he had made and the dark track of earth it left behind as it was rolled, led two years later to the artist gathering the last of the snow he found in rural Yorkshire and making a snowball from it, which he repositioned under a hedge, making of it a trespasser in a snow-free landscape. Three years after that, Goldsworthy created a summer snowball from snow he had collected and stored in his mother's deep freeze the previous winter. Its unexpected appearance in the Italianate Garden at Tatton Park in Cheshire both bemused and gladdened visitors, surprised to find time and seasons confused with a snowball materialising under a summer's sun. Next, he became interested in what a snowball gathered as it was rolled, how it retained the debris of the land its snow had covered, debris that became more evident, part of its story, as the snowball melted. For an exhibition in Glasgow in 1989, Goldsworthy purposefully filled eighteen snowballs with an assortment of foraged fragments: pine needles, flowers, pebbles, sticks. As each snowball thawed, it released its hidden treasure and the display changed from one of sentinel snowballs to a carpet of nature's bounty.

Goldsworthy has made snow arches, cleared patches of snow to disclose the black soil beneath and etch out patterns on heathered hillsides, and gouged out circles in hillocks of snow in Japan to create peephole vistas of the world beyond. He works largely with his bare hands and whatever tools he can improvise from his surroundings: branches, stones, twigs. His is a tactile as well as a visual art, with what he calls 'the shock of touch' as vital as his sense of sight. His handling of the powdery softness of snow, the sensation of it stiffening as he squeezes and sculpts it, the freeze of his fingertips, the often-harsh outdoor conditions, all of these are part of his creative process.

We can easily forget about the sensory nature of making; how intrinsic touch is both to our pleasure and our creative pursuit. Snow is especially sensual. We experience its cold as we compact it and press it into shape with our hands, as our palms smooth its surface. Its coldness numbs our fingers as we work, affecting their flexibility, making them tingle when warmth returns. Goldsworthy is alert to snow's sensory qualities. It is an essential aspect of his artistry: a creativity that is not only triggered by imagination but registered in physical sensation.

Goldsworthy is also interested in exploring nature's transmutability, in how the weather and the changing seasons can alter the look and feel of the materials he uses and the presence of his sculptures in their surroundings. What he creates is deliberately ephemeral, intentionally making sculptures that are vulnerable to decomposition even before they are completed. It lends his work an urgency that demands artistic focus. And in snow he finds an irresistible medium, transformable but mercurial. It is impossible to predict when and how his snow sculptures will alter as they thaw. This is art made fleetingly, claimed temporarily by an artist's hands and then returned to nature. Every winter we wait for the snow to come, never knowing if it will fall, how long it will last, whether there will be enough of it to allow us to make a snowman. And global warming is bringing a dramatic alteration in the distribution of snow. Those hitherto snowbound regions that rely on snowmelt for irrigation will, with its decrease, face snow droughts that will endanger harvests. Those regions predicted to experience heavier snowfalls will have to contend with life-threatening avalanches and snowdrifts and a catastrophic disruption to daily life. The days of our reliance on snow to bring us winter's recreational delights are numbered. And the joy of building snowmen is in danger of becoming a nostalgic memory as snowfall becomes ever more unpredictable across the world, as its appearance heralds danger rather than delight.

What is true of snow is also true of sand. Its forms are fleeting. We traipse out to sandy beaches with hope in our hearts and merriment on our minds, bringing chirping children who dangle buckets and spades expectantly in their hands. We know that the castles and moats we are about to construct, the sand sculptures and sand graves we will oversee, will be claimed, washed away by the incoming tide. But that does not deter us. We design, labour over, embellish and mould sand marvels that only we – and a few passers-by – will ever know existed. It is their very temporariness that enhances their making. These are personal, unique, familial acts of imagination that only we will experience.

And on the shores of today's seaside towns, people of all ages inscribe personal messages on sandy beaches – declarations of love and loss writ large – to be taken by the tide. This is writing that is physically exerting, stretching a hand that clutches a broken branch or a seaside spade as far as they can reach to pen the letters, moving up and down, across and below, to mark out text without obliterating what is already written. I have photographs of my own hand-scrawled messages written in the sand on seaside holidays with my family. It is their scale that is so pleasing: the vastness of the sandy canvas, the largeness of the letters, so big they can be read from the sky. It is liberating to know that the words we write will be erased by nightfall, submerged and then smoothed away by water's ebb and flow. And it is the very impermanence of what we etch in sand that has made it an important element of spiritual rituals for different indigenous groups around the world.

The transience of any symbolic imagery created in sand ensures that it only exists for the duration of a sacred rite. The Navajo Native Americans use coloured sand to lay down ancient patterns and motifs on the ground, coded designs that reference myths, visions and beliefs, chosen for their relevance to specific ceremonies. For them, once a drawing is completed, it becomes a living, sanctified entity, a portal through which benign spirits can enter and evil spirits depart. Whoever is in need of mental or physical healing is instructed to sit on the drawn, sanded patch of ground from dusk to dawn as a shaman calls upon spirits to effect a cure. As he does so, it is believed that the spirits residing within the sand drawing will absorb the negative forces that beset the sufferer. And when dawn breaks and the ritual has ended, the drawing is destroyed to ensure that the toxic energy it now contains will be discharged.

In Oaxaca in southern Mexico, where ancient traditions have become fused with Christian devotion, they make *tapete de arena* or a sand rug as part of their funerary rites. When the coffin is removed for burial, an artisan creates an elaborate holy image from sand, on the site where the coffin stood. It remains there for nine days of mourning, during which family and friends adorn it with flowers: roses for women and marigolds for men. It is thought that the making of the sand rug and the vigil that surrounds it aids the passage of the soul to heaven. After nine days the image is obliterated, the sand gathered up and taken with the flowers to the cemetery to be scattered over the grave.

Sand rugs have now become a feature of the Day of the Dead festivities, incorporating the iconography of grimacing skulls and dancing skeletons. They line the streets, decorate altars and are displayed outside cemeteries as a welcome to the souls who have departed.

Tibetan Buddhist monks also destroy the intricate and beautiful sand mandalas they have taken days, sometimes weeks, to create. For them, the act of making and the act of erasure are intrinsic parts of a devotional practice that encourages spiritual focus and harmony between the monks themselves and their temporal and celestial worlds. Before work begins, the site for each mandala is consecrated to mark it out as a sacred space. While the mandala is a visual metaphor for the universe and the cosmos, each separate section of it holds symbolic meaning. Its central circle signifies unity, while its four squares represent the core values of Tibetan Buddhism: love, compassion, joy and equanimity. And its creation is a meditation, amplifying the spiritual awareness of those who make it. The destruction of a mandala does not end its spiritual efficacy, rather the sand is taken to a river or the sea and scattered on the water as an offering to its residing spirits.

For some indigenous people, the tradition of writing in sand has evolved as a way to tell and curate ancestral stories, reassert beliefs and map human and supernatural territories. In Australian aboriginal culture, the Dreamtime or Dreaming, an ancient philosophy based on the interconnectedness of people, place, flora and fauna, is expressed through song, dance, rituals and art, including sand drawing. With no written language, those aboriginals living in Australia's desert and coastal regions convey and preserve their creation stories by marking them in sand images, using a complex vocabulary of symbols passed on through generations. For these artists the process of making rekindles an ancestral spirit energy and re-energises a living, if threatened, culture.

A similar practice takes place in the archipelago of Vanuatu, the cluster of eighty-three islands in the South Pacific, where islanders also create sand drawings to transmit knowledge and safeguard ancestral stories. Amongst a people with over 130 different vernacular languages, visual messaging is a vital way for common history and beliefs to be communicated. Through symbolic imagery that evokes myths, cosmology and song cycles, they protect and transmit a shared heritage. How the images are drawn is as important as what is depicted. A maker never lifts their finger from their drawing until it is complete. They trace lines of connection between the past and the present, between kinship groups, between natural and human worlds in one continuous line, ensuring that the starting point is also the end point. And they never revisit the edges of what begins as a gridded outline nor go over an existing line. Similar rules are evident in the sand drawings of the Chokwe people of Angola, who illustrate their proverbs, fables, riddles and ancient tales in visual ciphers, arranging a series of evenly spaced dots and weaving lines between them as their makers recite traditional tales of the Flying Bird, the Spider in the Web, the Stork and the Leopard and more.

Sand is not only used as a surface to write or draw on but is also utilised as a malleable material to mould into sculptures. Once, on an Italian beach, bored by sunbathing and too timid to tackle the strength of the incoming waves, I began to carve a mermaid, heaping up mounds of sand to sculpt her curved scalloped fish tail and generous breasts. I used a shell to gouge out the waves of her hair, a drag of seaweed to add a decorative garland around her head. When a trio of nut-brown elderly women in designer bikinis, teetering on high heels and glinting in jewellery strode past, I became uncertain, nervous that my rudimentary artwork would be considered somewhat risqué on a family beach. They stopped, gesticulated, laughed and exclaimed, transmitting their admiration and delight at my work-in-progress in excited Italian. They seemed pleased to have this icon of siren sexuality, albeit made from sand, lying languorously in their midst.

It was at the end of the nineteenth century that sand sculpture emerged as a seaside feature, with sand commandeered as a profitable creative resource. And it was an American, Philip McCord, who led the way in 1897, sculpting from sand a poignant statue of a drowned mother holding her dead child in her arms. The statue in Atlantic City won much admiration from passers-by, who showed their appreciation, so the story goes, by tossing coins at its feet. A new boardwalk industry began to flourish, with artists and artisans trying their hand at moulding sand into extraordinary sculptures, competing with each other, experimenting with the malleability and longevity of dampened sand.

Today's sand sculptors, both amateur and professional, are increasingly ingenious. Over recent decades, there have been experiments with different kinds of sand, with the ratios of sand to water, and even other additives to develop a modelling material that is more robust and impervious to the erosion of water and wind, lasting for months, even years. It enables professional sculptors to move beyond the seashore and install their creations in the lobbies of grand hotels, in city parks and shopping malls. Scenes from popular fairy tales and from history, and the architectural glory of hilltop castles and futuristic cities can all be realised in sand. But while the making of such monumental art from tiny sand grains – from something so fine that it slides through your fingers – is incredible, its displacement from the sea-salted shores to air-conditioned interiors seems counter-productive. The allure of sand lies in its natural environment, its natural form. The small, child-crafted sandcastle, crumbling to ruin on a sandy beach, has a far greater emotional pull.

It was the fragility and the mercurial nature of beach-made art, the inevitability of its erosion, that the director Danny Boyle – celebrated for such films as *Trainspotting* and *Slumdog Millionaire* and the mastermind behind the London Olympics opening ceremony in 2012 – harnessed to produce an emotive contribution to the commemorative events devised for the centenary of Armistice Day in 2018. Boyle's vision was to install sand-made works on thirty-two beaches along the length and breadth of Britain's coastline, transforming them into sites of remembrance. Into their sands were etched portraits of real people selected by the communities they had once belonged to, people who had served in the war, many of whom had lost their lives. With the technical and artistic support of the company Sand in Your Eye, each of the thirty-two communities collaborated in the creation of a sixty-metre-high portrait of an identifiable local hero whose life they had researched. They also stencilled and shadowed each shoreline with silhouettes of soldiers, nurses and munitions workers: military personnel laid out in serried ranks, others peopling the sand in ghostly outline. As each community gathered on the sand to stand beside the images of those who had given their lives or offered their service to safeguard the generations that followed, they amplified the event further by singing wartime songs, reciting war poems, writing personal messages on the beach and lighting lanterns in the dusk. And, as the tide came in closer to trespass on and erase the images of the long dead, a poem, 'The Wound in Time', specially commissioned from Carol Ann Duffy, then the Poet Laureate, echoed on every beach. Its final line – 'Your faces drowning in the pages of the sea' – was heard in a whip of wind as the tide crept over the portraits and gently washed them away.[4]

The film animator Jessica Langford, a longtime friend of mine, was inspired by the fluidity of sand and used it as her medium for her evocative short film, *The Gift*, commissioned by Channel 4.[5] Inspired by the Japanese legend 'Urashima Taro', *The Gift* tells the story of a young girl who rescues a seal. He carries her down into his undersea world where she is presented to the Fish Prince and, as a reward, he clothes her in a sealskin so she can stay with them. Initially enthralled by her life in the ocean's depths, in time the girl longs for home and asks to be taken back. As a parting gift the Fish Prince gives her a beautiful scallop shell. On her return home, the girl discovers that years have passed since she left. Her family is gone and her house has become derelict. Alone and bereft, she prises opens the scallop shell only to find herself by the sea again, changing into an old woman. But, as the waves wash over her, she magically metamorphoses into a young seal. The shell was a gift of time.

Jessica animated her film by drawing with sand on a light box directly under a fixed camera. Curious to know how she created not just the images, but their dreamlike drift from one to the other, I go to visit her. She shows me the small light box she used for the film: a sheet of glass, backlit and covered with finely grained sand. In their illumination, each grain of sand appears like a glimmering bead, its edges gleaming. She illustrates how, by adding more sand, she can darken her images to create shadow and better modulate mood and atmosphere. Ruffling her fingers through the sand, Jessica demonstrates how she can stir up waves or, with a fingertip, trace out a fish swimming in the water's curves. Then, smoothing her palm across the sea, she creates, in an instant, a wide expanse of beach that, with one simple movement, becomes moonlit as she clears a small circle of sand to make an orb of light.

The Gift lasts for only nine minutes and encompasses 7,000 sand drawings, twelve for every second. It took Jessica five years of planning, storyboarding, trialling camera set-ups and creating drawings for her to produce her haunting film. And it was through her exploration of the fluid quality of the sand itself that she determined how best to capture the illusion of constant movement, to realise her intent to create a mystical film whose scenes ebbed and flowed like visual tides. For her, it was a creative exploration of the singular expressiveness of sand, experimenting with the potential of its drift and its luminous quality to capture a fragile transience that is the essence of the story she wanted to tell and, as she came to realise, the essence of sand itself.

Our natural world offers us its resources as a gift. We do not need to buy creativity. We do not need sophisticated technical equipment to make something both glorious and gladdening. We collect our snow from a winter's earth, harvest sand from sun-warmed beaches, claiming these natural treasures as our own. And what nature offers us is not just its raw materials for creativity but a site of memory. While the things we make from its bounty might be short-lived, the memory of our making persists, as Andy Goldsworthy observes, 'remain[ing] in the places where they stood'.[6] We remember and can revisit the places where we made a snow statue or a turreted sandcastle. But the natural world is under threat; it may be, in the future, that the landscapes we hold in our mind's eye will retain ever fewer resources. For most of us snow will come less frequently, linger for less time and there will be less of it. Our beaches are becoming more polluted and, with sea levels rising, some areas of our coastline are in danger of being eroded. The joy that snow and sand bring is a fleeting delight but it is one that might become ever more ephemeral, tinged with nostalgia for what used to be a plenitude of pleasure.

5
Bubbles, Blow Books and Kites

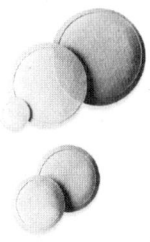

Then He proportioned him and breathed into him of His Spirit, and made for you the hearing, the sight, and the hearts
Qur'an, 32.9

The Amazing Bubble Man is appearing in a fringe event at the Edinburgh Fringe Festival and, as the reviews for his previous shows are euphoric, I buy a ticket in the hope of some unusual entertainment. The auditorium is packed and the babble of the audience's excitement pierces the air. I am surprised to see how many small babies are in attendance, lounging languorously on their parents' laps, seemingly impervious to the mayhem around them. But, as the house lights fade, there is a sudden, instantaneous and communal quietening as Louis Pearl, the Bubble Man himself, dives onto the stage in a warm rush of enthusiastic energy.

Louis Pearl is a consummate performer, confident in how to conduct the tempo and mood of his show. He begins intentionally slowly, creating his first bubble tentatively, trying to steady it as it emerges trembling from his cylindrical hoop. Surveying its wobble nervously, he waits for it to settle, before cautiously blowing it free. He and we watch as the translucent ball of rainbow light floats above his head like a contented sigh, following its path as it soars. We witness its end as it tragically, and inevitably, bursts. And, as we clap its ascent and mourn its pop, it feels as if life and death are being played out before our very eyes, both materialised in the fleeting delicacy and sudden demise of a single beautiful bubble.

For the next hour our belief in the fragility of bubbles is tested, however, as the Bubble Man makes soapy spheres that join one to the next to create ghosts of caterpillars that dangle from his hands, as he blows a bubble inside another bubble and blows both inside yet another bubble, as he fills a larger bubble with a community of bubbles, fills another with smoke and puts an entire child inside a bubble. Surely this is not possible. Surely a bubble has to burst on impact with another. Is it not destined to pop at the lightest of touches? And how is it possible for a bubble to bounce, be square, be filled with snow?

From time to time, a bubble does burst mid-act, and the Bubble Man tries his trick again, this time successfully, to be rewarded with ever more congratulatory applause. His extraordinary performance is accompanied by the auditory encouragement of us all, his audience: by our oohs and aahs, our clapping and sighing, our laughter and involuntary gasps. For the grand finale we are treated to an avalanche of bubbles, to an auditorium filled with their cascades and drifts. They rise and fall above and around us, until we are enveloped in their swirling, floating, crystal orbs. Fired up with a newly awakened sense of bubble possibility I, like many others, queue up to buy the unique, more robust, bubble elixir that Louis Pearl himself has concocted and the bubble dispensers that he has also invented, that promise more and bigger bubbles. When I get home, I introduce our dog Midge to my newly purchased toy and, as it pours out a crescendo of bubbles, I watch him leap and turn and snap and jump at this ever-unreachable waterfall of luminosity. That summer it becomes our satisfyingly unpredictable new delight.

When we dip a ringed wand into a bath of soapy water and breathe lightly on its coated surface we not only release a pretty iridescent sphere but produce a symbol of the fragility of life. It was the Roman scholar Marcus Terentius Varro who, in his *De Re Rustica*, written in the first century BC, coined the proverb *Homo bulla* (Man is a bubble).[1] And a number of Dutch artists of the Golden Age adopted his adage as a visual metaphor. The engraver Hendrik Goltzius entitled his 1594 depiction of a cherub blowing bubbles while leaning on a skull and bones, *Allegory of Transience: 'Homo Bulla'* and annotated his work with the words '*Quis evadet?*' (Who evades?) implying the death that awaits us all.[2] The 1651 self-portrait of the Dutch painter David Bailly is a lament on his mortality and shows the artist sitting by a table strewn with objects symbolic of loss: a spilt glass of wine, a spent candle, decaying flowers and fugitive bubbles.[3] And Jan Steen insinuated into his 1663 painting of merry revelry, *The Dancing Couple*, intimations of encroaching decay and death in the form of shattered shells, crumbs of bread, broken eggshells and, in the corner of the courtyard, a small boy blowing bubbles.[4]

While later French painters, most notably Édouard Manet and Jean Simeon Chardin, also chose to include bubbles in their work as visual allusions to the futility of pleasure and the inevitability of human decline, it was the painting *Bubbles* by the English artist John Everett Millais that became iconic.[5] This portrait of Millais' grandson, dressed in green velvet with his head haloed in golden curls, shows him clutching a bubble pipe and bowl, seemingly mesmerised by the diaphanous orb rising above his head: a tender portrayal of childhood innocence. But, if one examines the painting more closely, one realises that Millais also intended it to be a reflection on the brevity of life, with the insertion of a potted plant in full leaf standing in the shadows and an empty broken pot lolling by the boy's side. *Bubbles* was adopted as a marketing image for Pears soap, where it was touted as a representation of purity and, by association, cleanliness. Its advertisers disregarded its underlying poignant message and it was left to satirical cartoonists to reclaim its true intent. Millais' portrait was lampooned by them, and others in subsequent decades, to pass ironic judgement on the frailty of political power, with leaders such as Gladstone and the German Kaiser replacing Millais' grandson in a wry pastiche of the original painting.

The ephemerality of bubbles reminds us of the brevity of life, but bubbles are also optimistic. They emerge like human breath made manifest: breath that is infused with hope. Each time we blow away the thistledown of dandelion heads and make a wish, or we blow out our birthday candles and think about what we most want in life, when we blow up balloons for parties, we are investing in good fortune, petitioning unseen, unknown forces to bring us luck.

Ancient myths abound with tales of breath as a life-giver or life-destroyer. In Celtic mythological sagas are the stories of the Irish druid Mug Ruith, for whom breath was a weapon of power. Wearing a speckled mask of bird feathers, he traversed the skies, racing across the clouds in a winged flying machine. Assailed by enemy warriors, he simply blew on them to turn them to stone. When set upon by other malevolent adversaries, one puff of Mug Ruith's breath was enough to change his attackers into mirror images of himself, whereupon they attacked and murdered each other. In ancient Greece it was believed that breath was synonymous with the soul and the scriptures of Christianity, Islam and Judaism all record that God breathed life into man. Buddhists revere breath as a vital energy, the cradle of inner harmony, and Indian philosophers designate *prana* or 'life breath' as a universal energy that flows through our animate and inanimate worlds.

Breath is thought to kindle life, to be the wellspring of changing fortune. And it is unsurprising, therefore, that breath has been long exploited by magicians to add mystique to their conjuring. One of the oldest props in a conjuror's armoury was a 'blow book'. For those audiences in earlier centuries who gave greater credence to the ability of a conjurer to call upon supernatural powers, the blow book was not viewed simply as an entertaining illusion but as a remarkable feat, and it was the magician's breath that was thought to be the mystical agent of change.

A magician holds up a book to an audience and, rifling through it, shows that all its pages are blank. The book is closed, the magician blows on it, intones an abracadabra and reopens it to reveal, to the astonishment of his spectators, that the book is now filled with black-and-white illustrations. Again the book is closed, blown on once more and reopened, and, miraculously, its pictures have become coloured or even transformed. Not only can monochrome images turn mysteriously to colour, but sketches of comical caricatures can be changed in an instant to delicate drawings of flowers, or a portrait of a man can transmute to one of a woman – or a monkey, or an angel – at the flick of the conjuror's fingers and the blow of their breath. In the performance of a blow book it is the magician's breath – the brief audible hiatus – that marks the moment when the magic happens. It acts as a sensory distraction during which an audience's attention is diverted from what they see to what they hear.

The spellbinding act of a blow book's transformation has never failed to astound me. It seems so deliciously impossible. When I worked in repertory theatre, a magic show would sometimes be shoehorned in between the run of plays. And, as I worked backstage, I was able to closely observe magicians manoeuvre their props as they rehearsed. But I was never able to catch the trick of a blow book. When I discovered that its secret did not solely rely on a deft sleight of hand, nor on the manipulation of the book itself, but was dependent on the way the book was crafted, I became curious to try to make one myself. It posed an unusual creative challenge. I began with research. Knowing more about the history of blow books would, I felt, equip me with some insight not only into their physical charms but, more importantly, into the secret of their manufacture.

I discover that blow books, these marvels of illusionary entertainment, are centuries old. In 1550, the Italian polymath Gerolamo Cardano wrote in his compendium of Renaissance philosophy and knowledge, *De Subtilitate*, of how it was possible to present the illusion of 'changing forms in one and the same book, with the earliest one always vanishing'.[6] If it seems magical to me now, how must blow books have seemed in an age when books themselves were a rarity, when pictures were largely confined to church or court interiors. In the sixteenth century, a blow book would have been an extraordinarily exotic novelty, confounding spectators not only with its presence but with its wondrous, mercurial qualities.

Thirty years after Cardano wrote of them, it was an English Member of Parliament, Reginald Scot, who furnished us with an account of a blow book's showmanship, recording in his *Discoverie of Witchcraft* how an itinerant entertainer would brandish:

> . . . a booke, whereof he would make you thinke first that everie leafe was cleane white paper: then by vertue of words he would shew you everie leafe to be painted with birds, then with beasts, then with serpents, then with angels, &c:[7]

Scot also provided detailed instructions on how to create a blow book. His purpose was twofold. Rather than providing guidance to those interested in replicating a blow book's transformation, his primary intent was to expose the bogus nature of the trick and disabuse his readers of a conjuror's magical power. Writing at a time when there was increasing denunciation of practices that meddled with the darker arts, Scot had witnessed the rise of the zealous, often vindictive, crusade against those suspected of being involved in ungodly activities and in witchcraft – the majority of them women. The title page of his manuscript lists the principal transgressors. They include witches and conjurors, enchanters and soothsayers, alchemists and figure casters, and idolators and dreamers. With witch hunts gathering pace, Scot also hoped that his book would counter the growing witchfinder frenzy and stem the victimisation of innocent people by debunking the superstitions that underlay people's belief in sorcery.

Scot's directions on how to make a blow book, while complex, seem ripe for emulation. I decide to test them out, over four centuries later, to see if they still stand up to scrutiny. Not being familiar with the finished object, and dependent on instructions written with all the verbosity of sixteenth-century pedantry, I commence with a degree of uncertainty, but Scot's tutorial starts simply enough:

> Make a booke seven inches long, and five inches broad, or according to that proportion: and let there be xlix, leaves; to wit, seven times seven conteined therein.[8]

I duly fold enough sheets of paper to realise the requisite number of pages to fashion, as Scot commands me, a small booklet. Now that I have something satisfyingly concrete in my hands I feel more confident. I know that, for the blow book to work, its illustrated pages must be interspersed with others that are blank. Reading on through Scot's guidelines, I discover that the book's fore-edges are to be systematically and differently notched so that the blank, monochrome and coloured sections can be easily located and distinguished by the magician's touch: a ploy that will be imperceptible to the audience.

The magician will simply feel for the notches and free those pages that are to be shown while holding onto the others. But, while I understand the theory, the practicalities remain somewhat obtuse and I have to revisit Scot for enlightenment:

> ... so as you may cut upon the edge of each leafe six notches, each notch in depth halfe a quarter of an inch, and one inch distant ... .[9]

Maths has never been my strong point. It is, therefore, with an uneasy foreboding that I measure and mark the proscribed notches and, with more than a little trepidation, that I pick up my craft knife. Then, hesitating, unsure of the shape and the placement of each notch, I peruse Scot's text yet again:

> ... Cut off with a pair of sheares everie notch of the first leafe, leaving onlie one inch of paper in the uppermost place uncut, which will remaine almost halfe a quarter of an inch higher than anie part of that leafe ... .[10]

Now I am lost. Despite having the paper prototype of my blow book in front of me, I am bamboozled by too much mention of too many notches. Corroboration is needed and some reassurance. With both in mind, I enlist the help of my neighbour Adrian, a man much practised in making things; a man who, single-handedly, renovated an old school into a stylish home with polished-cement kitchen worktops and ensuite bathrooms. Armed with my book, pencil, craft knife, ruler and Scot's instructions, I seek out his advice. Adrian ponders on the problem and he ponders again. What is so admirable about Adrian is his considered approach to craftsmanship. He thinks his way through a process, teasing it out, rehearsing procedures in his head to arm himself with a strategy before he picks up a tool.

He examines my book, flicks through its pages, excises some notches, rearranges the book's layout and, eventually, leans back with a glint in his eye. He has caught the gist of its exacting mechanics. It is, he explains, all to do with pressure and placement. One hand grasps the book's spine at its fold while the other ruffles through its pages but, by holding it at specific points, with each section separated from the others by the nature and position of its notches, it is only those that are to be viewed which are freed. He demonstrates and it works. He suggests I make another book using coloured paper to signify each section. That way his hypothesis can be better tested. I go home and search out some coloured paper and begin to create another book, but I foresee that the making of this blow book is going to become a protracted process. My spirits dip at the thought of the coming hours spent measuring, marking and slicing off snippets of paper all over again.

Sometimes life is too short to take the long way round and the urge for unadulterated creativity has to be curtailed because of lack of time. So I cheat. I dispense with Scot's instructions and Adrian's guidance and order a custom-made blow book online. Then I copy the layout of my purchased template, emulating its notched pages with meticulous care. I assuage my artisanal guilt by resolving that my illustrations can at least pay a modicum of homage to the sixteenth century. I make my book, marking the pages designated as black-and-white with a 'B' and those that appear in colour with a 'C'. I check my version against the template and check it again, knowing that one wrong cut, one misplaced illustration, and the trick will be ruined. All seems perfect and, with its pages stitched together along its spine, the book is ready for illustrating.

My research has discovered only one extant sixteenth-century blow book, conserved in the New York Public Library. Referenced simply as Spencer Ms.180, the book was made in Italy and contains a series of small watercolour paintings depicting romantic encounters, court tournaments and diabolical apparitions. Its identification as a blow book came just twenty-five years ago, detected by Louise George Clubb, the Professor Emerita of Italian and Comparative Literature at Berkeley University in California. When she first saw the book, although delighted by its rare portrayal of Renaissance fun, she was intrigued by its peculiar construction and by its intermittently scalloped edges. Suspecting that it was more than a mere picture book, she invited the American magician Ricky Jay, an aficionado of the history of magic in general and an enthusiast of blow books in particular, to examine it. He confirmed that it was indeed a blow book, the oldest yet discovered.[11]

So, with Spencer Ms. 180 and the Italian Renaissance in mind, I unearth a series of postcards I once bought in Italy. They portray young gallants from the Siena *contrade*, or district clans, each sporting their emblematic costume, each carrying their heraldic banner. I choose seven and draw their outlines in black ink on separate pages, then redraw and paint them in colour on another set of pages, leaving the rest of the pages blank. My blow book is done. Somewhat nervously I pick it up and clutch its spine tightly in my left hand. Then with my right I flick through the pages from back to front. All are blank. I move my hand to the bottom outer corner and flick through again and am delighted and amazed when only the black-and-white images appear. I shift my hand to the outer top corner, flick through once more and, magically, they have metamorphosed into colour. And, while my blow book is but an echo of an historical illusion, I must confess that, even to my modern eyes, my rudimentary replica is as captivating and as mysterious as its original.

However, it is not just human breath that can be used to entertain us, but also the breath of nature: the wind. In past centuries, shaman used flutter books as part of their healing rituals. Inscribed with incantations, these were books that were placed in the open air for the wind to rifle through and transport the petitioning texts to the gods on high. The sacred writings on Tibetan prayer flags – flags that are symbolically coloured with blue for sky, white for air, red for fire, green for water and yellow for earth – contain 400 mantras. They are hung diagonally on high mountain passes and outside hilltop monasteries to flap in the breeze and create a wind-borne spiritual vibration through which positive energy can be distributed more widely, the natural surroundings purified, and compassion and wisdom dispensed. When the prayer flags disintegrate, they are left to be absorbed by nature and so continue their advocacy. In Buddhist temples, revolving prayer wheels are filled with thousands of individual paper petitions, and the daily turning of the wheels, the circulation and animation of air that such turning provokes, ensure that these human entreaties will be energised to merge the spirit of their prayers with the air itself.

As well as the ornately crafted wheels found in Buddhist temples, there are other versions sold on the streets of China. These are pinwheels, simply made, their spokes of sorghum stalks wrapped round with recycled paper. But they have the same intent as their more sophisticated equivalents: to let the wind catch them, spin them, help to blow away past and present worries, and carry the wishes whispered by their owners nearer to the gods. I encountered these wheels of good fortune when I visited China in the late 1990s and spied a seller on a street corner in Chengdu clasping a large paper column studded with whirling pinwheels. I bought one and, with his permission, took a photograph of him and his clutch of colourful whirring wheels, his treasure trove of incipient happiness twirling against a deep-blue sky. Now framed, the photograph hangs in our bedroom as a beacon of optimism. And it is easy to forget that, here in Britain, we have our own crafted hopes, in the form of hand-held pinwheels, or windmills as they are more commonly called, those blow toys bought at seaside towns and from tourist gift shops. But we rarely equate them with anything more than a plastic souvenir or a toddler's amusement. Yet their origin lies in deeper terrain, as dispersants of dreams.

But it is kites, the most beautiful and most majestic of sky-borne talisman, that best articulate human aspiration. Thought of in many cultures as the external souls of men and gods, kites dance across the sky like spirits. Whether diamond or delta, bird or bat, box or Bermuda, each variation of a kite – and they are manifold – intoxicates its operator. Watching the kite in your care and under your control – whether home-made or bought – lift into the air, tracking its chase of colours through the sky, is enthralling. It is like having a conversation with the wind. You coax your kite aloft with a breeze's encouragement but, once it rises, it is the wind that claims it. The challenge is to not relinquish it to the wind's dominance but to make it respond to your tug and steer. This is what you, and others, have designed your kite to do – to find speed and balance in the wind's gust. It is human skill and strength that makes this an equitable challenge. You and the wind encounter each other, not necessarily as competitors vying for the upper hand, but as collaborators searching out an equilibrium that will enable the kite to fly higher and travel further.

The history of kites reveals that they have a spiritual, social and emotional history that defies the simplicity of their design. In the centuries before powered flight, what lay above in the heavens was an enigma, a vast unknown territory where the gods – or other, possibly malevolent, spirits – resided. This belief in a distant otherworld, accompanied by a belief in the power of those above to direct the fortune and fate of humanity, made it necessary for people to not just placate but to petition unseen gods. Kites, with all their symbolic iconography, fashioned as birds or other creatures, were thought to act as envoys, taking people's prayers closer to the gods, who, pleased with their beauty, would be inclined to be compassionate. While humans remained tethered to the earth, they sent their kites up as spiritual representatives, risking their fate on unpredictable winds.

I have always harboured a love of kites. It is not an affection born of childhood nostalgia. I have no memories of running along a sand-hot beach, a kite string clutched taut in my outstretched hand, nor of me racing up some grassy knoll whooping with delight as my paper kite lifts into the sky. Quite the reverse. As a child I was firmly anchored on home ground: rooted to patterned carpets. My mother, tasked with round-the-clock childcare, had little time or inclination for outdoor activity. She believed in the safety of the interior and, to this end, decreed that I and my siblings should play indoors or, if school holidays found her over-wearied by maternal surveillance and arbitration, within the confines of the garden, where our quarrelsome squealing could reassure her of our continuing survival.

It was when I left home, in the early days of a more independent life, that kites began to impinge on my consciousness. Kite-making featured in one of the volumes of a comprehensive craft compendium that I purchased for a song in a local discount store. 'The Family Creative Workshop' was a series of American books aimed at hippies, instructing young social optimists in the making of a range of sustainable essentials required to furnish the new age: how to knot your own hammock, build a canoe, tie-dye a kaftan, fashion a fretboard dulcimer and make your own kite. At the same time, I was making regular visits to Berwick Street in London to search out affordable fabric for costumes during my theatre days. Berwick Street lies cheek-by-jowl with Chinatown, where painted parasols, gold-fringed lanterns and embroidered slippers hang outside small shops, alongside delicate bird and butterfly kites, in a riot of colour. In my late twenties I displayed some of these Chinese paper kites at home to add cheer to the walls of my less-then-salubrious bedsit. And, at some point, I made my own kite, gouging out notches in lengths of dowelling, crisscrossing and tying them together tightly before stretching red and yellow taffeta over their surface. I purchased the necessary kite accoutrements – a central T joint, slit end caps, standoff fittings and a fly line – from a specialised store in London and strung together a tail of jaunty red and yellow bows. As far as my memory serves me, the kite was never flown. Rather, I recall, it simply joined its Chinese counterparts on the wall to brighten my drab surroundings.

In later life, however, there was kite-flying: picnics with friends, with home-made kites burling in a summer's breeze. Then later, as parents on windswept beach holidays, watching our children race along the sand clutching kite strings that threatened to pull them into the sky while, above them, trails of bright colour swooped and rose like exotic birds flying on a slipstream. Later still, I was commissioned to create some large-scale kites for a local festival. I appliquéd a mythological Celtic bird, its contours edged in gold and stitched tongues of dancing red and orange flames. I sewed a hedgerow of spring leaves and embroidered a gossamer cobweb with tiny silver insects trapped in its filaments. When they were launched and were caught in a shaft of sunlight, the kites appeared as luminous as stained glass, gliding upwards and onwards like magnificent messengers sent to entertain the gods. From the simple kite I first made with its snaking tail of red and yellow bows, to the later, larger kites I crafted that carried pictures up into the sky, it is the romance of kites that beguile, the knowledge that they can travel further than we could ever go. While they sit quiet and still on the table as we make them, in the sky they can dance, twisting and twirling, choreographed by a mercurial wind.

Kites have become ubiquitous throughout the world, enjoyed for individual and community sport. With a chronology spanning more than 2,000 years, their story, far from being a colourful thread in the history of children's play, is one that belongs principally to an adult world of religious ritual and adventure, scientific experiment and exploration, warfare and ancestral worship. In ancient times, most particularly in Asia, kites were despatched as prayers and portents, as supplicants to invisible gods and as talismans to dispel misfortune, bestow blessings and invoke rain. And, in some cultures, the spiritual agency of kites has persisted.

Kites have a valued place in Japanese culture, where there are hundreds of different varieties of kites, reflecting the rich diversity of family, village and regional identity, with designs made distinctive by their shape, method of construction, use of colour and their purpose. Forbidden by the shogun government, which ruled from the twelfth to the mid-nineteenth century, to depict real people or events, kite-makers adopted the practice of employing bold, dramatic colours to capture the dynamism of fictional samurai warriors, kabuki characters, mythical heroes and, increasingly, manga personalities. There are a plethora of Japanese kite-making and kite-flying rituals that have evolved over the centuries. In some regions the grandfather of a newborn baby makes a kite as a protection, painting onto it the face of a legendary god or an auspicious creature with a fearsome expression as a deterrent to evil spirits. The kite is hung above the child's cradle until they are old enough to be taken with their family to launch the kite together in a collective hope for future good fortune. It is thought that the higher the kite rises, the more it prevails in a forceful wind, the more successful and stronger the child will be.

On Mishima Island in the Sea of Japan, the kite made for an infant depicts a demon, often with a tassel attached to his eye. Denoting a tear, it acts as a talisman to ensure that the child will grow up to be sympathetic. In farming regions, at harvest time, a stalk of rice is attached to the kite's string in gratitude to the bountiful gods, in anticipation that they will appreciate the gift and ensure a good harvest the following year. Meanwhile, the *daruma* kite is painted with the image of a Buddhist monk and flown with a specific request in mind. Only when the wish is granted does its kite-maker paint in the monk's eyes. A similar practice accompanies some of the kites the Japanese make for their New Year celebrations, flown to disperse hopes for the coming year amidst the deities of the air. Only at the year's end – and only if the gods have realised a maker's dreams – does its creator put the finishing touches to their kite.

While the majority of Japanese kites are celebratory – made to welcome a new baby, to mark the New Year, to give thanks for a good harvest – some have a more sorrowful intent. On the island of Hachijo to the south of Tokyo, at the site of the suicide of the twelfth-century archer and warrior Minamoto no Tametomo, his life and death are immortalised through a kite flown in his name. And a kite, illustrated with the portrait of an old man weeping, commemorates the persecution of the Ainu people, made as both a lament for a nearly extinct culture and a way to conserve its history.

In Korea, people also make kites for newborns, with the child's name and date of birth written on the kite's bamboo frame, accompanied by blessings for its future. But while, as in Japan, the family go together to share in its launch, once set aloft this kite's line is cut so that it flies free to seek the gods' protection and secure an auspicious life for the baby. Korean kites, inscribed with people's past travails and future dreams, are also released at the lunar New Year, with their tails tied with twists of flammable paper. Once ignited, the kite's string burns to ash as it rises to gain the attention of the gods. Should it fail to fly or fall to the ground it cannot be claimed for fear that whoever takes possession of it will inherit the cares of the past. A similar ritual exists in China. Known as the Day of Broken Kite Strings, it is part of the ancestral rites of remembrance, when kites contain messages of family fealty to safeguard the wellbeing of the deceased in the afterworld.

Ancestors are also remembered through kite-making and flying in Guatemala when, for 1 November, All Saints' Day, and 2 November, All Soul's Day, people make *barriletes* – massive kite wheels fashioned from thousands of pieces of tissue paper. Appearing like giant mandalas, the kites are created to honour the dead and are inscribed with messages and decorated with a collage of images that relate family and community history. Increasingly, they also bear commentaries and slogans about communal social issues such as pollution, corruption or inequality.

As well as being used in ritual ceremonies and traditional family celebrations, kites have also been a source of simple, recreational pleasure, sent up into the sky as joyful messengers to please the gods and those who witness their trembling ascent. Some are designed to offer aural diversion to go with their visual appeal. Japanese kites are often fixed with an *unari*, a simple bamboo cylinder with holes that makes a low, murmuring sound in the wind, much like a wind flute. The Arabic writer Al-Jahiz, born in Iraq in AD 776, tells of the paper kites adorned with tiny bells that tinkled in the wind as they flew. And during the Five Dynasties (AD 907–60), the imperial Chinese craftsman Li Ye is said to have devised a musical kite that was furnished with a bamboo flute to fill a summer's sky with drifting melodic harmony. Devising greater audible pleasure in kites has continued with the addition of whistles, hummers, buzzers and other music-making elements to amplify their presence and that of the wind as they play with each other in the heavens.

The history of kites, however, reveals their deployment not solely as wondrous delights but as instruments of war and divination. In China, in 200 BC, General Han Hsin flew a kite over the ramparts of a city he was besieging to gauge the necessary length of the underground tunnel he planned as a secret passageway through which his troops might breach his enemies' defences. It was a successful strategy. And when Emperor Wu, the seventh emperor of the Han Dynasty, found himself and his people trapped during a siege of AD 549, he commanded his craftsman to fashion him a bird kite with its wings inscribed with pleas for rescue. The kite was to be flown to his allies, but it is chronicled that the kite was so birdlike that the emperor's enemies shot it down before it could reach its destination.

In Europe, kites were used as predictors of battles, with a kite's continuing flight auguring victory and its swoop denoting uncertainty. They were also deployed as martial weapons. In 1405, in his manual of warfare, *Bellifortis*, the German military engineer Konrad Kyeser described and illustrated what he called 'a flying dragon'.[12] This vast, winged dragon kite was made from red silk and linen, with a fearsome head of bulging eyes and sharp-toothed jaws, its tail undulating in multi-coloured streamers. It was carried into battle by three horsemen, two of whom lifted the dragon high on poles while the other held a reel of cord that was unravelled as the trio rode towards their advancing adversaries, to terrorise the advancing army. This vision of an unearthly monster was made even more terrifying by the dragon kite's *pièce de résistance,* a bottle of mineral oils secreted in its mouth that was ignited by a mechanism on the kite line to release fire and smoke from its gaping grimace. A century later, the Italian mathematician, physicist and astronomer Giambattista della Porta wrote a guide to scientific experiments in which he described how to make what he called a 'fire-drake'. His accompanying sketch of a man with a diamond kite seems innocuous enough were it not for della Porta's directions that its tail was to be packed with gunpowder and tied with multiple crackers so that it exploded in the sky to frighten all those who witnessed its conflagration. Della Porta also advocated tying a lantern to a kite's tail to dupe onlookers and make them believe that an inauspicious comet had arrived in their midst.[13] This book was to be the inspiration for a young, inquisitive Isaac Newton. As a boy, he followed della Porta's instructions and duly knotted a lantern to the tail of his kite, which, when he launched it one dark night, convinced his petrified neighbours that they were being visited by a portent of doom.

Kites themselves can be combatants in aerial battles and there is a long history of flying fighting kites, particularly in Asia. These are kites whose lines have been coated in abrasive powder made from broken glass or porcelain, or even inserted with small blades. Men and boys from local neighbourhoods compete with each other to keep their kites aloft while their opponents try to cut their lines. It is a skilful and popular sport with widespread participation. One kite battle that draws large crowds takes place in Hamamatsu in Japan where, for nearly 500 years, neighbourhood teams have warred with each other, flying locally designed, locally made kites, each calligraphed with their children's names. These are kites of community, family, identity and place. Today, over 150 neighbourhoods compete and thousands gather to witness the spectacle. In Korea, the lunar New Year is the kite-fighting season and its heavenly battles attract thousands of spectators. In Indian cities, and over the skyscrapers of Thailand, they fly their kites from urban rooftops in similar battles. The popularity of the sport has spread but, increasingly, there are concerns about safety for those who participate. Some countries have banned kite-fighting altogether, while others have restricted when and where kite-fighting can take place. And more and more, kite-flyers are being encouraged to settle for forcing kites down or line-touching as a less dangerous approach to elimination.

In Afghanistan, kite-flying was banned altogether by the Taliban between 1996 and 2001, deemed a distraction from Islamic devotion. It triggered the novelist Khaled Hosseini to extend a short story he had written into a novel. *The Kite Runner* was a controversial, if award-winning, encapsulation of the tragic and tumultuous trajectory of Afghanistan's recent history. It tells of the relationship between two boys, their strengths and frailties revealed through their escapist kite-flying. In the book kites become a metaphor for hope and loss and, in its later chapters, a symbol of reclamation.[14] And when the Taliban lost its stronghold over the country, one of the most poignant signs of liberation was the sight of kites once again billowing in the skies. Since the Taliban regained control in 2021, some kites are still being flown but not with the same exuberance and only in the hands of men and boys. Kite-flying events are now organised outside of Afghanistan to register support for the thousands of displaced Afghan refugees and solidarity with those still there, particularly women, who are now forced to live restricted lives under Taliban rule.

Elsewhere, however, kite-flying is still a flourishing recreational activity. Weifang in China is dubbed the 'kite capital of the world' and it attracts thousands of people to its annual International Kite Festival, a showcase of traditional and innovative kite design, both technical and artistic. With over fifty countries represented, Weifang's festival promotes and conserves the rich diversity of kite-making not only through the kite-flying events themselves but through workshops, exhibitions and a dedicated kite museum that has now been established in the city. It is kites that have become the main source of Weifang's economic regeneration through its expanding kite industry, with an estimated 600 companies and thousands of local people earning their living through some aspect of kite production.

*

In Europe and America, kites were late to make an appearance and their function has been, generally, more prosaic, with kites recruited as scientific tools to measure distance or air temperature, to experiment with electrical charge or to test the possibilities of accelerated travel and human flight. In 1752, Benjamin Franklin, the American inventor and political philosopher, used a kite to test his theory on how to harness electricity. Tying the string of a silk kite with a metal key and conductive wire, he flew his kite during a thunderstorm and was delighted when it attracted an electrical charge from the storm, perceived as a visible spark. As he related, this was an experiment through which 'Spirits may be kindled'.

And it was the potential of kites that, in the nineteenth century, exercised the mind of a Bristol schoolteacher and Methodist preacher, George Pocock. He envisioned a future in which kites might become an expedient and inexpensive way to propel the horseless carriage. For his first experiment, he sent his young son hurtling down the snowbound slopes of Bristol Downs on a sledge drawn by a kite. The adventurous voyage was gleefully recorded by Pocock in an 1827 treatise in which he documented the trial: 'on letting go of the string, the sledge was instantly hurried away so unexpectantly, and with a velocity so great, that all attempts to overtake it were quite fruitless'.[15] He made no mention of his son's response to the experience. Instead, heartened by this success, he sacrificed his eleven-year-old daughter Martha to the scientific cause and, when he sent her up into the sky in a wicker chair tied to a kite, he was delighted to watch her sailing over the Avon Gorge, over 30 metres above the ground.

By 1822, George Pocock was ready for his first demonstration of kite-drawn travel. By then he had invented what he called a 'charvolant', a lightweight, large-wheeled carriage drawn by two huge kites with a T-bar acting as an improvised steering control. His family were, yet again, dragooned as guinea pigs. George and his wife, with some of their eleven children, sped out of Bristol in their carriage at the extraordinary speed of 20mph, managing to overtake and outstrip the stagecoach travelling from Bristol to Marlborough. They arrived at their destination twenty-five minutes ahead of the coach despite it being given a fifteen-minute head start. George was jubilant, vindicated, and he swiftly patented his device.

Five years later, he published his treatise suggesting that kites should be employed not only to accelerate carriage travel but to speed the voyages of ships, and that kites could be utilised to convey heavy goods up heights and down rivers. Despite Pocock's kite-driven charvolant winning the approval of King George IV and the enthusiasm of sportive young bloods, it never attracted commercial investment. An 1828 London newspaper was doubtful of its future, drily observing: 'As the thing stands, what has been done is amusing and displays great ingenuity, but we rather doubt the possibility of applying the power to any purposes beyond that of diversion.'[16] But George Pocock remained undeterred and stayed loyal to its inventive charms. He continued to use his charvolant for intrepid family excursions, bowling down the streets of Bristol and circumnavigating its neighbouring environs until his death in the 1840s, convinced, as he declared in elegiac prose, that:

> This mode of travelling is of all others the most pleasant: privileged with harnessing the invincible winds, our celestial tandem playfully transpierces the clouds, and our mystic moving car swiftly glides along the surface of the scarcely indented earth; while beholders, snatching a glance at the rapid but noiseless expedition, are led to regard the novel scene as a vision rather than a reality.[17]

At the start of the twentieth century, Pocock's experiments were followed by those of the Italian-born, London-based engineer and inventor Guglielmo Marconi. In 1901 he successfully used a sail kite attached with a wire antenna that was tethered to the ground to pick up the first audible transatlantic radio signal from his base in Newfoundland, Canada, sent from his team in Cornwall, England. In the same decade that Marconi was trialling wireless transmission, the American showman and aviator Samuel Franklin Cody was also experimenting with kites to see if they could be used to more easily detect enemy artillery, tow boats and lift human beings. A contemporary pamphlet advertises the Cody War Kite as suitable for signalling and reconnoitring purposes, 'constructed of a special silk which is practically invisible when flying high'.[18] And today, kite-makers are embracing technological advances, using LED lighting and 3D digital printing to orchestrate spectacular sky ballets that seduce the eye and fill the air with sound. Through their inventiveness kites can travel faster and higher and be synchronised to fly together in choreographed, syncopated, visual harmony.

But, increasingly, the visual impact of kites is being rivalled by drones, those propelled automata that can cluster and be programmed to create astonishingly mesmeric images in the sky. One recent New Year's Eve, a friend sent me a short video of a drone display over one of the Scottish isles. I watched, transfixed, as a graceful stag leapt over the hills, silhouetted by a star-studded sky. It was both beautiful and memorable: technology married with pictorial poetry. And it seemed to me then that kites might be relegated to nostalgia, considered to be mere quaint relics as other, more mechanical means are invented to excite our visual appetite. And yet, for all their beauty, for all their poetic expression, what is lacking from drones is both the personal and the hand-made appeal of traditional kites. They are devoid of the spiritual metaphor that has underwritten the voyages of kites to the heavens above. Through history, it has been kites that have conveyed the fears and aspirations of the human race, that have sought connection to what lies beyond us.

Blow books and bubbles, prayer wheels and kites, devised to harness human breath and the air around us to create moments of wonder. And, as the bubble bursts, the prayer flags disintegrate and our kites tumble from the sky or are sent heavenwards when their string is released, we relinquish them to the elements, glad of their brief existence which, for a short while, was glorious.

6
Dressing Up

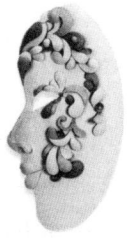

Clothes make a statement. Costumes tell a story
Mason Cooley

When I was young we had a dressing-up box. It was not strictly a repository of fancy dress but rather it contained a variety of clothes that because of their oddity or glamour were deemed worth keeping. I only remember a couple of fancy-dress outfits. One was a voluminous, brightly coloured clown's onesie that my father had worn for a rag day at his university when, clad in outlandish costumes, students cavorted through the streets of Glasgow collecting money for charity. Us children viewed his costume with suspicion as it seemed highly unlikely to us that our father – a sober-suited accountant, albeit with a twinkle in his eye – could ever have worn such a flamboyant get-up. There was also a beautiful eighteenth-century costume which, again, had belonged to him as a boy. It had been made by my grandmother, in the days when my father had graced the stage in dance routines that showcased the pupils of the dancing school he attended. Its jacket and breeches of cream brocade were exquisitely sewn and its velvet waistcoat, collar and cuffs seemed to us inordinately luxurious. I have a photograph of me wearing it once while pretending to saw a violin.

In truth, we rarely raided the dressing-up box or tried on the clothes it contained. Other items, such as a soft crêpe de chine blouse, which had tiny, covered buttons running from its wrists to its elbows, and a beautiful black evening gown whose skirt fell in soft tiers of frilled tulle were brought out from time to time, exuding a faint whiff of expensive perfume. They were exclaimed over, and our small fingers would feel out the cool of the crêpe de chine and its run of dainty buttons or fluff up the undulating flounces of the evening gown, but we never wore them. We understood instinctively that these were precious, the stuff of memories too intimate to share, our mother's private keepsakes. As we grew older, the contents of the dressing-up box were dispersed and disappeared bit by bit. They were replaced with serviceable blankets and crisply folded cotton sheets. But the dressing-up box has stayed in my mind as a remembered delight. Lifting its lid meant entering a world from before we were born, perhaps even before my parents were married. It was like looking through a small crack in their lives and glimpsing their younger, distant selves.

The wonderful thing about a dressing-up box is its randomness. It is a collection of clothes and accessories that have myriad stories stitched within their seams. Our children had one when they were small and, even now they are grown, remnants of it remain like flotsam of past, costumed fun. There is an array of wigs inherited from community pantomimes and a splendid velvet cap'n'bells headdress I made for Charlie when he acted the fool at a medieval banquet. There is the faded kilt that my father-in-law wore as a child, a skirt my daughter made on my sewing machine when she was about nine years old, a lace cravat, and a fairy dress in diaphanous rainbow hues with misshapen wings. The day my ten-year-old daughter announced to her twin brother that she was too old for dressing up, he was crestfallen. Without someone to share in the adventure of sartorial invention, to make incredulous at some imaginative disguising, his dressing up was robbed of fun. Gone forever was the mutual joy of rummaging through dressing-up paraphernalia and pulling out satin shoes or feather boas, tartan boots or sequinned scarves. Gone, too, was the thrill of wrapping himself in yards of silver net or donning a wig of golden curls, of seeing himself and his sister transformed into sparkling beings festooned in the stuff of fancy. I mourned as well. I used to love the sight of them traipsing downstairs in their absurd concoctions, tripping over their trailing trains of majesty and clattering through the kitchen in my cast-off high heels. For my son it meant the end to lace and velvet, to frills and fairy wings. And that made me, and him, sad.

There are myriad reasons why people dress up and a plethora of traditions and occasions that call for costumes: village fêtes and miners' galas, children's parties and charity collections, historical re-enactments and masquerades, fancy-dress balls and stag or hen dos, religious processions and carnival parades. And, across the world, there are diverse regional or national costumes that are worn to mark a distinct identity, to celebrate heritage and history. Some have become so recognisable that they act as national identifiers – the French beret, the Japanese kimono, the

Dressing Up

Scottish kilt – costumes that are often appropriated as fancy dress. All present the opportunity to throw off the everyday, prosaic self and adopt a more exotic persona. Dressing up is a collective, gregarious entertainment that demands an audience and fellow participants. Crossing the boundaries of class, culture and gender, costumes allow us to adopt fictional versions of ourselves. Yet, while it is transformative, it is also ephemeral: a fleeting alteration.

Fancy dress has its roots in pagan and shamanic rituals where it was believed that evil spirits could be despatched and human control asserted through unsettling disguises. Bizarre masks, flamboyant headdresses and tattered or beribboned, twirling costumes were all designed to signal a menacing opposition to interfering spirits. A trace of these older rituals lingers in the celebration of Halloween, All Saint's Eve, when malevolent forces are dispersed by encountering mirror images of themselves: humans dressed as ghouls and ghosts, devils and diabolic creatures. Guising, or trick or treat – the custom of visiting people's homes in disguise to perform a turn in exchange for a treat, usually sweets – originated in the medieval mummers' antics, when revellers would dress up as strangers and descend on people's homes or even grand palaces to challenge those present to a game of dice. The 'strangers' would entertain their hosts with a dance and be rewarded with hospitality: a convivial exchange. Today's Halloween still preserves the idea of barter and its connection to the spirit world, albeit that its costumes are inspired by the macabre, by characters in horror films, rather than fear of the supernatural. Our children demanded tomato-sauce-stained shirts for their Halloween excursions and went out dressed as

A Dead Schoolgirl or A Stabbed Boy, as a Corpse Bride or a blood-splattered zombie.

Dressing up has always been an intrinsic part of traditions that mark significant transitions: the old year to the new, winter to spring. May Day would bring a May Queen and her attendants prettified in white frocks and flowered garlands. Shrovetide, the Lenten eve, warranted revelry, periods of unabashed irreverence when, for a short while, social upheaval was permitted. At Shrovetide the lowest strata of society were allowed to assume the place of their betters and authorities could be ridiculed. Men would dress as women and women as men, the church could be lampooned without censure, and royalty and politicians satirised. As part of the hedonistic mayhem, social and sexual inhibitions were set aside. What was ignited was disruption and excess, a wanton release from constraint.

All such festivities demanded costumes, and the making of costumes has remained a constant in popular culture, although those created for parties, local pantomimes and town pageants now are very different from what was requisitioned for the elite fancy-dress balls of earlier centuries. People with restricted budgets and skills have always had to resort to their own ingenuity and concoct fancy dress from what could be easily and inexpensively rustled up: recycling old clothes and making judicious use of crepe paper and card. The wealthy, however, had no such constraints. With access to in-house seamstresses and couture houses, they could easily commission replicas of sumptuous historical or fictional fashion. But austerity in Britain following the First World War saw improvisation in costume-making become not just a necessity but a source of pride. A magazine of the 1920s and 30s, *Leach's Fancy Dress*, advocated the most basic of materials for costumes and also reflected the reality of working-class people's lives with suggested themes such as Pawnshop and Sacked.[1] By 1937, the royal photographer Cecil Beaton, writing on fancy dress in *Vogue* magazine, was advising that:

> Nowadays an effective grandeur can only be legitimately achieved with everyday utensils, and materials being used for purposes for which they are not meant. Steel wool pot-cleaners, egg-beaters, egg-separators, dishcloths, tin moulds and patent hangers all make excellent costume trimming.[2]

I remember when our twins were at primary school, the dread of their school projects and the costumes they required. The first we encountered was a project on the Romans. For its finale, a chariot race, the children were to arrive suitably clad in Roman outfits with their chariots in tow. Wedded to the idea that the creative use of basic materials would introduce my children to the transformative possibilities of the mundane world, I fashioned their Roman tunics from a length of old nondescript, beige curtain lining that I had found lurking in a cupboard. Chariots were constructed from large cardboard boxes, sprayed with silver. Their *pièce de résistance* was the addition of an eagle, the symbol of the Roman legionary standard, that we made from card and pasted onto the front of each chariot. Little did we know that as we were running up their simple tabards and gluing down our makeshift emblems, other parents were availing themselves of purple velvet to serve as sumptuous cloaks, creating armour from silver hand-scalloped card, and welding chariots of galvanised steel in their garden sheds. After their ignominious race across the school field, with their cardboard boxes flapping in the wind and crumpling in the rain, we realised that, if our children were not to appear unloved and uncared for, we would have to up our game.

And yet we resisted. It felt at odds with the spirit of joyful making, the triumphant recasting of the everyday into something unexpectedly and gloriously make-believe. As their years at primary school rolled on, we did what was necessary to send them off dressed as evacuees in the Second World War, as passengers on the ill-fated *Titanic* and as terrorising Vikings, but we kept things as simple as we dared. It was the local pantomime, however, that tested even my making skills to their limit. For it, costumes had to be created that suited the characters played by each of my neighbours. Not only that, but they had to be designed to enhance their physical appearance, disguising the girth of a robust farmer and inventing the waist of an elderly matron.

A consummate needlewoman, even I turned petulant when faced with the frustration of one of the Ugly Sisters' final costumes for our production of *Cinderella*. It had been conceived as a vast crinoline, layered with unopened packets of multi-flavoured crisps, an idea that seemed hilarious at the time of its conception but which quickly turned sour when I began the torturous process of its manufacture. When gluing, Sellotaping and stapling on the crisp packets proved futile, I turned to my sewing machine. The first row was sewn down easily enough, the second proved a little more troublesome, the third trickier still and the fourth impossible. Exasperated and defeated, I am ashamed to say that I hurled the costume across the room, a stream of expletives following in its wake. Once I had calmed down, I did retrieve it and grimly stitched the remaining packets on by hand, cursing each and every one of them. However, by the time the Ugly Sisters rustled forward to take their bow in front of an enraptured audience, my fury had long since ebbed and I rejoiced in the glorious foolishness of a ridiculous costume.

The sartorial challenge of school projects and local pantomimes pale into insignificance when compared to the elaborate costumes that carnivals demand, where visual imagination and structural ingenuity are key. In the Christian calendar, carnival heralded a final fling before the deprivations of Lent took hold. It was linked to other, more ancient traditions such as the Roman Saturnalia, the hedonistic festivities in honour of the god Saturn, and such medieval capers as the Feast of Fools and Twelfth Night. Over the centuries, carnivals have become popular throughout the world, customised to suit different cultures.

The Carnival of Venice can be traced back to the Middle Ages. When Austria took control of Venice in the nineteenth century, however, the carnival was forbidden, deemed too licentious for moral sensibilities. It was eventually revived in the 1970s by an Italian government keen to boost Venice's cultural appeal, and through it encourage economic regeneration. Venetian carnival costumes are exaggeratedly opulent, dramatising, even caricaturing, the elaborate court dress of yesteryear. Women wear vast flounced crinolines trimmed to excess in gold braid and jewels. Fanciful wigs harbour ribbons, flowers, feathers and diadems, nestled in white-powdered curls like perching birds. Sleeves are padded, slashed, puffed and frilled and ornamental accessories – fans, reticules and gloves – are de rigueur. Men sport brocaded and embroidered waistcoats, tricorn feathered hats, luscious velvet cloaks and tumbling lace cravats.

And then there are the masks, made from leather, porcelain, glass or papier-mâché, the trademark of the carnival. Originally designed to enable all classes to mingle freely and for participants to indulge in transgressive behaviour or covert assignations while retaining their anonymity, they have developed their own distinct visual code. Each style of mask has a separate symbolic meaning. The *moretta*, a small, plain black mask, traditionally made of velvet, is reserved for women. It has no mouth hole, allowing its wearer to remain silent and maintain their mystique. The *gnaga* resembles a cat with cup-shaped ears and vertically slit eyeholes. Usually highly ornate, it only covers the upper part of the face and was principally adopted by homosexuals who, thus disguised, escaped censure. The *bauta* mask is also worn by men. With an oval framing the face and a projected nose that covers the mouth, it not only obscures its wearer's facial features but distorts their voice to secure greater anonymity. Other masks are borrowed from the Italian commedia dell'arte to match a costumed persona.

About three million people flow through the narrow alleyways of Venice during its carnival to glimpse the splendour of its revellers. Some Venetians wear costumes that have been conserved from past centuries and past carnivals.

Visitors can commission or hire costumes from one of the city's ateliers to ensure that they are suitably dressed for their attendance at one of the carnival's many magnificent balls, where dressing up in historical costume is obligatory. Despite the expense of ball tickets – over £1,000 for some – and the additional cost of costumed finery, the romance of participating in the Venice Carnival continues to seduce.

Venice's annual carnival might have the monopoly on historical glamour and grandeur but other carnivals – those in Rio de Janeiro, New Orleans, Basel and Goa among others – are as exuberant, with costumed excesses of vibrant colours, elaborate headdresses and multitudes of sequinned, feathered and beaded adornments to create riotous spectacles. These are carnivals as a form of mass theatre, with participants adopting the role of street performers. Open to all, they heighten the celebration of individual and group identity as ebullient expressions of visual, communal energy. Many also bolster the presence of those habitually marginalised from centralised activity, providing them with a rare place on the public stage, as with the multicultural carnival of Trinidad and Tobago, shaped by centuries of colonialisation. France, Spain and Britain brought an influx of enforced labour from Africa, China, India and Portugal to the Caribbean and they also imported the pre-Lenten Catholic tradition of carnival. It was, however, an event reserved for the privileged, with enslaved and indentured workers forbidden from taking part. It was not until their emancipation in 1834 that the wider community of Trinidad and Tobago could participate in the festivities; when they did, they seized upon carnival as a medium through which to express their own diverse identity and their newly forged liberty. Extravagant costumes mimic fabulous, exotically plumaged birds, with vividly coloured wings and headdresses. These are costumes as affirmations of freedom. The bejewelled and sequined bikinis worn in parades, the ropes of scintillating, iridescent beads that are draped over the dancing participants, are not gaudy displays of abandonment but rather theatrical statements of liberation. It is through their costumes that the people of Trinidad and Tobago lay conspicuous claim to the city streets, filling them with a dazzle of colour and the symbolic glitter of light.[3]

The Carnival of Cayenne in French Guiana was also imported by colonisers and also excluded enslaved people, but they defiantly organised their own event that referenced their indigenous culture and it is this carnival which has persisted. Participants dress up as mystical gods and supernatural spirits, personifications that help them to keep faith with a distant land and conserve a fragile heritage. The trajectory of the Notting Hill Carnival in London, however, has a different genesis. Those Black Caribbean immigrants who made their way to Britain in response to the post-war appeal for labour found themselves confronting racism and exclusion from the country's mainstream culture. When race riots broke out in 1959, Caribbean talent was showcased on television in an attempt to breach the divide between the Caribbean and British communities. In the 1960s, that initiative became fused with another scheme, to foster community unity through organising an outdoor platform for the performing and visual arts of the Caribbean and Black diaspora.

With a parade that now stretches for nearly five kilometres and attracts an audience of over two million, the Notting Hill Carnival is a joyous, spectacular event with extraordinary costumes and heart-pounding music: a manifestation of local vitality. But it has maintained an undercurrent of protest and resistance expressed sometimes overtly in campaigning placards or covertly in its exuberant volatility. And an undercurrent of racial tension still exists. The event continues to be disrupted by violent incidents, in confrontations between participants and the police. There are still multiple arrests. And increasingly there are calls for it to be abandoned. But Leroy Logan, a former superintendent in the Metropolitan Police and chair of the Black Police Association, writing in the *Guardian* newspaper after the 2024 carnival, when there were eight stabbings and over 300 arrests, suggests that heavy-handed policing, inadequate planning with community groups and the number of revellers corralled into such a small area, are all factors in the continuance of anti-social incidents. He advocates relocating the carnival to a larger outdoor space and placing more emphasis on greater, and earlier, community engagement. While the violence that erupts at the carnival is not pervasive, it remains as a living memory, and as a prod to the continuing attention and respect needed to safeguard and foster community cohesion.[4]

The ceremonial masquerades of West Africa that have inspired the carnivals of formerly enslaved people around the world have a unique costume repertoire of their own, one that entwines spiritual heritage with secular concern. Ritual masks and costumes are made and worn for rites of passage and to mark the changing seasons. They draw on a complex visual language that disseminates ancestral history, mythical beliefs, moral education and Christian faith. These costumes symbolically embody spiritual guardianship: they articulate the dual identity of their wearer and the spirit they adopt when wearing them.

In her book *Maske*, the American photographer Phyllis Galembo has captured the extraordinary presence of such costumes. Made from diverse but simple materials – fur, straw, sisal, cotton – and ornamented with shells, baubles, sequins, animal skulls and beads, they are infused with an ebullience that is expressed not just through colour, but through an accumulation of texture. These are costumes conceived as body masks, with the whole body, including the face, obscured. The wearer is totally encased in intricately patterned, knitted or patchworked garments or enshrouded in matted tufts of grass or thick tasselled yarn, with the head covered by a symbolic mask that signifies a supernatural force or a totem animal. One of Galembo's photographs captures the extraordinary presence of a group of four participants from the Egbung village in Nigeria dressed for the Agot masquerade. They wear top-to-toe, boldly coloured, differently patterned tents of cloth with only two slits cut as eyeholes. Their hands are bare. Three of them have their cloth-enveloped heads topped with wooden carvings: one with a golden tiara, another with a crucifix, and the third with the figure of a man and a snake. The cloth tents are ornamented with thick multi-coloured fringing that loops around their necks and across their costumes. While the sharp, bright colours evoke a costume designed for celebration, the small, pierced eyeholes and the heft of the heavy fringing are unsettling.

Seen in movement they are figures that would appear like mysteries, travellers from an elsewhere land.[5]

While these outdoor festivities are symbolic of communal release, the elaborate balls that proliferated in earlier centuries were the exclusive indulgence of the elite. The wearing of magnificent attire was a long-practised form of propaganda used by royalty and the nobility to articulate supremacy. Until early in the seventeenth century, sumptuary laws had prevented all but the highest ranks of society from wearing luxurious cloth and trimmings. For court tournaments, masques and other court revelries, costumes were interpretative, made as symbolic disguises to elevate their wearers into personifications of intangible ideals: embodying the virtues and attributes of ancient mythical gods, or fictional heroes. So it was that France's sixteenth-century king, Francis I, made his entrance at a court masque clad in a flowing ensemble that represented the deities of Diana, Mars, Mercury and Minerva; similarly, in 1640, the six-year-old Charles Emmanuel II, Duke of Savoy, appeared costumed as Love for a court ballet at the castle of Chambéry, wearing a winged robe of cloth of silver and gold.[6] But it was balls that allowed the aristocracy to exercise and proclaim their conspicuous wealth and, in that, costumes were key. Balls offered a release from the formal limitations of court etiquette and, if masked, allowed a welcome behavioural freedom.

While balls were a constant feature of the social calendar of the great and the good from the seventeenth century onwards, it was in the nineteenth century that costumed balls became a conduit for solidarity among the upper classes.

With industrialisation accelerating, and agitation not just for reform but for revolution on the rise, aristocratic privilege was under threat. The Earl of Eglinton took it upon himself to organise a rousing antidote to upper-class despondency. In 1839, on his Scottish estate in Ayrshire, he invested in a three-day 'triumph', a vainglorious medieval tournament and banquet with over 2,000 participants drawn from the cream of high society, all costumed in medieval splendour. It was a doomed escapade. On the first day, the skies opened, bringing torrential rain. Pavilions collapsed, banners drooped and the field became a quagmire. The panoply of umbrellas held over the heads of prancing horses and processing participants ruined the illusion of medieval, chivalric magnificence.

Not to be disheartened, Queen Victoria followed his lead and in 1842 hosted a medieval costume ball at Buckingham Palace for 2,000 guests. Ostensibly to boost the silk trade of Spitalfields, the ball was, in reality, an attempt to restore the elite to a moment of settled privilege, prestige and power. The queen chose as her theme the fourteenth century, when Edward III ruled England. With his wife, Queen Phillipa of Hainault, the couple were regarded as compassionate stewards of royal and familial stability and Queen Victoria decided to model herself and Prince Albert on her favoured predecessors, with the artist Sir Edwin Landseer commissioned to capture the grandeur of Victoria and her consort. Despite the instructions issued to her guests that they were to dress authentically, we can discern from the portrait that the queen did not follow her own dictat. Rather her costume, while referencing the decorative detail of her earlier medieval counterpart, conforms to contemporary fashion. Below her tight, corseted wasp waist she wears a multitude of petticoats under a skirt of heavy velvet, with her train of glittering gold, bordered with ermine, trailing out behind her in a long sweep of majestic excess.

The historical nostalgia nurtured by Queen Victoria's balls – her medieval revelry of 1842, her Georgian ball of 1845 and her Stuart-inspired ball of 1851 – was emulated by what had become a new aristocracy in America. Those elevated to societal power through wealth or celebrity turned to the culture of past and present nobility to exercise and promote their privileged status. To this end, the Manhattan millionaires, the Bradley-Martins, organised a costume ball in 1897 at the Waldorf-Astoria Hotel in New York, where its ballroom was transformed into a replica of the Hall of Mirrors at the Palace of Versailles. Eight hundred guests were instructed to deck themselves out in the lavish splendour of outfits from the sixteenth to the eighteenth century. Mingling with figures from bygone European courts were a plethora of French kings and Tudor courtiers, a chivalric knight in full gold-inlaid armour and a court jester. The banker Orme Wilson's costume epitomised the magnificence on show. Dressed as a cavalier from the court of Louis XIII, he wore a lilac brocade coat, a royal purple velvet cloak lined in white satin and embroidered in gold, purple silk breeches, lilac silk hose, diamond buckled shoes and a plumed hat. Some of those attending amplified their costumes with authentic historical touches: a great-great grandfather's velvet waistcoat, the chain of an old Italian nobleman, a gown dating from the sixteenth century that had been passed down through generations. Old and rare lace was much in evidence and one guest flaunted jewels that had once belonged to Marie Antoinette's daughter. These were claims not just of power but of pedigree: heritage appropriated through expensive sartorial frippery. The *New York Times* recorded the names of the ball's invitees, detailing their fancy dress: the fabrics, colours and accessories of their costumed attire. It made for sensational reading, a tantalising glimpse into the private and extravagant world of the self-appointed elite.[7]

That same year, the Duchess of Devonshire held a ball in honour of Queen Victoria's Diamond Jubilee. 'Pre-1815' was the requested dress code. It was a conscious choice, resetting the clock back to the year of Britain's triumph, its victory at the Battle of Waterloo, a small grasp at past glory. But the women who attended the ball, and its hostess, seemed to have more contemporary issues in mind. Many costumed themselves as historical female monarchs: Catherine the Great and the Empress Theodora, Guinevere and Cleopatra, Marguerite de Valois and Elizabeth I, Britannia and Anne of Austria, Marie Antoinette and Jane Seymour. The Queen of Sheba, and even Titania, Shakespeare's Queen of the Fairies, were also present. The hostess dressed herself as Zenobia, Queen of Palmyrene, the rebel ruler who captured Egypt and conquered Roman provinces in the third century. At a time when the suffragette movement was in its ascendancy, women had become more voracious in their campaign for their right to vote. Of those attending the ball, there would have been some, if not all, actively involved in the movement and it seems plausible that these women used their costumes to parade and assert women's political power.

Dressing Up

This was a time when photography was the new, exciting medium and for her ball the Duchess of Devonshire arranged for a photographic tent to be erected in the grounds of her estate to ensure that each of her guests was captured in their historical finery. A commemorative album was produced that seems now like a memorial to a lost world. Within two decades, a swathe of the British upper class, the inheritors of its heritage and continuity, would be wiped out in the trenches of the Great War.

The photographic record of another ball, held at the Russian Winter Palace in St Petersburg in 1903, is equally poignant. It includes images of the Tsar and Tsarina posed with their assembled guests in a bluster of costumed grandeur, dressed in the elaborate garb of the seventeenth-century Romanov empire. Come the revolution of 1917, many of them would meet a tragic fate. The Grand Duke Andrei Vladimirovich forced into hiding and exile; the Grand Duke George Mikhailovich shot; and many more compelled to flee and to be forever disempowered. In time, the Tsar and the Tsarina were imprisoned and, with their children, eventually executed.

As well as being immortalised in their ball costumes, the wealthy amused themselves by creating, and being photographed, as tableaux vivant or living pictures. They recreated art masterpieces, scenes from history or literary classics, improvising stage sets and rehearsing postures that evoked the mood of the original. It was a diversion that Queen Victoria was especially fond of and throughout the 1880s she dragooned her many offspring into a diversity of costumed tableaux as entertainment when holidaying at Balmoral Castle in Scotland. Some were inspired by Sir Walter Scott's novels, others by Shakespeare's plays. A series entitled 'India' registers her ongoing entrancement with not just the nation but also her Indian attendant, Abdul Karim. For those lacking the theatrical resources of the British queen, such tableaux were generally created from found materials and improvised backdrops. There was a penchant for tragic, emotional scenarios such as 'A Slave's Lament', 'The Gambler's Wife' and 'The Waning of the Honeymoon', depicting swooning women and despairing men in attitudes of abject distress.

The photographic experimenters of the age – Lewis Carroll, Octavius Hill, Robert Adamson and Julia Margaret Cameron – excited by the poetic potential of the medium, could not resist heightening the drama of their photography with posed costumed tableaux. Julia Margaret Cameron photographed her sitters as biblical or heroic characters such as King Ahasuerus and Queen Esther, or the Maid of Athens. One of Cameron's sitters recalled the countless, tedious hours spent posing in costume while the photographer sought the perfect image, remarking that if her 'intention was to represent Zenobia in the last stage of misery and desperation, I think she succeeded'.[8]

For such photographs, the traditional attire of other nations was often adopted, a cultural appropriation that over the ensuing centuries has attracted increased censure. The nineteenth-century plant hunters Reginald Farrer, Joseph Rock and George Fraser might be excused for wearing indigenous dress, as documented in photographs of the time, their motive being to blend in with their surroundings and escape the scrutiny of marauding brigands while they explored the hinterland of China and Tibet in search of botanical novelties. But the motivation of others is more suspect. The 1780 painting of the Canadian politician Lieutenant John Caldwell dressed as a Native American and that of the Scottish explorer Captain Colin Mackenzie in 1842 attired in full Afghan dress attracted criticism. Some condemned the men's posturing as arrogant, an ostentatious display of power in blatant disregard of the cultures they emulated. Others judged such portraiture to be authentic acts of admiration, a wish to identify with people whose cultures enthralled the two men. Cultural appropriation was becoming a sensitive issue and, by 1927, the London Missionary Society, aware of the controversy it could arouse, decreed that indigenous dress from other countries was only to be hired out for educational purposes.[9] Now, assuming the skin colour or traditional costume of another culture is no longer considered droll or diverting but roundly condemned as racist.[10]

Caldwell and Mackenzie had access to their costumed grandeur through their travels, but for the Victorians at home the growing enthusiasm for dressing up fanned new market opportunities. For those lacking imagination, there were helpful publications on hand. *Fancy Dresses Described: A Glossary of Victorian Costume,* published in 1876 by Arden Holt, an apparent nom de plume for a variety of authors who penned the eight editions of the book that appeared over the ensuing years, was one of the most popular guides for amateur costumiers. In it, the particulars of a wide variety of costumes are organised alphabetically and detailed.

It is both a comprehensive and imaginative guide. Uncowed by the sartorial challenge posed by dressing up as Beer, a fawn-coloured skirt with brown bands to mimic barrel hoops is recommended, its shoulders accentuated with bunches of barley. For Spelling Bee, an orange skirt with letters of the alphabet scattered around its circumference is suggested. In case the letters prove insufficient for immediate identification, the embroidered addition of the names of popular dictionaries, such as Webster and Johnson, and a bee perched on the head is advocated. While there is guidance on how to re-create the raiment of past nobility, the working classes are not overlooked, with the costumes of an Irish Potato Gatherer, a Washerwoman, Haymaker, Ratcatcher, Rural Postwoman and Fishwife included. And should dressing up as some*thing* eccentric, rather than some*one* quaint be preferred, the costumes for A Wastepaper Basket, Cigarette, Toilet Table or the new-fangled Telephone are all described.[11] At the London department store Debenham & Freebody, you could have any of Holt's costumes made to order or, if you preferred, be supplied with its pattern and the required materials to make it up at home. This was just one of a wide range of costume pattern books that became available.

Such was the clamour for costumes that a plethora of suppliers began to offer specialised stock: haberdashers started to provide an extensive range of fancy-dress accoutrements; shoemakers to advertise that they could dye shoes to match your chosen costume; theatrical costumiers like Nathans in London rented out the costumes that hung on its rails redolent with history and theatrical fantasy; and haute-couture houses, for a sizeable fee, could equip you with jewelled and embroidered fancy dress that was guaranteed to turn heads.

By the start of the twentieth century, although conventional historically costumed balls continued to be organised, there was an appetite for more adventurous disguises. In her book *Costume: Fanciful, Historical and Theatrical*, published in 1906, Eliza Davis Aria, an English fashion writer and gossip columnist, heralds the trend with the observation that:

> We have passed the days and nights when we yearned to represent some tragic figure – when to appear as Marie Antoinette or Mary, Queen of Scots seemed the pinnacle of delight. Gone too are the times when the representation of a lampshade would exhaust the inventive power of the many, and fled are our desires to coquette as a Columbine or flit as a fairy in white tulle![12]

A more hedonistic costumed revelry began to emerge, epitomised by the Chelsea Art Club Ball, which took place each year at the Royal Albert Hall in London from 1910 until 1958. Themed and designed by artists, including such luminaries as Augustus John and Alfred Munnings, the ball represented an imaginative leap into visual performance, with giant floats, created by art students, circulating amongst the party-goers. In 1919, its theme was *Dazzle*, to honour the camouflage of the British and US Navy warships of the First World War, conceived by the British artist Norman Wilkinson. Its costumes were cleverly rendered in the ships' geometric patterning, with modernist designs that echoed the Cubist movement in art. Over the following decades, the Chelsea Art Ball descended into such bacchanalian excess and drunken mayhem that it found itself banned from the Royal Albert Hall. It moved back to its own premises, where its annual ball continues to test artistic imagination on an annual basis.

Another reason to dress up gathered momentum during the nineteenth and twentieth centuries. As fashion became more consciously gendered, men were increasingly excluded from the sensory delights of wearing lace and silks, frills and organza. They were expected to dress themselves in suits that were constructed with tailored severity, in fabrics that rarely strayed beyond a muted palette. It seems to have encouraged a growing eagerness in men to abandon such sartorial restraint, albeit temporarily, and adopt greater freedom through cross-dressing. The myths of the ancient world are redolent with cross-dressing deities. And, throughout the centuries when women were not allowed to perform in public, ceremonial events and theatrical entertainments were exclusive to men, and it was men who took on the female roles. It was only men who performed in the Japanese kabuki theatre, with the male actors who dressed as women onstage also expected to maintain their female attire offstage.

There are many accounts of Renaissance court festivities involving the sexes exchanging sartorial identities. Even in the censorious moral climate of sixteenth-century Calvinist Scotland, nobles took part in tournaments dressed as women, and Mary, Queen of Scots, not only appeared at a masque 'clad in men's apparel' but strutted the streets of Stirling in men's clothes.[13] All of Shakespeare's female characters were originally performed by male actors, with cross-dressing a frequent trope in his dramas. Through the centuries there have been countless stories of women disguising themselves as men to become pirates, soldiers and sailors. And since the 1880s, for the Up Helly Aa annual Viking celebration in Shetland in Scotland, its male squads have frequently donned women's clothes, dressed alike as Chinese Ladies, Tennis Girls, Suffragettes or Fairy Princesses. Manchester's police force, however, was scandalised when in 1880 they raided a fancy-dress ball in a temperance hall in the Hulme district and found no women present but rather a considerable number of men who 'were in female attire, the costumes being of the most gorgeous description, with bracelets, &c.' Forty-seven men were arrested and subsequently charged with soliciting and encouraging acts of immorality. They were fined and bound over to be a good behaviour for a year or face imprisonment.[14]

Cross-dressing was not unlawful until 1893. But when it was encountered in less than salubrious surroundings it was thought to betray sexual deviancy in general and illegal homosexuality in particular. The eighteenth-century Molly Houses – private houses or taverns where gay and gender-queer guests could meet, socialise, indulge in sexual encounters and dress in drag – were subjected to sporadic raids. When the police flushed out the clientele at Margaret Clap's establishment in 1726 they found men who were:

> 'completely rigged in gowns, petticoats, headcloths, fine laced shoes . . . some had riding hoods, some were dressed as milkmaids, others like shepherdesses with green hats, waistcoats and petticoats and others had their faces patched and painted and wore extensive hoop-petticoats'.[15]

Some clients were arrested. While Margaret Clap was imprisoned for hosting a house of ill-repute, three of the men were hanged for sodomy.

In America, in the latter half of the nineteenth century, queer masquerades were a regular feature at the Hamilton Lodge in Harlem and elsewhere in America. The American surgeon Charles H. Hughes, writing in 1893, reported on a Black drag dance in Washington D.C. where men were:

> 'lasciviously dressed in womanly attire, short sleeves, low-necked dresses and the usual ballroom decorations and ornaments of women, feathers, ribboned headdresses, garters, frills, flowers, ruffles etc.'[16]

It was in Washington DC that William Dorsey Swann, a Black man born into slavery, provided a social space for drag queens. In 1896, when one of his parties was raided by the police, more than a dozen men, including Swann, were arrested and convicted. Courageously and audaciously, Swann appealed, speaking out in defence of his fellow supposed transgressors. It was the first time a gay man had confronted and questioned the homophobic prejudice of the prevailing political and legal systems and demanded justice. While Dorsey Swann did not win his appeal, he became an icon for gay rights and defiantly continued to host drag parties and balls, emboldening others to do the same.

The coming of Prohibition in the 1920s, and the more censorious crackdown on what was thought to be deviant behaviour, saw the American drag scene move further underground. But in June 1969, when police raided the Stonewall Inn, a safe house for the gay and drag community, and used strong-arm tactics to evict and arrest those present, they were met with resistance. Three days of rioting ensued and gay liberation activists mobilised. The campaign for gay rights became overt. And most of the annual Pride events now held throughout the world are scheduled to take place in June to honour those who first fought for gay equality at Stonewall. While the gay movement was gaining ground, however, drag queens of colour continued to face greater discrimination. While white, Black and Latino communities hosted individual drag ball events, for those balls that were racially inclusive, people of colour felt pressured to 'whiten up' if they were to have a chance of winning any of the competitions that were an intrinsic part of the programme.

In 1982, the drag queen Crystal LaBeija took umbrage at the patent racial prejudice that existed in the supposedly inclusive drag ball scene. She established an alternative ball, one that not only organised events and competitions but provided support and mentoring for what was a marginalised community. Other people of colour were inspired to follow her lead and the word 'House' was coined to describe the social infrastructure of this new movement. Many of the Houses were named after haute-couture houses such as Dior, Gucci and Chanel, and they have developed their own distinct repertoire of spectacle. Costume competitions have a range of categories that span a wide gender fluidity and visual diversity, encompassing such themes as Butch Queen, Femme Queen, Transmale Realness, Body and Bizarre. The flamboyant costumes participants create are not merely elaborate theatrical adjuncts to catwalk performances but powerful statements of the determination to be seen and acknowledged. And each House offers advice in performance skills, issues a code of conduct and is organised like a family, with an appointed Mother or Father and with Children as its members. They provide a caring network for those excluded from mainstream society because of their queer identity and give people a sense of belonging not only to the House itself but to a history of queer culture: its traditions, defiance and resilience.

But it has been the phenomenal global popularity of the TV show *RuPaul's Drag Race* – first screened in 2009, now in its seventeenth season, with franchises around the world – that has fanned a wider public appreciation of fun and fanciful drag costumes, the alluring theatricality of dressing up. Each season includes Design and Ball Challenges, when contestants compete to fabricate something extraordinary from given materials. These might be an eclectic range of fabrics but, more often than not, they are given much more demanding and eccentric materials, with sweets, pretend money, sleeping bags and fruit supplied to elicit originality and creativity. The contestants rarely disappoint, combining imagination with sartorial artistry to assemble fantastical outfits that are both memorable and remarkable. From a sculptural, flared dress made from playing cards to an elegant flowing gown composed entirely of strips of liquorice, RuPaul's contestants have raised the bar in costume ingenuity. What began as a show that was part of a subculture has emerged as a showstopper that attracts millions of viewers worldwide. Its appeal lies not just in its glamorous and outrageous costumes, however, but in how contestants reveal their un-costumed selves to tell their story. In doing so they expose their vulnerabilities and demonstrate their strengths, both creative and emotional. *Ru Paul's Drag Race* makes for compulsive viewing for an audience invited to be not voyeurs, but sympathetic admirers.

While the drag scene has brought a new sartorial flamboyance to our screens, it is cosplay – that cavalcade of costumed fandom that originated in people's enthralment to science fiction – that has generated widespread participation. When, in 1939, Forrest J. Ackerman and Myrtle R. Douglas appeared at the first Science Fiction Convention in New York City dressed as futuristic characters inspired by H.G. Wells's film *Things to Come*, they had no idea that they would ignite a movement that was to gain such momentum. Over the following decades, the scope of get-togethers in costumed camaraderie, dressed as favourite fictional characters, has broadened to encompass not just characters from sci-fi novels but others drawn from comic books, fantasy films, anime, video games, history and popular culture.

Although Ackermann and Douglas started what became a growing trend, there were precedents. In 1877, Jules Verne, the French author of *Journey to the Centre of the Earth* and *Twenty Thousand Leagues Under the Sea*, held a costume ball in Amiens with his guests dressed as characters from his novels. And at the Royal Albert Hall in London in 1891, a fund-raising bazaar and fête was themed on the 1871 science-fiction novel *Vril: The Power of the Coming Race,* by Edward Bulwer-Lytton, with visitors encouraged to dress as its winged superhuman protagonists. Its heroine, Princess Zee, graced the event wearing a black satin gown and a silver tiara that gleamed with the glare of electric light.

Making Matters

The donning of a cosplay costume has a deeper significance for its wearer than simply paying homage to a favourite character. Cosplayers see themselves as part of the story. Their ambition is to inhabit their character, with some striving to become their character's clone, not just through replicating their appearance but by adopting their voice, mimicking the way they move and borrowing the words and phrases they use. Cosplay is essentially a social, performative art through which participants revisit and re-encounter the personalities and plot lines of their favourite books, films and TV series together as visual reinforcements of a shared infatuation. Interaction and mutual appreciation within the cosplay community are integral to the experience. To this end, people are passionate about the authenticity of their chosen costume. The meticulous care some cosplayers spend on their costume creations often demands a high level of artisanal skill if a spaceman, a Stormtrooper or a White Walker from *Game of Thrones* is to pass muster.

Such attention to detail also prevails in the world of historical re-enactments, where it is not only the look of the costume that matters but also the techniques employed in its making and the materials from which it is made. Some people go to great lengths to achieve verisimilitude, even learning traditional crafts in order to be able to produce more authentic replicas of the clothes of earlier centuries. In more recent years, cosplay has also been appropriated by cinema impresarios who have restyled blockbuster movies as costumed sing-alongs, with the re-screenings of *The Rocky Horror Picture Show*, *Frozen*, *Grease*, *Mary Poppins* and *The Sound of Music* attracting large audiences of costumed fans.

Dressing Up

The arena of political protest is increasingly witnessing elements of cosplay, with the iconic ruby-red cloaks and white caps of Margaret Atwood's dystopian novel *The Handmaid's Tale* being adopted in different parts of the world at different times to campaign for women's rights, in particular for repeal of laws against abortion. Dressing up to gain more attention for political demonstrations is not new. The Rebecca Riots in Britain in the nineteenth century saw male agricultural workers wearing women's clothes to protest against unfair taxation. Mock processions were organised that same century in America, with workers lampooning the authority of politicians and the military in costumed ridicule, brandishing farming tools as faux weapons. And each year, the Procession of the Species in Olympia, in the state of Washington, sees thousands of people gather for its annual Earth Day celebrations, to demonstrate in support of greater environmental protection, wearing home-made costumes that replicate flora and fauna from the natural world, thronging the streets with an intoxicating parade of iridescent butterflies, bicycling bees and flocks of birds.

Such costumed protests are a contrast to the splendour of the masked balls that continue to be popular not only in Venice each year but in Vienna, where 400 balls are organised annually. Debutantes still attend Queen Charlotte's Ball in London. Established in 1780, it continued unabated until the 1970s and, after some decades of absence, has recently been revived. Alongside such grandeur, there remains a continuing enthusiasm for the less impactful but still ingenious improvised fancy dress of local fêtes, village galas, annual pageants, cricket matches and festival finales.

From the explicitly political to the quirkily local, from the glamorous to the comical, dressing up in costume responds to the human desire for transformation, to materialise, just for a little while, a different, more dramatic self.

I have driven just half an hour away from home to attend the Comrie Parade, the last event in what has been a fortnight of community-led frolics in the village. For this, the grand finale, local costumed groups are to process down the street in floats as they have done for decades. It seems that everyone who lives here has turned out to cheer them on. Despite the incipient rain, the narrow pavements are spilling over with families, friends and neighbours. The sound of a pipe band stirs the crowd to attention and down they come, kilts swinging, filling the afternoon air with the swell of their bagpipes and the thrum of their drums.

More music, more clapping, and the rumble of the first float is heard in the distance. It trundles past, an agricultural lorry crammed with locals disguised as bygone farming folk and farm animals. There are shepherds dressed in smocks, a pig snuffling through a pink cardboard snout, two large rams, their fleeces reimagined from bales of straw, and a number of horned cows of variable shapes and sizes. A medieval castle is next, its painted stone walls emblazoned with a frieze of heraldic shields. From its ramparts, fair maidens with long flowing locks threaded with artificial flowers throw out sweets to the assembled audience while small, sleepy squires in emblematic tabards peer over its walls to survey their realm. For 'Keeping Christmas in Comrie', a splendid silver-edged sledge is driven by a cheery Santa Claus, suitably recognisable in a bright-red

Dressing Up

outfit and long white beard, waving magnanimously at the crowd. On his accompanying lorry is a motley group of Christmas characters. A snowman with a crinkled hat stands cheek-by-jowl with a large human Christmas pudding and child elves with paper-pointed ears. A boat appears next, peopled by volunteers of the RNLI lifeboat charity, its sea captain keeping a watchful eye over any sign of fraternisation between his crew of yellow sou' wester-clad deckhands and his gorgeously sequinned mermaids.

The fourteen floats that pass by are characterised by their jolliness, by the fun of silly decoration and cobbled-together fancy dress. This is not shop-bought entertainment. This is pure home-made and home-grown delight. And, as the spectators cheer them on, applauding and hooting, and the costumed merrymakers wave, dance, blow bubbles and call out hellos to friends in a happy moment of community celebration, it seems to me, more than ever, that there is joy in creative improvisation, that for all the sophisticated diversions and on-screen distractions that our modern world tempts us with, it is the palpable pleasure of a community making and having fun together that endures to become cherished as a local tradition.

7
Puppets

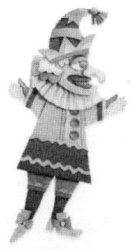

A puppet is the artistic soul set free
Frank Ballard

I was a teenager when the Berlin Wall was built, the wall that divided the east of the city from the west and separated families and friends. Over the next twenty-eight years more than a hundred people were to die along its length. In 1964, the American satirical news series *That Was the Week That Was* aired a three-and-a-half-minute piece that expressed the poignancy of what the wall's presence meant to those who had to part there, a hand ballet by the American puppeteer Burr Tillstrom that was subsequently screened on British television. There was no set, no costumes, no strings, only a small cloth as a prop. Instead, Tillstrom used just his hands and forearms to choreograph sorrow, fear, fury and loss in the story of a couple saying a forever goodbye at the wall. There was no indication of their age or gender. They might have been a mother and son, two lovers, neighbours or brothers – they represented all those who had been forced apart. Through hands that curved to an embrace, that caressed each other in care, became entwined in love and were straightened in resolve, Tillstrom transmitted heartbreak. His short drama made me cry. While I was too young to fully comprehend the politics that lay behind the building of the wall, uncertain even of where the wall was in the world, I understood its tragedy and found it haunting. The piece lurked in my memory like a lament and fostered in me a heartfelt sympathy as acute as if I had witnessed such partings in real life. When the wall was eventually demolished in 1989 and I watched the jubilant crowds clambering over that tumbling, graffitied barrier, sitting triumphant astride its ruins, I remembered Burr Tillstrom's plaintive presentation – the tender cradling, the last wave of longing – and I cried again. It seemed to me then, as it did when I first saw his performance, that he grasped – quite literally – human vulnerability in his hands.[1]

Many might question whether the manipulation of a pair of hands can be designated as puppetry. But puppetry is wide-ranging and generous in its scope. It denotes anything that can be endowed with recognisably human traits. Whether it be a carved figure able to move flexibly on strings or a kitchen utensil provided with a voice, both have a place in the charisma of puppetry.

Puppetry is the art of transcendence. It relies on the human capacity, even desire, to suspend disbelief and embrace other worlds, worlds that are peopled by crafted beings whose movements and manners are manipulated. Yet, despite their evident artifice, puppets somehow seem able to manifest an intimate, honest and direct expression of the human condition. They project feelings that we understand. Puppetry entices us to make an emotional connection and become invested in an unreal world.

I learned how articulate puppetry could be early on in my career in the arts when I served on an Arts Council of England committee and visited, with other panel members, the Cannon Hill Puppet Theatre in Birmingham to decide whether it merited a continuance of funding. Its consideration at committee had proved vexatious, with some dismissing the Puppet Theatre as a place of whimsical entertainment that catered more for the liberation of parents from childcare than for the progress of creative innovation. It was, they insisted, hardly art. With no consensus reached it had been decided to despatch representatives from both sides of the divide and I was considered to be sufficiently non-partisan to provide an unbiased opinion.

The Puppet Theatre had been founded in 1968 by John Blundall, the mastermind behind some of the most iconic *Thunderbirds* puppets. And it was John who now greeted us assessors with an apparent lack of enthusiasm. A somewhat mournful man at the best of times, it was with desultory graciousness that he led us through the various spaces that comprised his domain: the show gallery of puppets, the small theatres, the workshop. Spying a short length of rope left lying on a table in the workshop, he retrieved it, intent on tidying it away. But, as he lifted it up, he instinctively formed its uppermost end into a small loop and nodded it in our direction. He had made a puppet. He turned its head and inclined it slightly in what was clearly a quizzical gaze. Then, with a flick of his wrist, he caught the rope's other end in his hand, twisted it upwards to fashion an arm and gestured a small, shy, hesitant wave of welcome.

The most illuminating aspect of his impromptu performance was that John hardly seemed part of it. He remained his slightly dour and somewhat defensive self while conjuring conviviality and curiosity in the rope puppet he held in his hands. He was merely its conduit. The lesson, for that was what it was, was certainly unplanned but it made me realise that puppetry was not simply about showing but about revealing, and that John Blundall had an unnerving, innate capacity to recognise and evoke the dormant personality of an inanimate object. He was both an animist who respected the spirit of things and an animator who could make it visible. I argued strongly that day for continued funding and John later insisted that it was my impassioned defence that had saved the Puppet Theatre. But, in truth, it was his victory.

John's transformation and personification of a small length of rope into a cheerful character who responded to our presence opened my eyes, and my heart, to the appeal of puppetry as a portal to worlds not just of the imagination but of emotive agency. What we had witnessed was certainly engaging because of John's expertise as a puppeteer, but it was much more than that. It was a demonstration of a symbiotic relationship, a unique alliance between a puppeteer and their puppet: separate yet interdependent. And it introduced me to the unexpected and seductive power of puppetry: how the familiar can be made strange and the fantastical seem familiar.

Inspired by John and working at the time as a community artist in Northampton, I organised a puppet festival at which he was its main attraction. I watched as he breathed life into a colander, a pair of chopsticks, a set of keys; as he introduced more sophisticated marionettes that, with exaggerated gestures, grotesque faces and bizarre costumes, acted out stories of defiance, mischief, resilience, fearlessness and compassion. I also watched his audience and how the swarms of over-excited children and anxiously shushing parents quietened surprisingly quickly when the house lights faded and the first puppet made its entrance. How the most recalcitrant and boisterous of teenage boys left off their swagger and joshing and became rapt, mesmerised by posturing puppets and the trials and triumphs they experienced. It was as if the puppets John personified, fashioned from bits of wood and scraps of cloth, reflected their own silliness, and – perhaps more importantly – their seldomly voiced sensitivities. They elicited in these boys an immediate empathy and encouraged in them a rare attentiveness.

Since that Northampton puppet festival, I have acquired a plethora of puppets, bought or made for no other reason than the charm of them. There is a latex glove puppet of a sheep that I found in a village jumble sale, a pair of delicately carved Javanese shadow puppets, a Rajasthani marionette of a handsomely bearded Lothario who conceals a beautiful woman under his robes. A turn of the wrist sees his lover jump up behind him on horseback to ride into a romantic sunset. A glove puppet of Captain Hook, resplendent in a red velvet coat and lace cravat, was a gift from an actor friend when he played the role in *Peter Pan*, and a stringed puppet of an elderly, bespectacled man in a shabby suit was bought in Prague, a city famed for its puppet art. Towering over them all is an antiquated wooden Chinese puppet, another gift. His embroidered headdress and fringed silk sash mark him out as an official at the Imperial Court, his lips perpetually curved in an obsequious smile.

Puppets

There are also the puppets I have made over time. Tiny cloth finger puppets of carnival characters; a disconsolate jester dangling on strings, whose grimace belies the jolly tinkle of his cap'n'bells; and a beaked-nose woman with bedraggled black hair and a ragged gown, who made an appearance as a witch at Halloween and – re-attired in tartan – metamorphosed into Jean Armour, Mrs Robert Burns, to entertain guests on Burns Night. All these puppets have served their time as distractions on gloomy, rainy winter days when my own and visiting children had need of laughter. They have played their part in taking children – and me – to a more imaginative elsewhere.

Made from the simplest of materials or constructed with an intricacy of strings and jointed parts, puppets are diverse and the puppetry repertoire expansive. It can be as straightforward as the show devised by a puppeteer friend of mine, Andy Jones, during the pandemic lockdown. With glove puppets made from hessian he performed his play alone behind his large sitting-room window while his audience sat watching, sheltered from the rain, in a gazebo on his small front lawn, listening to the unfolding drama through outdoor speakers. His puppets became an escape from anxiety. Whimsical, mischievous, beleaguered and triumphant, they battled against the odds to survive in a show that was both pertinent and playful. But puppetry can also be as sophisticated as England's National Theatre production of *War Horse* in 2007, a dramatisation of Michael Morpurgo's book of the same name for which the Handspring Puppet Company from South Africa devised moving portrayals of the horses sent to the battlefields of the First World War. Each horse was manipulated by three puppeteers, two inside the horse's frame and the other, on the outside, animating its head and ears. They not only communicated their horse's emotional state through visual and aural cues – the swish of a tail, the pricking up of ears, the quiver of fear – but conveyed its distinct physical character, its weight, suppleness, strength and frailty, through its puppeteers' own movements. In what the company calls 'emotional engineering', they created innovative ways to capture the communicative nuances of a horse's body language. But from the simplest to the most sophisticated, all forms of puppetry share the same intent: to mirror human foibles and investigate human integrity.

Puppets straddle the world. They are found, in myriad forms, on every continent and in most countries and their ancestry is ancient. Some are unique to specific places – the Vietnamese water puppets, the armoured marionettes of Sicily and those of Italy's commedia dell'arte characters. Others have been introduced through cultural exchanges across borders or through colonialisation, creating hybrid puppetry that merges indigenous stories with stagecraft that has been adopted from elsewhere. Still more have become icons of popular entertainment, as with Jim Henson's Muppets.

But puppetry has always maintained a radical substream. The character of Ubu Roi, in Alfred Jarry's controversial play of the same name, was first conceived and performed as a puppet. The folk singer Pete Seeger used puppets to accompany his early protest songs when he toured America with the Vagabond Puppeteers. Dario Fo and Franca Rame, the Italian left-wing theatrical campaigners, often deployed puppets in their dramas to confront corruption and injustice. And, in the 1960s, the American puppeteer Peter Schumann founded the Bread and Puppet Theater, which became a celebrated platform for political dissent and debate. Its use of giant processional puppets as campaigning tools inspired others and there are few current political demonstrations that do not feature a huge puppet caricature of a politician.

It is intriguing, therefore, given its history and its diversity, that puppetry has rarely been acknowledged by or absorbed into the higher echelons of theatrical drama. But it has had its literary and artistic champions including Joseph Haydn, George Bernard Shaw, George Sand, Johann Wolfgang von Goethe, Maurice Maeterlinck and Max Reinhardt. Whether finger, glove, string, rod or shadow; small or large; two-dimensional or three; made of wood, cloth, wire, papier-mâché or plaster, puppets are mediums through which the gods can be appeased, human foibles exposed, old legends reprised, challenges confronted and current issues disseminated. Referencing mythological tales and real life, puppet performances address human power and prejudice, dreams and disappointments. They have a settled place in the undertow of culture as a salve and a revolt.

A puppet can embody our thoughts and emotions and sometimes reveal something more of ourselves. It is because of this that puppets are increasingly being used as part of a therapist's toolkit. In what is called 'cognitive behavioural play therapy', puppets can establish a useful distance between a therapist and the child, young person or adult they are supporting. With each having a puppet as their intermediary, emotions, experiences and memories can be revisited vicariously and more safely through role play. The therapist uses the conversation between the puppets to address issues that are too traumatic to broach directly and suggest strategies for dealing with them. The tactility of puppets is comforting and the interaction with them creative, and both help to establish a non-threatening atmosphere and elicit a trust in confidentiality that facilitates communication. While it might be too challenging to voice fears or distress directly to another person, the responsiveness and unjudgemental presence of puppets can provide an engaging channel for self-expression and exploration.

Wordless and inanimate until set in motion by its operator, a puppet is dependent on its maker for its character: a character that remains unresolved until its making is complete and the performance is in action. Only then does its personality and attitude fully reveal itself. Most puppeteers make their own puppets. And those who have inherited a cast of older puppets, often passed down through many generations of the same family, re-costume or re-characterise them to suit their own interpretation. The relationship between a puppeteer and a puppet is surely one of the strangest and most compelling of interactions: a co-dependent transference of energy. But while a puppeteer is a puppet's creator, guardian and agent, in performance he or she is generally unseen and, even when visible, most often subsumes their identity to that of their puppet.

Although most puppets are manipulated by a solo puppeteer, others, as in *War Horse*, require a team to express their full emotive charge. Lacking an actor's flexible facial expression, puppets are limited to gesture and posture to transmit their personality and feelings: their communication must be explicit, clear and direct. This is especially true for the puppets used by itinerant showmen, which must have immediate appeal if they are to attract the attention of passers-by. The characters they portray, therefore, are often already familiar to an audience: stock personalities such as the fool, the rejected lover, the conceited braggart and the cunning trickster. And many of the older puppet shows were retellings of popular folk tales, epic poems or well-worn legends. Those puppeteers who have inherited their storylines, skills, style and comic business, passed down through the male – and, much more rarely, female – line, jealously guard them as the preserve of their specific families. Dynasties of puppeteers have evolved who can claim a puppetry ancestry that is centuries old: a puppet tradition unique to each family, conserved, replicated and developed by each generation. This has ensured that, while the illiterate ancestors of present-day puppeteers never wrote down their scripts or stage directions, the nature and mores of older puppet dramas have survived, despite the ephemerality of the shows themselves. They are preserved within an aural, visual and tactile memory.

Puppets have a long history. String-manipulated clay figures have been found in the tombs of ancient Egyptians and stringed dolls discovered buried with those interred in the Sacred Valley of the Incas, thought to have been put there as companions for the afterlife, to protect, serve and entertain the dead. Many of the oldest forms of puppetry were ritualistic, puppets operated by shamans to communicate with deceased ancestors or to pacify and amuse the gods. Some performances took place in temples with the gods as the only audience, others took place privately in people's homes to confer blessings, enact exorcisms, heal the sick or contribute to funeral rites.

The precise origin of puppetry is still being debated. A puppet show was recorded by the Greek historian Herodotus in the fifth century BC and puppets are thought to have existed in the ancient cultures of China and India. What is certain is that, while already present in parts of Asia and Africa, by the fifteenth century puppetry had become popular throughout Europe. The Catholic Church used puppets as spiritual avatars to add appeal to its religious festivals and feast days. Troubadours and minstrels adopted them to animate their romances, comedies and epic tales. But, over time, a schism appeared between spiritual and secular puppetry. The more sacred, ceremonial, formal and literary-inspired forms were claimed by the elite – be that religious or royal – to be performed for educated audiences within temples or at court, with a greater emphasis placed on the aesthetics of the puppets themselves. To the common people was left booth-staged or cart-laden puppetry. Rougher, more raucous, irreverent and often sententious, it took its place as an outsider art.

An example of elite puppetry can still be found in Japan, where its highly stylised *bunraku* is much respected. Thought to have emerged in the sixteenth century, its puppets have jointed limbs and are manipulated by a complexity of strings to produce an emulation of human beings that is extraordinary and spectacular. A ten-year apprenticeship is required to master the movement of a puppet's feet, another ten to manoeuvre its hands, still more for an apprentice to reach the accolade of master puppeteer. The metre-high main characters, carved from wood, can alter their facial expressions and register emotion through the mobility of their eyes. They can pick up and discard objects and even seem to breathe. The discipline of the performance, its rigid conventions, and the chanted scripts proclaiming the heroics of triumphant battles and the tragedy of unrequited love reflect the gravitas of the literary classics on which *bunraku* is based. Two or more puppeteers, clad and masked in black, group around each puppet to realise choreographed subtleties of gesture and movement that, with the accompaniment of the chanter's operatic narration, create dramatic and emotional intensity. At the height of its popularity, in the late nineteenth century, there were hundreds of *bunraku* troupes performing throughout Japan. The formality of *bunraku*, however, has fallen out of favour with today's audiences, who find its high-flown literary dramas less illuminating and relevant to modern life. Now there is only the National Bunraku Theatre left to carry the flame and stay true to the unique qualities of this ancient form of Japanese puppetry.[2]

In Britain, Punch epitomised the puppetry of the people and became the people's puppet hero. Born in the seventeenth century, at a time of social unrest, he became a cipher for rebellion. With his wife Judy, who joined him a century later, Punch enjoyed a meteoric rise to popularity. Despite his misogyny and immorality, he was embraced as a comical curiosity both by the working class and a burgeoning middle class as a diversion for holidaying families and as a harmless amusement for children. Yet he seems an unlikely character to be taken into the hearts of a sentimental

British public. A sociopathic serial killer, graceless, vain and shameless, Punch's antics, if you can call them that, include duplicity, physical violence and the murder of a doctor, constable, hangman, his own wife and their baby. Hardly, then, the stuff of children's entertainment. Originating in the Italian commedia dell'arte character of Pulcinella, Punch has notable equivalents in other countries, other irreverent rogues with a penchant for whacking opponents – Petrushka in Russia, Mester Jackel in Denmark, Karogö in Turkey, Jan Klassen in the Netherlands, Kasperle in Germany and Polichinelle, and later Guignol, in France – but none of these are as vicious as Punch, none as transgressively spiteful or as contemptuous of others. They generally remain within the pantomimic boundaries of mischievous behaviour. What all these puppets share, however, is that they all became iconic embodiments of a national spirit. And, as such, were exploited to political ends.

During both the First and Second World Wars, Punch and his European counterparts were sent to the front to entertain the troops and to city streets to perform jingoist dramas to boost morale. With Punch donning a soldier's uniform and wielding a gun rather than his usual truncheon, and with plays such as *Guignol in the Trenches* and *Kasperle at the Outpost*, puppets were recruited into war service.[3] But their popularity and their palpable rebellion against authority could also be dangerous for those in power, which led to censorship and, at times, proscription. When, in a newly revolutionary France, a version of Guignol was found to be too aristocratic for republican tastes, his puppeteers were guillotined. And in 1830s Lyon, when Guignol was suspected of being deployed as an agitator in support of striking silk workers, his puppeteers were banned from using any improvised dialogue and had to submit their scripts for pre-approval. In occupied Czechoslovakia during the Second World War, the Third Reich closed puppet theatres and put shows involving Kasperle under close surveillance. But their draconian actions only served to intensify the power of puppetry as a weapon of resistance. Basements were commandeered as puppet theatres, Hitler or Himmler lampooned as the hangman or the devil.[4]

Puppetry became a buffer from terror and a bolster to an oppressed national identity. Nowhere was this more evident than in German concentration camps during the Second World War. From Dachau, Auschwitz and Ravensbrück emerged stories of puppet shows produced in the harshest of circumstances, with POWs scavenging materials from the sparsest of resources: threadbare uniforms, food sacks and scraps of paper. In Ravensbrück the Polish actress Jadwiga Kopijowska and the artist Maja Berezowska produced a traditional *szopki,* a musical nativity puppet play, to entertain the children. But they inserted cultural references that were undetectable to their prison guards, choosing traditional Polish carols that had underlying themes of patriotism and survival and adding new characters – a Polish mother, a Polish soldier and a camp inmate – to voice their experiences of war and incarceration.[5] The pioneering Czechoslovakian puppeteers Jan Malik and Josef Skupa used allegory to disguise the subversive nature of their POW puppet plays. Over a hundred Czechoslovakian puppeteers were to die in the concentration camps. Of the reputed 1,300 puppet troupes operating in the country in 1936, only a quarter survived Nazi occupation. It is testimony to the value its people placed on puppetry that by 1947 1,200 puppet theatres were back in action.[6]

Sometimes those in power simply appropriated popular puppet characters to promote their own propagandist agendas. Russian revolutionaries put Petrushka centre stage. Already costumed in a red shirt, his attire pronounced him Lenin's man and he strutted the boards spouting revolutionary slogans in productions such as *The Crown and the Star* or *Death of the Imperialist Hydra*.[7] More sinister was the Nazi adoption of Kasperle. In 1938, the Third Reich established an Institute for Puppetry, *Reichsinstitut für Puppenspiel*, organised through its Hitler Youth and Strength through Joy departments.[8] There was little joy, however, for the exponents of the Kasperle puppets, who were instructed to submit their existing puppets for examination to gauge whether the length of their puppet's nose betrayed any Jewish traits. In Nazi hands the prototypical Kasperle puppet underwent its own assimilation and the size of its nose was reduced and its hair made blonder to ensure it was more identifiably Aryan.[9]

And during China's Cultural Revolution of the 1960s and 70s, which saw an elimination of old traditions, those puppets thought to perpetuate superstitious beliefs or glorify the imperial classes were burned by the Red Guard cadres. They were replaced with puppets costumed in modern dress, who celebrated the toil of workers and peasants and promulgated a Maoist ideology. Some villagers and travelling puppeteers, unwilling to relinquish the craftsmanship of their ancestors, buried their puppets or hid them as best they could. When a group of academic researchers travelled through China in 2008/9 to see what remained of its puppetry heritage, they found that some forms were all but extinct. Only one style of marionette theatre and one glove-puppet troupe survived in northern China. Of the sets of gilded costumed string puppets, unique to villages in the hills of central Fujian, only two partial sets remained. In Shaoyang City in Hunan only a single sixteenth-generation glove puppeteer retained his set of puppets from a village that, just a century before, harboured over 110 puppet sets. It was not just the loss of the puppets that was tragic, but the loss of their stagecraft, of theatrical traditions. For some it was only memory that served as a source of reconstruction. For others, those who managed to retrieve the puppets they had buried or hidden during the Mao purge, restoration was possible and older puppetry traditions could be revived.[10]

In the latter half of the twentieth century, the traditional savage story and aggressive character of Punch met with increasing unease. He was modified and his show made more acceptable to a modern audience. The bullish and brutal thug who had traipsed largely uncensored through British popular culture for five centuries became reformed, his violence replaced by play fighting. Today there are over 250 Punch 'professors' (the name given to Punch puppeteers) still active in Britain and, through the annual Punch and Judy Festival at Covent Garden in London, he continues to give voice to the people, albeit with more geniality. Judy, his wife, is also being reappraised through *The Judy Project* at the University of Exeter, a research programme that is exploring her history and her diverse manifestations over the centuries.[11] Not only are the roles and gendered attributes of female characters in traditional and contemporary puppet theatre receiving greater attention, but female puppeteers of the past are being rediscovered and in increasing numbers to take their place in the annals of puppet history.

And it is women who are taking centre stage in today's story of puppetry. They are pursuing, in greater numbers, the potency of puppetry to promote the social issues that affect their lives. Until more recent times, it seemed that very few women had played a part in puppet performances except, sometimes, as unseen singers or, occasionally, dancers. With sparse documentation on the nature of early puppetry, most of which was written by men, it is hard to know whether women were totally absent or if their participation went unrecorded or was even erased. But now the role of women in puppetry has become an increasingly fertile area of research, development and practice. When in February 2023 I booked tickets for the Manipulate Festival in Edinburgh, an annual event that explores contemporary animated film, puppetry and visual theatre, the first show I saw intrigued me, not because of the show itself, interesting though it was, but because in its audience of around thirty people, there were only four men.

Many of the oldest forms of puppetry excluded women as makers and practitioners and, often, even as audiences. Deemed 'unclean' because of their menstrual cycle, women were seen as potential polluters of puppets' spiritual agency and forbidden to touch them. In many cultures, where women were not only seen as inferior but were restricted to domestic lives, they were unable to attend or participate in public cultural activities. *Women and Puppetry: Critical and Historical Investigations*, published in 2019, is a compilation of fifteen essays on the role and practice of women puppeteers, past and present.[12] Essentially, it is a story of discovery, reclamation and reinvention, and documents how some endangered traditional forms of puppetry are only being safeguarded through the intervention of female puppeteers.

The Japanese puppeteer Nakauchi Masako, the great-great-great-granddaughter of a medium, has reclaimed her shamanistic heritage. Having persuaded one of the last remaining masters of the ritual *hakomawashi,* an itinerant form of spiritual puppetry, to take her on as his apprentice, she has revived the age-old New Year custom of visiting 1,000 homes in remote rural regions. Travelling a route bequeathed to her by her puppet master, she visits each home to dispel the negative forces of the past year and, through her puppet's blessing, usher in a more auspicious future. Hers is a practice that not only preserves an ancient form of puppetry but continues to provide the social communication that was an intrinsic part of the tradition, conveying news, information and solicitude to the houses she visits.[13]

And increasingly women are becoming puppeteers in forms of puppetry that, traditionally, have been restricted to men. In Kerala in India, Rajitha Ramachandra Pulavar is bringing the indigenous shadow play of *tholpavakoothu*, a devotional practice dedicated to a female deity, to wider audiences. *Tholpavakoothu* has always been temple-based and attended solely by men but, as the daughter of a respected puppet master, her familial connection has enabled her to be accepted as a puppeteer, albeit outside of the temple building. She has used the opportunity to provide insights into women's experiences. It is a courageous path. Despite facing outrage from some on social media, she remains determined to utilise her puppetry platform for the benefit of women, not just the gods, and slowly her commitment is winning support.[14]

Other women puppeteers are also acting as catalysts to bring women's issues centre stage, particularly those subjects thought too controversial for live theatre such as female sexuality, gender inequality and domestic abuse. And as puppeteers they play a vital role in disseminating information that modern policy-makers want to see embraced more widely: most urgently those that deal with children's education and healthcare. In West Africa, the traditional male-only puppetry linked to voodoo rituals and secret societies is being adapted by women to address the most difficult of subjects – genital mutilation, and the dangers of HIV/AIDs.[15] The Iranian puppeteer Maryam Moini's 2014 show *Maryam*, performed at the 15th International Puppet Festival of Tehran-Mobarak, dramatised the complex emotions surrounding abortion. With puppets personifying alternative versions of herself, she used them as provocateurs to express, through physical eloquence, what could not be openly discussed.[16] And the Turkish puppet-maker and operator Candan Seda Balaban, with her co-project-designer, the writer and director Yigit Sertdemir, has tackled the rarely aired topic of female sexual fulfilment. *Modes of Pleasure,* which was performed by an all-women ensemble in Istanbul, is a show that would certainly have been banned if performed by live actresses, but it was made more palatable through the humour and poignancy of puppetry.[17]

Women's increasing involvement in puppet theatre is both opportune and timely. As well as becoming guardians of older styles of puppetry that are in danger of obsolescence, women's participation is becoming less contested by men, who are unenthusiastic about continuing to perform as female puppet characters, seeing it as emasculating, and who consider puppetry an unrewarding profession economically. It has enabled women to slip into the breach without too much impediment. And their conservation and, in some cases, rekindling of older forms has helped to boost the tourist agendas of those countries seeking to emphasise distinct national heritage through the promotion of traditional arts and crafts. Rajitha Ramachandra Pulavar's involvement in traditional Indian shadow puppetry not only ensures that *tholpavakoothu*, as practised by her family through generations, is conserved but that it reaches new audiences.

Shadow puppetry is surely one of the most magical and mesmerising manifestations of the puppet arts. Backlit silhouettes appear behind a white screen and, depending on their proximity to it, their scale and definition can be altered, allowing them to become as large as giants or as insubstantial as ghosts. Some are simple figurative cut-outs made of black card or leather, others are highly decorative with intricately carved features and moveable limbs operated with rods, partially coloured with paint or inserts of opaque gel. Like other forms of puppetry, shadow puppetry is embedded in sacred, shamanic rituals. Over centuries these ethereal puppets were used as spiritual mediators to unite the living with the dead and the supernatural with the temporal universe. And they continued to thrill secular audiences, who were duped by the spectral appearance of shadow figures, seemingly conjured from thin air, which were, in reality, materialised through optical machines and projected on screens of smoke or semi-transparent cloth.

The nebulous presence of such shadow figures was both a source of horror and entertainment for nineteenth-century audiences when phantasmagoria became a staple attraction in European theatres. The materialisation of spectres and demons, ghosts and ghouls was amplified with sensory accompaniments: the crack of thunder, the whisper of disembodied voices, the arid smell of decomposition. This was an age that peddled terror. The showman Etienne Gaspard Robert pioneered projection techniques that had his audience shuddering in their seats. In republican France, his ghostly cavalcade of historical, long-dead figures unnerved the authorities, who feared he might bring the French king, Louis XVI, back to haunt them. His theatre was summarily shut down and, by the end of the nineteenth century, people's susceptibility to such theatrical deceptions had diminished.

Their fascination with shadow play, however, persisted. Hand shadows became popular as home entertainment, and a plethora of publications began to appear illustrating how to forge a silhouette of a rabbit twitching its ears or a bird flapping its wings on a darkened wall.

These simple shadows made with the human hand were a far cry from the ancient art of shadow puppetry practiced in Asia, most eloquently in *wayang*, the shadow puppetry of Indonesia and Malaysia. It is an intrinsic part of their spiritual and animist culture, viewed as a sacred and elevated form of theatre. Its key narratives are based on the ancient Indian epic poems, the *Mahabharata* and the *Ramayana*, stories of mythological gods, love and war, intrigues and betrayals, reunions and reconciliations, but their migration to Southeast Asia brought about a reinterpretation of dramatic style and an intensification of spiritual agency. What emerged has become a distinct form of shadow puppetry, rooted in mythology but accommodating current concerns through satirical commentary. Devised over a thousand years ago as an entertainment for the gods to be performed privately within temple walls, the *wayang* has evolved into a public drama, though still respectful of its religious origins.

A *wayang* performance can last for up to nine hours. It takes place at nightfall and continues until dawn. The puppets, their staging and the way the play is presented are symbolic. As many as 200 puppets can be used in a single performance, some with interchangeable heads that register different emotions. The screen they perform behind signifies the sky and its illuminating oil lamp the sun. The trunk of a banana tree, into which the central rods of the puppets are put when they are not in motion, symbolises the earth, while the staging itself is a metaphor for the cosmos. Traditionally the *dalang*, or puppet master, has inherited his skill and knowledge through generations of the same family. His is a multifaceted and complex role: he acts as shaman, storyteller, director, stage manager, musical conductor and curator. While he is the intermediary between the puppets and their audience, he remains unseen. He has to narrate the epic tales from memory, give voice to the puppets and cue the sound effects created by the accompanying musicians. He also has to be adept at improvisation, able to intermix his telling of familiar dramas with his own astute and satirical interjections that touch on topical issues and inject comic entertainment.

It is the *dalang* who sets the play in motion, beginning with a mantra as a salutation to the first, anonymous puppet master and as a blessing on performers and audience. The first puppet he displays is the *kayon*, a large leaf-shaped image employed to indicate a shift of time, place or mood. It can also signify non-figurative elements such as a mountain or a river, a weapon or a flame. The puppets, cut from blackened leather, are stained in coloured pigments and gilded in gold. They have delicate filigreed hairstyles and headdresses, and costumes detailed with carved ornamentation. Emanating from a Muslim culture that eschews any representation of the human form, the bodies and profiles of *wayang* puppets are deliberately elongated, their heads and facial features purposefully delineated in elaborate curves to emphasise their otherness. And each puppet portrays a specific character trait, such as wisdom or masculine strength, or signifies a distinct social status. About 50cm tall, inclusive of their central rod, with two other rods attached to their wrists and arms jointed in two places, they are designed to execute a wide repertoire of expressive gestures. As well as the mythological characters, a jester, Semar, and his clown assistants act as a chorus to bear witness to the unfolding drama. It is these puppets who underpin the sacred stories with a secular and comic subtext. At the end of each performance those characters who have died or disappeared during the drama reappear to be blessed with holy water. This ensures that their spirits will not escape to haunt either the audience or the other puppets.

Some years ago, I attended a week-long workshop to learn about the craft of making a *wayang* puppet. After an induction into its spiritual significance and an introduction to the use of the *kayon* and key characters, we were invited to choose one to replicate in thick black card. I chose Arjuna, a knight. Adventurous and brave, refined and quiet, he is bare-breasted and wears an intricately patterned sarong that billows out behind him. His long curled black hair is caught up, sweeping from the nape of his neck to the top of his head in an elegant curve. His facial features and limbs are elongated, his arms slender, his fingers delicate and his body is painted in gold, with the design on his sarong ornamented in daubs of white and blue paint.

Apart from the complexity of his hair and his sarong he seems simple enough. It will, I think, be a straightforward task to cut away morsel after morsel of black card with a sharp knife. But I soon realise that, because of the curvature of the design, it is tricky to maintain precision. Each of the small repeating spirals that pattern his sarong have fretted edges with tiny flowers sprinkled within them; the curls of his hair are delicately registered through narrow, curved incisions. The beauty of *wayang* shadow puppets is their flow. Their visual presence is not merely decorative but deliberately undulating. Each small cut is made on the curve and must be smooth and evenly spaced so as not to interrupt the eye. I find it is impossible to work with any speed and difficult to maintain such intense concentration.

My hand tires with the repetitive action of cutting at a slant. My eyes, constantly fixed on a black expanse, blur and lose focus. It is all too easy for my knife to slip.

Until you follow the process of another maker you cannot fully appreciate the level of skill and the amount of patience that is required to make what they make. It is only when you try to do what they do that you understand their mastery. It takes me the whole week to carve my shadow puppet and, even then, it is primitive compared to the exquisite puppets the workshop leader has shown us. While not exactly slapdash, mine lacks finesse. It also lacks something else: dedication. The making of a *wayang* puppet is, for its artisans, a devotional act, underpinned by religious faith. Their reverence is an intangible quality but one that imbues their craft with a visual equilibrium, a harmony expressed and transmitted through the puppet itself. My puppet has none of the eloquence nor sensitivity of those it is modelled on. While it is recognisably Arjuna, he lacks grace.

Shadow puppetry exists throughout the world, each culture evolving its own distinct style: the comic antics of Karogö in Turkey, the shadow-dance dramas of India, the mythological shadow stories of China. And it was when I went to China in 1995 that I first became aware of its shadow-puppetry traditions. I had come to the Sichuan University Museum in Chengdu to research the embroideries of the Miao, one of China's minority clans. Having sketched the stitched patterns on the symbolically crafted, embroidered Miao cloths that were on display, I wandered through to the other galleries, where I was beguiled by an unexpectedly diverse collection of shadow puppets. They were so beautiful, so intricate, that I felt compelled to sketch some, carefully replicating the contours of an exuberant goose, its scalloped feathers tinged with colour, its webbed feet firmly planted on an absent ground. I traced the image of a king prawn whose spine was shaded in russet hues, and whose long appendages seemed to quiver above bulging black eyes, despite it being stilled behind glass.

With no notion of what part they played in what drama, the sensitivity of their craftsmanship and the allure of their luminosity made them seductive. Made from oiled paper, painted in translucent – and, as I later learned, symbolic – colours, these were multi-jointed puppets designed to maximise movement. In the glow of lamplight they would have seemed like figures that had just stepped out from stained-glass windows, their colours softly illuminated. Later, I bought a tiny shadow-puppet head just 8cm high. Old, and carved from animal skin that had been scraped and thinned until it became transparent, it turned out to have been made in Sichuan in the nineteenth century. It is the head of a courtier. With his elaborate hairstyle, his tiny row of teeth gleaming below a handsome, twirling moustache, his corkscrew topknot fringed at its edge, he evokes an artisanal attention to detail that is extraordinary. When I researched further, I found that it was not only key characters that were afforded such creative labour but also stage scenery, furniture and animals. A tree would be gracefully leafed in a filigreed canopy of entangled branches; a desk cluttered with open books, a vase of spring flowers and a plethora of small, delicately rendered ornaments; and a horse would have its decorative, embroidered trappings faithfully reproduced in miniature exactitude. These were puppets designed to cast not only shadow but reveries.

By the mid-eighteenth century, Chinese shadow puppets had migrated to Europe, where they became known as Ombres Chinoises. While they were adopted, they were also altered. European puppeteers eschewed the toil involved in the lengthy creation of coloured and carved animal-hide puppets and replaced them with simpler silhouettes, generally cut from black cardboard or zinc. The most famous venue for shadow puppetry was Le Chat Noir, a cabaret club, the first of its kind, established at the end of the nineteenth century in Montmartre in Paris. Attracting radical artists, writers and composers – including Toulouse-Lautrec, Verlaine, Debussy and Satie – regular patrons banded together as Les Hydropathes (those who are afraid of water) to embrace an artistic life through an alcoholic haze.

The puppeteers turned to technology to fashion dreamscapes: glass panels painted with perspective illusions to provide a depth of field, electric light to modulate tone and atmosphere. Through their adult-centric shadow theatre they forged a new visual concept. With their intangible representations they reimagined the mood of historic events: Napoleon's retreat from Moscow, designed by the Russian-born illustrator Caran d' Ache (Emmanuel Poire), as a series of fifty dramatic tableaux that captured the triumph and humiliation of the French emperor; *Le Marche d' Etoile*, conceived by Henri Riviere, which re-envisaged the devotional procession to the crib of the newly born Jesus as a pilgrimage by the disabled and disadvantaged. The images that survive of Riviere's production show the poetic quality that the shadow artists at Le Chat Noir were able to achieve. Using figures that decreased in size to maximise the illusion of perspective, the imaginative use of colour-filtered light, and the skills of multiple puppeteers, Riviere created haunting images of the lame, the poor, the elderly and the desperate struggling to reach Bethlehem across a parched desert. With the death in 1897 of its founder, the impresario Rodolphe Salis, interest in Le Chat Noir and shadow puppetry declined. But its existence has remained like an echo in the cultural consciousness of Parisians. And, even today, most toyshops in Paris will display and sell miniature versions of Ombres Chinoises.

I am waiting in the school hall of Bannockburn Primary School for a group of 8–12-year-olds for whom I am to run a summer-holiday workshop. It has been organised by Stirling Play Services, a small, hard-working team tasked with providing disadvantaged children with social, creative and fun activities after school and in the holidays. With fifty children signed up for my four-day workshop, I suspect that the experience will be challenging.

The children arrive in a babble of voices, discarding lunch boxes and jackets as they crowd into the hall. The crescendo of banter and bravado makes the room shrink. The swell of their excitement and the blast of their energy is palpable.

'What's all this then?' A boy, hardly taller than my elbow, picks up a pile of neatly laid canes. He eyeballs me as he clatters them back down on the table.

'They're for the puppets,' I say with a bright, bright smile.

'Good luck with that, then,' he retorts, and moves on to finger the felt-tip pens.

His friends guffaw. One grazes his hand over a heap of fabric remnants.

'I dinna sew,' he says to no one in particular. 'I dinna like sewing. It's girls' stuff.'

'My mum sews,' another volunteers.

'Aye, well, she's not here though, is she?'

The Play Services team calls order and manages to corral the marauding children into some semblance of attentiveness before signalling for me to begin my spiel. I tell the children that in the next four days they will design, create and perform a shadow-puppet play for an audience of family and community members, that they will write the script and make the puppets and set, and that they will be the puppeteers. There is a collective grunt of unease, of incredulity. I try to gain purchase and credibility, knowing I have to come up with something fast if I am going to snare their interest, secure their confidence and encourage the will to try.

'What will our show be called?' I ask.

'Rubbish,' shouts one, and I earmark him as the jester of the pack and resolve to give him a task that will surprise and engage him.

'Mickey Mouse, Alien, Sesame Street.' The suggestions come hard and fast. 'Sleeping Beauty,' whispers a small girl still clutching her lunch box. 'Enrique,' proffers another. There is a communal rustle of recognition and I sense ignition, a small spark of interest.

'Tell me about Enrique,' I say.

The children stay quiet. Even the girl who has suggested the name is silent.

'Is he a boy or a cat or some kind of animal?' I ask.

'He's a singer,' the girl pipes up.

'He's Spanish,' adds the boy sitting next to her.

It turns out they are talking about Enrique Iglesias, the son of Julio Iglesias, the footballer turned singer, whose album *Vivir* is fast becoming a summer hit.

'Enrique it is,' I declare. 'Let's send Enrique on a journey. Where will he travel to?'

'Let's send him to China,' says a voice.

'China it is.'

And with a name and a place agreed, I divide the children into four groups, each one tasked with coming up with a separate scene, each supported by a member of the Play Services team. They imagine a talking bird who takes Enrique on a magic carpet to China. They imagine a strange, flower-thick jungle, a wise man with a giant sunflower as a compass, a beautiful pagoda and a rainbow that Enrique will slide over to get back home. It never ceases to amaze me how quickly children enter non-reality, how easily they free-float to fantastical worlds where all is possible.

With the scenario for the play sketched out, we make a giant list of all that is needed in the way of characters, scenes and props. And, after a demonstration of how shadow puppets are made and what they look like behind the screen, the children get busy with black card and coloured gels, setting to work with zeal now that they are in charge. The hall becomes a buzz of business: children drawing, scissoring, taping sticks to puppets, creating sound effects, rehearsing narration, trying out their characters behind the screen. They discover their capacity to create. This is craft not chipped away by poverty, nor roughened by deprivation. Rather, in the unfamiliar and simple world of shadow puppetry, these children find dexterity and finesse that are all too often elusive. I listen to the murmur of their absorption and know that I no longer have to keep a wary eye on the careless, the belligerent or the bored.

On the final afternoon, as the audience starts to arrive, I go backstage to where the puppeteers and technical team are whispering with mounting anxiety. I tell them that all they have to do now is to show how talented they are and entertain the crowd. Then I sit down with their parents and neighbours, their brothers and sisters, and tightly cross my fingers. This is the moment of sweet surrender, when I hand over my leadership to them and their creative aplomb.

And what aplomb! Bannockburn's *Enrique* is narrated faultlessly by two small girls, with puppets shadowing the screen in a captivating story of adventure. And, as the rainbow arched over the stage and Enrique reached home, as the strains of an actual Enrique Iglesias song – 'Al Despertar' (Upon Awakening) – signalled the end of the show, there was loud and sustained applause and fifty bashful children filed out to take a bow. They grinned as the applause continued, aware that they had created something magical and meaningful, that they were the authors of a mesmerising memory for them and for their audience.

8
Pinholes and Peepshows

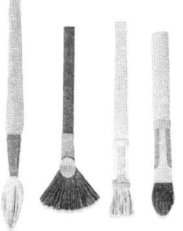

This is the eye, the chief and leader of all others
Leonardo da Vinci

I am standing in my garden with the actor Simon Callow. We are in our late twenties and on the brink of real careers. I have just been appointed Arts Project Officer in Northampton, to the delight of my mother, who is relieved that I finally have a job title she can share with her friends. Simon is in rehearsal for Peter Shaffer's play *Amadeus* at the National Theatre. He is to play Mozart, a role for which he will later receive the Laurence Olivier Award for Best Actor, a role which will catapult him into the theatrical limelight, bringing him fame if not fortune. But at this moment, in the garden, we have no inkling of what fate has in store for us.

We are standing stiffly, side by side. I am wearing a long, self-sewn skirt made from Laura Ashley fabric. Simon is rakish in a loose linen shirt as befits his newly acquired style of louche, urban theatricality. We are not smiling. Rather we are staring gravely ahead. What the photograph does not show, what it cannot reveal, is that the object of our rapt attention is a biscuit tin perched on the garden wall.

It is one of those large square tins bought at Christmas that are filled with cheese crackers, the biscuits that no one ever eats. I have decanted its stale contents and painted its silver interior black, jabbed a tiny hole in the centre of its lid and covered it with black tape. Inside, on the bottom of the tin, I have placed a sheet of photographic paper before sealing the tin's lid with more black tape. It is this biscuit tin that is perched on the garden wall and, with Simon rooted to the spot allotted to him, I have ripped off its small tab of tape and run to his side. Our eyes are fixed on what is now a pinhole camera.

This experiment in very early photography finds me uncertain as to the necessary exposure time. But I know that it is generally longer than one estimates and, given that the day is overcast and cloudy, I suggest to Simon that we allow twenty minutes. So we wait, tight-lipped as our Victorian forebears would have done, aware that any twitch, any glimmer of a grin, will risk blurring the image. Just as the first of that afternoon's rain begins to fall, our time is up and I race to the wall to replace the tape over the camera's aperture. We descend to the dark of my cellar and the red glow of the darkroom lamp I have installed there. We crouch over the tin and I carefully remove the paper and slide it into its prepared bath of developer. We watch as the ghost of us gradually appears. Then I quickly fish out the paper, dip it into its bath of fixer, and hold it out gingerly between the tips of my fingers. Simon and I peer at the image of ourselves stilled in the garden: two slightly blurred figures caught at a moment of change.

Pinhole photography was one of the mainstays of the community arts movement in the 1970s. At a time when photographic technology was developing apace, it seems curious that young artists like us should have reclaimed one of the simplest forms of visual media to create and display images of contemporary community life. But we wanted to bring communities affordable tools of self-expression and exercise our ingenuity in the face of limited funding. We thought we were being anarchic. We zealously set up community darkrooms in public toilets. We commandeered vans, blacked out their windows and taped their interiors with sheets of photographic paper to capture expansive panoramas of local vistas.

Some decades on, when the community arts movement had become more reliant on Arts Council grants and had accumulated more sophisticated resources, there was a national conference exploring its history and current practice. My fellow organiser and I thought it would be fun to begin the proceedings by auctioning off past memorabilia by way of a warm-up. We held up photographic evidence of embarrassing liaisons forged at earlier get-togethers, articles written with idealistic zest that claimed creative fulfilment could ameliorate marginalisation for the disenfranchised, and posters designed to spark a cultural revolution. Accompanying the toe-curling lots was a roughly printed small manual on pinhole photography, covering such intricacies as multiple portraits, zoom lenses, and the construction of pocket cameras from tobacco tins. There were no bidders, no claimants. By then we had all moved on. But I still have that pamphlet, a remnant of optimistic days when we thought we could change the world.

The pinhole camera has an illustrious heritage as the descendant of the camera obscura, an optical device which, in earlier centuries, garnered a controversial reputation as an occultist's tool, an artist's shortcut and an agent of Catholic proselytisation – surprising condemnations given that it was simply a way to project and reproduce images. Its possibilities excited the Italian artist-genius, Leonardo da Vinci, who was much exercised by the painterly effect of light and shadow. In his 1450 notebook, he recorded his experiments with a camera obscura:

> ... if the façade of a building, or a place, or a landscape is illuminated by the sun and a small hole drilled in the wall of a room in a building facing this, which is not directly lighted by the sun, then all the objects illuminated by the sun will send their images through this aperture and will appear, upside down, on the wall facing the hole. You will catch these pictures on a piece of white paper, which placed vertically in the room not far from that opening, and you will see all the above-mentioned objects on this paper in their natural shapes or colours ... [1]

Champions of da Vinci have been scandalised by any suggestion that his knowledge of how to replicate imagery through projection might have tempted him to use his camera obscura as a drawing aid, to forgo the labour of sketching out his masterpieces by eye. It is more than probable that the great engineer, experimenter and artistic innovator would have seized upon such a novel method not just to speed up production but, more importantly, to ensure greater exactitude of perspective. In his book *Secret Knowledge: Rediscovering the Lost Techniques of the Old Masters*, the artist David Hockney makes the case for not only da Vinci but other artistic luminaries, including

Vermeer, Rembrandt, Caravaggio and Velazquez, taking advantage of the expediency of this device to achieve an enviable verisimilitude in their paintings.[2]

Da Vinci, certainly, was not the first to test the potential of the camera obscura. Far from it. Mozi, the Chinese political philosopher, had experimented with it in the fifth century BC, Aristotle explored its use a century later, as did Anthemius of Tralles, the Greek mathematician, another 700 years on. In the tenth century, the Arab physician Ibn al Haytham had toyed with the phenomena, and even had an interior space specially constructed with a small hole in one of its walls to allow him to study the effect of projected light. But, for all these early optical explorers, there was a vexing drawback. The image the camera obscura replicated was inverted and upside down. And, at a time when glass itself was of primitive quality, the projected pictures lacked clarity, appearing as ghostly versions of their original. However, what was limiting for some was exploited by others, namely those magicians and purveyors of the supernatural, who used the camera obscura to conjure terrifying spectres and mysterious apparitions, much to the annoyance of the Catholic Church, which thought it should have the monopoly of inexplicable visions.

The problem of distortion was eventually solved by the Italian scholar and polymath Giambattista della Porta in the sixteenth century. He perfected the camera obscura, furnishing it with a convex lens and an angled concave mirror. An image could now be projected the right way up and the right way round. While della Porta was lauded by some for his inventiveness, he was viewed with deep suspicion by the Catholic inquisition, who regarded his interest in optical devices with as much distrust as they did his other questionable enthusiasms for palmistry, demonology and the magical arts. His 1558 book *Magia Naturalis* included recipes for a witch's balm that cured acne and mind-distorting drugs to assist communication with divine forces, as well as a description of a magic lantern which, when fuelled by the fat of a slain hare, was said to entice even the most modest woman to strip naked. Unsurprisingly, the book fanned the outrage of the Catholic hierarchy and provoked censorship.[3] It fell to the seventeenth-century Jesuit scholar and mathematician Athanasius Kircher to rescue the camera obscura's credibility and have it reinstated as a valid scientific and artistic tool. He sought to expose the bogus nature of its 'unreal' images and dent the zeal and plausibility of those hailed as conjurors of phantoms.[4]

As the quality of glass improved and advances in producing brighter light occurred, it became possible to project sharper and clearer images. The discovery of limelight in the 1820s – an intense white light realised by directing a flame at a cylinder of lime – was revolutionary. For the first time images could not only be projected in vibrant colour but they could also be viewed from a greater distance without losing their clarity. Camera obscuras began to appear in the drawing rooms of wealthy Victorians and larger versions were installed in seaside towns and cities throughout Britain as novel visitor attractions. A few of these still survive to enthral today's tourists, including one in Edinburgh, housed in its World of Illusions Museum.

Keen to explore its appeal, I took myself off to Edinburgh. When I had climbed the five flights of stairs to the camera obscura, I was ushered into a small rotunda where an audience was gathering, grouped around a large concave disc. As the lights dimmed, the operator began to slowly turn the disc. On it appeared a busy road with people going about their everyday lives, walking hither and thither, negotiating traffic, greeting friends and drinking coffee in pavement cafes. I suddenly realised that what we were seeing, in real time, was Princes Street, Edinburgh's main thoroughfare, and the streets around it, a mile and a half away. Shoppers, unaware that we were spying on them, were hurrying along, catching buses; commuters were trundling their cases to and from Waverley Station; here a cyclist was chaining up his bike, there a mother was stooping to pull a blanket over her baby in a pram. It seemed astonishing that, right in front of us, was the minutiae of a distant world, projected so clearly. As the disc turned, the operator zoomed in on different people, choosing who to spend time with and who to overlook. Then she gave the children in the audience a sheet of plain paper and showed them how they could use it to scoop up a passer-by. Oblivious to their capture, individuals were gleefully separated from their companions, removed from the urban hustle and bustle to appear isolated on a drift of white. With a final panoramic flourish, the operator rotated the disc one last time to let it sweep across Edinburgh's cityscape and, with that, the session was over. I tumbled out into the light feeling strangely triumphant at having been, for a short while, an unseen and unknown voyeur of other people's lives.

The peepshow proffers an opposite view of the world from that of the camera obscura. It provides a different visual thrill. Rather than using a small hole and mirror to capture what lies beyond, a peepshow's aperture enables the eye to trespass on a scene within a small box. What is revealed is not a projected image but rather a crafted microcosm: events and places reimagined by artists in illusionary perspective. The original 'perspective boxes', or 'show boxes', were generally small enough to be handheld and had a single peephole, although there were also larger versions, constructed as cabinets, created with multiple spyholes. They all contained expansive scenes in miniature glory: the funeral of the Duke of Wellington, the Battle of Waterloo, the Palace of Versailles, the torment of hell. Peepshows were designed to surprise, captivate and astonish. The ingenious use of perspective gave the impression of greater depth and transformed two-dimensional pictures into three-dimensional panoramas.

It was not only *what* was seen but *how* it was seen that heightened the appeal of peepshows. The exterior of a simple box or sturdy wooden cabinet did not betray what lay within. Such mystery added to their allure. Moreover, when viewed, a peepshow required concentration. With just one eye focused on the scene before them, a solitary spectator escaped into an interior world without distraction. This was an exclusive entertainment, its spyhole only accessible to one person at a time (or, if made with multiple apertures, a limited audience). A peepshow was, essentially, an individual, immersive and private indulgence and, as with my experience of Edinburgh's camera obscura, it offered a diversion that was tantalisingly voyeuristic.

It is Leon Battista Alberti, the fifteenth-century Italian Renaissance artist and author, who is cited as the originator of the peepshow, devising it as an example of perspective ingenuity. With scenes painted in translucent colours on small panes of glass, he found clever ways to manipulate the direction and density of his light sources. He employed coloured filters to diffuse the light so that day could change to night, calm to storm, and starlit skies and moonlit mountains appear as if by magic. To those who experienced one of his peepshows, who were the first to peer into recognisable landscapes miniaturised and captured in a box, it must have been truly a thing of wonder.

Peepshows, or showboxes, became collectable novelties commissioned by fifteenth-century court royals and connoisseurs, acquired as extensions of their Cabinets of Curiosity, their Wunderkammers, and made, like them, as large wooden cabinets with a number of holed panels through which different realistic or fantastical vistas could be discovered. There were others that were devised as curios, shaped like eggs. Made of marble, they were operated by a side knob which, when turned, revealed different images. Others had multiple mirrors to amplify the sense of depth, or additional strings and levers to engineer the movement of characters and other scenic features. Still more used the difference between projected and reflective light and perforated or pinpricked backdrops to reveal stars studded in a midnight sky or palace windows being lit by candlelight. And some panels were painted on both sides to enable a character to disappear, or an angel to materialise, by the simple shifting of light from front to back or vice versa.

But, despite such technical resourcefulness, it was the manner in which the interior of a peepshow was painted, the play on perspective and the deployment of trompe l'oeil, that produced the most intriguing effects, no more so than in seventeenth-century Dutch perspective boxes. One, a masterpiece of peepshow creativity, is conserved at the National Gallery in London. *Interior of a Dutch House* was created by Samuel van Hoogstraten, a Dutch painter of the Golden Age.[5] He provided two separate apertures and jettisoned one wall of his five-sided box as an experiment in sophisticated visual trickery. At first glance his interior appears confusing, a jumble of multiple views and distorted images. But, when the eye begins to settle on the interior's specifics, to look through the box's various vantage points, what it contains comes into focus. A dog, painted flat on the floor and up part of a wall, surprises you when it sits up in three-dimensional clarity as your focus changes. Other objects – an upholstered chair, a broom leaning idly against a wall, an empty wine glass on a table – similarly startle you by their sudden metamorphosis from two-dimensional reality to a lifelike appearance.

There is much to be discovered in van Hoogstraten's showbox: the woman sitting quietly reading in a corner; the shadow of a visitor glimpsed through the glass of a door; the content of gilt framed paintings, created as miniature anamorphisms, their detail seeming distorted until the eye and aperture lens are properly aligned. In this visual adventure, the viewer is forced to shift both viewpoint and focus room by room if all is to be noticed. When van Hoogstraten's work was exhibited in London in 1656 it caused a sensation, and the diarist John Evelyn recorded: 'all the artists and painters in town came flocking to see and admire it'.[6] And a later artistic admirer of peepshows was Thomas Gainsborough, the celebrated portrait painter, who was inspired to devise his own. Using oil-painted moveable transparencies lit from behind with candles, he softened the light on his small rural scenes by diffusing it through a screen of fine silk. Here were miniature and picturesque landscapes that captured not just light but mood and atmosphere to compose what a contemporary curator at the V&A Museum called 'a moonlit nocturn'.[7] It must have been intriguing for Gainsborough to experiment with encapsulating his atmospheric landscapes in layers of painted glass rather than layers of paint, to see the change in tonal quality when they were modulated by light projected through a silk screen. When his eye peered through his box's single aperture, the experience of his crafted art would have had an intensity lacking when he viewed his art at distance on a gallery wall.

I had marvelled at peepshows when I saw them for the first time, as imaginative small worlds devised by children under the guidance of an artist friend. Using recycled shoeboxes, she had helped them to make miniature landscapes that, when spied upon through a small hole, seemed like secret discoveries. So when, some years ago, a request went out for people in my glen to contribute to a local Christmas event in the village hall, a Treefest, which would showcase a range of eclectic, home-made whimsical or bizarre Christmas trees – large and small; real and artificial – I decided to transform an old shoebox into a peepshow. I cut out a large rectangle from the box's lid and replaced it with tracing paper, and made a small hole in one of the box's shortest sides, the size of a five-pence piece, just big enough for an eye to peer through. I thought I would expand the brief and rather than settle for just one tree I would present a winter wonderland forested in snow-clad fir trees. I plucked a couple of sheets of white paper from the printer tray, creased them a little and glued them onto the floor of the box to counterfeit a carpet of snow. Then I scrunched up more white paper, loosened it out to mimic the peaks and troughs of a snowy mountainside and stuck the sheets intermittently to the box's internal walls so that they billowed and flattened at strategic points. With scissors I snipped out tiny fir trees and a single stag, glued them in place, and strung a lace of LED lights haphazardly through my paper forest. When I closed the box, switched on its lights and peeped through its hole, what I discovered was enchantment, a magical miniature evocation of a winter's idyll, a tranquil snow-covered landscape with just one solitary stag caught momentarily in its shadows.

In the seventeenth and eighteenth centuries, the peepshow, or 'raree show' as it was more commonly called, became a popular attraction. Throughout Europe and the Far East, particularly in China and Japan, itinerant showmen and women peddled entertainment, carrying peepshows on their backs. The French Savoyards, with a performing animal in tow, became popular figures of romantic roguery, immortalised in figurines and prints.

In Britain, the portability of peepshows made them useful as a way for disabled veterans of the Napoleonic and Crimean Wars to earn an income. Easy to erect, quick to dismantle, showmen pitched their peepshows on city pavements and village greens and touted for business at local fairs and markets. As purveyors of wonder, these showmen also had to be performers. Peepshows were audiovisual experiences. Their appearance had to surprise and delight, but their promoters also had to be engaging storytellers and masters of sound effects. It was through their theatrical bravado that they whetted the appetites of those still fingering the coins in their pockets.

It should come as no surprise, given the voyeuristic nature of peepshows, that over time they were exploited as private titillations of sexual caprice. At the end of the nineteenth century, with the invention of Edison's kinetoscope and then the mutoscope (ways of producing photographic images in sequence at a fast pace to simulate movement, the prelude to moving pictures), came What the Butler Saw machines, installed as popular seaside attractions in amusement arcades. A penny in the slot would reward you with a short, grainy, black-and-white 'film' of a girl undressing or lovers embracing. These were not pornographic by modern-day standards – the girl would never remove more than her outer garments, never reveal more than a frilled petticoat or, at its most risqué, voluminous bloomers; the couple would remain fully dressed with only the urgency of their embrace betraying an illicit passion – but they were naughty, nonetheless. By the 1970s peepshows had been absorbed into the shady world of red-light districts, where a coin in the slot would buy you a few minutes of a live striptease performed behind glass.

While erotic peepshows were diverting for a minority, less provocative peepshows continued to appeal to a wider public and over the centuries have persisted in a variety of forms, reinvented in response to different cultural challenges. In Egypt in 2021, the Mahatat, an arts collective, brought together artists, architects, storytellers and musicians to resurrect and reinvent the *sandooks* or peepshows of the past that had been a regular feature of everyday street entertainment. They devised novel showboxes – a mirrored geodesic dome, like a huge disco ball, decorated with Islamic patterns; and a revamped ice-cream cart painted in pastel shades – as street installations that suggested familiarity but were also enticingly fanciful. They interviewed cab and minibus drivers, collecting contemporary stories and urban myths to dramatise in miniature. These were peepshows that presented audiences with a visual experience that, while rooted in the past, was still capable of being revelatory and relevant.

And when the Covid pandemic led to a decrease in theatre audiences, as people became more nervous of prolonged close proximity with others in enclosed spaces, Japan's Moonlight Mobile Theatre designed a new kind of auditorium for their dance performances. They built a rotunda encircled with small individual cubicles. Each member of the audience sat in solitude, facing a door in which there was a peephole and a letterbox through which they could view the show. Called 'mailbox' theatre, this was an innovation that solved the problem of social distancing while simultaneously encouraging audience members to concentrate wholly on what they were watching. With the rotunda having an audience capacity of only thirty, every show presented in it was a sellout. Its exclusivity proved to be as enticing as it had been for those earlier hand-held or boxed-cabinet peepshows.

Across time, peepshows have displayed great versatility. They can encompass a small, crafted landscape in a box or a full-sized circular auditorium. They can display fairy-tale tableaux or erotic thrills. And they can harbour depictions of historical events or intimate tragedies. What all these have in common, however, is that they stemmed from the explosion of interest in optical devices, the increasing desire to view the world differently, and in that they provided – literally – an alternative perspective on life.

I have come to Exeter to peruse the remarkable and comprehensive collection of optical devices and cinematic printed ephemera and artefacts garnered by the Scottish-born film-maker Bill Douglas and his fellow enthusiast and friend, Peter Jewell. On Bill Douglas's death in 1991, Peter Jewell donated their shared assembly of over 7,000 items to Exeter University, and in 1997 it was housed in a dedicated building, The Bill Douglas Cinema Museum. I arrive to a hospitable welcome from the museum's curator, Dr Phil Wickham. He has arranged that the sixty and more items I have requested to see are ready for inspection. Some are piled high on trolleys in the study room while others are available to view in the museum's galleries. He leads the way.

When the first trolley is wheeled to my side, I experience the familiar fizz of anticipation. There is nothing more exciting than seeing things in the flesh that you have only read about or seen as pictures in a book. While these descriptions and images might give you an impression of shape and size, only in their materiality can you appreciate the scale, the patina of age, the physicality of them. I pick up a pocket-sized paper diorama, Tim's Telescopic View, a concertina that, once opened out, reveals a series of separate but interconnected three-dimensional scenes. It was produced in 1977 for Queen Elizabeth II's Silver Jubilee, celebrating and illustrating her 1953 coronation, viewable through its small aperture. This historic event is captured in all its glory. Here are the streets decorated with long red banners, the tight press of the phalanxes of uniformed servicemen and the jostle of flag-waving crowds. I am looking down the Mall, through Admiralty Arch, to the famous fountain and, behind it, to Buckingham Palace. Emerging from the palace is the Queen herself, waving from her golden coach led by eight white horses, her progress protected by the Queen's Guard, resplendent in red tunics and tall bearskin hats. That such a small rectangle of paper can contain such a wealth of detail and capture the essence of ceremonial magnificence is paradoxical. Yet this physical reduction somehow enhances the visual impact while, surprisingly, its enforced focus seems to emphasise its specifics.

The majority of dioramas featured topographical scenes: celebrated vistas and distant lands made more palpable by the layered impact of their paper perspectives. The nineteenth-century traveller, author and botanist Maria Graham, Lady Callcott, made her own dioramas to share her experiences of Chile. Cleverly designed, with an aperture in its frontispiece created by leaving a void between the arching branches of her painting of a large tree, she transported those who peered into her creations to an exotic land of fertile plantations, moody mountains and sandy shores. Hers is only one of the 400 paper peepshows that are part of the Gestetner Collection in the V&A Museum in London. It includes other home-made pieces: fragile relics of an earlier age when looking and making were central to an expanding exploration of, and engagement with, the wider world. *How* something was made and viewed, not just *what* was seen, however, was what excited people. The advances in colour printing in the first decade of the twentieth century, the reduced cost of print both to produce and consume, and the potential of a newly acquired disposable income for the expanding, more leisured, middle classes all fanned the public's appetite for novel pictorial representations of real and imaginary places and people.

In the frenzy of visual curiosity that characterised the nineteenth century, the invention and popularity of optical devices seemed insatiable. Home-watched and, often, home-made, they were part of an expanding spectator culture that delighted in parlour recreations. The advent of affordable and brighter gas lighting allowed for evening entertainments to be enjoyed at home, pleasures that were fanned by Queen Victoria's much trumpeted domesticity with her Prince Albert. Moreover, new psychological thinking on child development expounded the benefits of shared family pastimes.

One of the most intriguing new-fangled devices to make an entrance was the kaleidoscope, a tube inserted with mirrors which, through its rotating top filled with shards of glass, could astonish its viewer with a medley of ever-shifting coloured patterns. While there is some evidence that kaleidoscopic effects were known to the ancient Egyptians, who used highly polished limestone arranged at different angles to watch dancers turn into moving mandalas, it was not until 1816 that a prototype of a manufacturable instrument was invented by Sir David Brewster, the eminent scientist and philosopher. His was an accidental discovery, happened upon while he was experimenting with the polarisation and refraction of light. Viewing objects at the end of two mirrors, he noticed that their reflected patterns rearranged themselves when he altered his viewpoint. Deciding to narrow his focus, he fashioned a drum with a hole at one end and a clear top at the other, inserting into it small pieces of coloured glass. When he looked through the hole and turned its top, he found that the glass moved into different arrangements with each turn, creating captivating, symmetrical patterns.

It would be nice to think that Brewster appreciated the beauty in what he perceived, that he was awed by the marvellous mercurial patterns he had produced, but seemingly that was not in his nature. According to his daughter, Margaret, her father was 'irritable, impatient, litigious and verbally aggressive'.[8] Hardly someone easily charmed by an idle pleasure. Brewster had higher hopes for his invention than mere amusement, patenting it as a device 'for exhibiting and creating beautiful Forms and Patterns of great use in all the ornamental Arts'.[9] It was scientific exactitude and artisanal potential, not personal visual wonder, that exercised him. Before his patent was granted, however, his discovery was copied and, recognising its marketable appeal, others made enviable profits through its mass production, with over 300,000 kaleidoscopes sold in America in the first six months of its availability.

Now, in the research room at the Bill Douglas Cinema Museum, I have an early model in my hand, made in heavy, black-lacquered metal. I hold it up and, as I turn it, moving motes of vivid colour group, disperse and rearrange themselves. I realise that its maker has deliberately included two large yellow capsules. They act as a controlling force, their heavier weight drawing the smaller pieces to them to create patterns that appear more consciously structured, although undisputedly random. It would have attracted keen interest: a revelation of not just what a kaleidoscope could show but how its contents could be manipulated, designed to offer a more intriguing visual experience. The plainness of the kaleidoscope in my hand, the severity of its casing, marks it out not as a toy but as an adult curiosity, born of a time when it would have been accorded scientific significance.

The kaleidoscope became the most persistent of these Victorian optical distractions. It is still popular today, marketed as a children's plaything, but in the hands of artists and kaleidoscope-makers it is a captivating tool of experimentation. In her book *Kaleidoscopes: Wonders of Wonder*, the American collector and promoter of kaleidoscopes, Cozy Baker, traces their history, their design, the variations of mirror assembly and their modern artistic manifestations. Over time their traditional contents, such as the small shards of glass scraps or translucent beads, have been supplemented with a more diverse range of objects – insect wings, coffee crystals, seashells, feathers and liquids. Mirrors have multiplied to effect ever more dazzling arrays of refracted imagery and are more cleverly angled to realise different formations such as spirals, honeycombs or squares.

The 1980s saw a revival of public interest in kaleidoscopes, particularly in the USA, which, by the millennium, had spawned over 40 American suppliers and exhibitors.

In response to this growing enthusiasm, Cozy Baker established the still-flourishing Brewster Kaleidoscope Society and established an annual international expo to provide information and advice on all things kaleidoscopic. And in Japan, as well as America, the flame of interest in kaleidoscopes has been rekindled. First introduced there by the East India Company, just three years after Brewster's invention, Japanese fascination with kaleidoscopes had waned over the centuries but, in the last two decades, has witnessed a revival. There are now numerous kaleidoscopic exhibitions mounted on an annual basis throughout the country. In 2004, a dedicated kaleidoscope museum was opened in Kyoto, which, as well as displaying traditional and contemporary models, presents a regular light show, organises workshops and hosts visits by celebrated kaleidoscope-makers. And kaleidoscopes have begun to be used as a form of therapy, placed in doctor's surgeries, in counselling waiting rooms and used in primary schools to induce a feeling of calm for those in need of soothing reassurance.

On the table, in the study room of the Bill Douglas Museum, I place a large black drum mounted on a handsome stand of turned and varnished wood. It is a zoetrope, which, with its decoration of Victorian paper scraps of pansies and pretty whimsical children, speaks of family fun. It is an early manifestation of moving pictures and a phenomenon in its time. Its rotating drum is notched evenly around its top rim and around its interior base a strip of paper has been inserted that, in a dozen small drawings, illustrates the progressive sequence of a clown juggling three balls:

a technique that was to later evolve, using celluloid, into cinematic stop-frame animation. As I rotate the drum and peer through the zoetrope's notches, the clown throws and catches, throws and catches.

I find an extant contemporary sketch of a zoetrope in use. A group of more than twenty people are grouped around a parlour table on which the zoetrope stands, illuminated by an overhanging lamp. I try to imagine what it must have been like for this original audience, seeing animated action together for the first time. For it was the zoetrope that introduced the possibility of communal viewing of moving images. When for centuries people and places had only ever been represented and observed in fixed pictures, it is unsurprising that the zoetrope was also named 'The Wheel of Life'. By the end of the nineteenth century, zoetropes had become a popular home entertainment and hundreds of zoetropic strips were produced, covering such diverse subjects as a couple waltzing, a galloping horse, a man balancing on a circus ball and boys playing leapfrog. It was the zoetrope that heralded the age of the scope. The stereoscope, megascope, cycloidotrope, choreutoscope, epidiascope and graphoscope and other innovative visual inventions, followed in quick succession: all variations and sophistications on light and picture projection. As the mid-nineteenth century wore on, the names of such novel optical devices became ever more fantastical and their functions ever more complicated – the anamorphoscope, the anorthoscope, the phenakistiscope, the praxinoscope, the zoopraxiscope – each offering a new way to witness the world.

But, while viewing devices became more sophisticated, optical inventiveness through simpler means could still captivate, as I discover when Dr Wickham, anticipating my interest, brings me a large box of Protean Views, named after the Greek sea god Proteus, who could assume different forms. Originally devised by the French photographer Louis Daguerre in the 1820s as a way to change the mood of a scene when viewed through a different light, protean pictures evolved into a novel way to change a scene entirely. While the technique was simple, its effect was atmospheric. A picture, printed on both sides of a piece of paper, its reverse only visible when held up to the light, changes when it is illuminated; its mutability enables the same scene to be captured at different historical moments merely through a shift of light. The box that Dr Wickham has furnished me with is crammed with sheafs of coloured sketches illustrating famous landmarks and beauty spots, cathedral interiors, historical events and dramatic scenes, all produced by William Spooner, a London-based printer in the 1840s. I pick up a lithograph and hold it up to the light. It changes. A picture of a church with its nave lit in a shaft of sunlight now appears shadowed at dusk, bathed in candlelight. I hold up another and a view of a restored Kenilworth Castle shifts in time to reveal its sixteenth-century splendour, with Queen Elizabeth I at its gates. Tourists idling over a spectacular view of Mount Vesuvius are superimposed onto the scene of its eruption in AD 79 with terrified onlookers watching aghast as the volcano spews out fire, flames and tumbling lava. My favourite, however, is of the solitary, exiled

Napoleon standing on St Helena's shore and watching the sun set over the distant horizon: a poignant portrait which, when light-filled, becomes a moment of memory – the Emperor of France returned to triumph, standing surveying his troops on another, now distant, shore. Protean Views became so appealing in their day that, for a while, they fanned a fad amongst genteel women to make their own, so much so that the pictures became known as 'Amelias'.

The delights of the Bill Douglas Museum seem endless. I wander through its permanent collection, enthralled by its cabinets entitled Shadow, Optical Illusions, Moving Pictures, Pioneers and more, trying not to become distracted by the visual temptations they display. But the expansive assembly of magic lanterns and their accompanying slides demand attention. The magic lantern came early to the history of optical devices. In 1666, we find the diarist Samuel Pepys being introduced to its charms, recording how a Mr Reeves brought him a lantern with pictures in glass 'to make strange things appear on a wall' which he judges 'very pretty'.[10]

Pepys was so impressed that he bought his own lantern at considerable expense. While his would have been the simplest of models, projecting hand-coloured pictures, the magic lantern evolved along with advances in the quality of glass and variations in lenses. By the nineteenth century, it was possible to present a dazzling show of brilliantly coloured images that could be enlarged with no distortion or fade, for families to enjoy at home or audiences to relish in community centres, churches and theatre auditoriums. This projection device offered an enthralling visual feast of large-scale imagery that, with the addition of clever mechanisms such as dissolves and pulleys, could appear animated.

A mainstay of popular visual entertainment in the nineteenth century, magic lantern shows persisted into the twentieth but have virtually disappeared today. What began as a simple, amusing visual entertainment created with a limited palette on hand-painted slides – with such themes as 'The Vagabond and the Swell', 'The Disappointed Fisherman' and 'The Courageous Lady Cyclist' – evolved into a media used extensively for both home consumption and public education. With a magic lantern show, a church service could be spiced up with vibrant illustrations of inspiring religious imagery. Tin Pan Alley, the American wellspring of popular music, could promote its latest sheet music through pictorial concerts. By the mid-nineteenth century, the Royal Polytechnic in London had become a popular attraction, drawing thousands to its spectacular visual shows in which multiple lanterns projected a dizzying array of images on a wide range of topics from astrology to zoology.

But it was the arrival of photography that made magic lanterns an essential prop for social, political and moral campaigning. Amateur actors were deployed on custombuilt sets to provide more realistic, and effective, representations of working people's lives – colliers, fishwives, factory hands – and ensure that the public became more aware of current issues. The Temperance Society in Britain took full advantage of these 'living photographs', depicting the depravity and despair caused by the evils of drink, with fictional scenes of poverty, abandonment and death. Its slide-show narratives such as 'The Gin Fiend', 'Ten Nights in a Bar Room' and 'The Drunkard's Reform' featured drink-sodden ne'er-do-wells, starving children and swooning mothers, with the final slide urging its audience to 'Sign the Pledge'. The children's charity Barnardo's commissioned slides that documented its rescue of street urchins and the Salvation Army amplified its message with a two-and-a-half-hour-long epic, 'Soldiers of the Cross', which traced the fate of the early Christian martyrs. Journalists made newsreels to report on contemporary catastrophes in alarming detail, geographers presented pictorial travelogues, commercial companies advertised their wares and political parties found a new medium for propaganda. As the nineteenth century wore on, no well-to-do home was without a magic lantern and people were encouraged to make their own trick slides, availing themselves of instructions found in magazines and books of the time.

I made lantern slides when I was a student at the Bristol Old Vic Theatre School. Although I was there for the theatre directors' course, the school had decided that the last thing I and my fellow trainee directors should be allowed to do was to be let loose amongst the impressionable acting students. Instead, for the first weeks, we were to receive a 'behind the scenes' education to gain insight into the challenges that faced different theatre departments.

First, we were installed in the carpentry workshop to learn the intricacies of building theatre sets and experience the terrors of the circular saw. Next, we were despatched to a tiny windowless room where one wall had multiple jacks plugged into ports and a tangle of trailing wires. There, like manic telephonists, we were taught how to plug in and pull out jacks to create soundscapes that might, one day, accompany the plays we directed. We layered up the acoustic drama of the brewing storm in Shakespeare's *King Lear* and attempted to capture the poignant end of Anton Chekhov's *The Cherry Orchard*, when the sound of a snapping string and a tree being felled slowly fades as the curtain falls. In the school's wardrobe department we stitched bonnets and repaired torn gussets, fashioned cravats and washed endless pairs of tights, and in the theatre itself we crawled along the rafters on narrow mesh shelves to tilt and angle theatre lamps and achieve the similitude of romantic moonlight or the sinister murkiness of a Victorian alleyway.

As a finale to our technical training, we were assigned tasks for an actual student enactment of Georg Buchner's *Danton's Death*, set during the French Revolution. I was told to make slides to be projected as visual commentary to the drama. They were to be sepia-tinted, appear as delicate ovals and, moreover, they were to be made of glass. The school's darkroom was duly unlocked and, after what I can only describe as a rudimentary induction on the technicalities of slide production, I was supplied with a box of clear glass slides and furnished with the date of my deadline. So it was that I began to experiment with the required photographic reproductions, but it was daunting. At first my images emerged blurred, my sepia-tinting proved too exuberant, my efforts to achieve a feathered outline for my ovals unsuccessful. But I persevered, caught up now in the challenge. And, over time, I mastered the process's intricacies, refined my images and, eventually, produced a serviceable set of slides. Ever resourceful, the head of the technical department used a wire coat hanger to improvise a cradle for holding the slides in place, which was summarily attached to a theatre lamp and, astonishingly, it worked. Danton rose to power, was usurped, tried and executed under my graceful images of eighteenth-century Paris.

At the start of the nineteenth century, wider knowledge – beyond one's own community and culture – lay largely within the pages of books, which the majority of people could neither read nor afford, or through the selective and often sentimental anecdotes of storytellers. By its end there had been a visual revolution. Through the invention and accessibility of peepshows, dioramas, zoetropes, magic lanterns and other optical devices, people were able to travel vicariously; to broaden their understanding of distant places, current events and other cultures and expand their imagination through novel visual representations. Such devices provided not just mental stimulus but the frisson of exploration, the sensation of discovery.

It was the image, more than the word, that fostered insights into more disparate human experiences, that illuminated the lives of others in distant places or those living in different circumstances, past and present, for those with limited access to worlds beyond their reach. And the potency of the image remains undiminished as the most seductive recorder, transmitter and interpreter of who we are and the world in which we live. TikTok, Instagram, Pinterest, Facebook, YouTube and other digital media have enabled people to collect and share images and visual information in new and ever more expansive ways. But compared to the privacy of the peepshow, where what was revealed was a microcosm of a real or fantastical world, a view of what lay beyond the spectator's direct experience, the images shared today are largely introspective, chosen as evidence of personal experiences and tastes, of intimate moments and selective interests. They face inwards rather than outwards. Paradoxically, despite our access to a much broader and diverse world of imagery, our gaze has narrowed. To see beyond our screens and, with friends, families and communities, engage with the small delights that people make allows us to savour a much more sensory and memorable experience of our world of wonder.

9
Lanterns

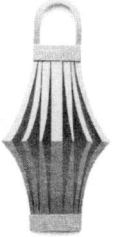

I am out with lanterns, looking for myself.
Emily Dickinson

I have come with my husband, Charlie, to Ulverston, a market town in Cumbria, to witness its annual lantern procession, which has been attracting large numbers of participants and a growing audience since 1983. The theme of this year's procession is 'Into the Garden . . .' and I have suggested to Charlie that we should make our own lantern and take part in the event. We could create a thistle, Scotland's national emblem, to trumpet our Scottish credentials. I have even done a rough sketch, a scrawl of struts and circles that I think will be simple for us to construct. Luckily there is a community lantern-making workshop taking place the night we arrive and I suggest we attend, make our lantern and have it ready for the procession the following evening.

The loveliness of the Lake District's lush green hills and glinting waters has slowed our progress to Ulverston and we arrive later than we intended. Having quickly checked in to our accommodation, we hurry to the workshop to find it well underway. Beneath a domed and whitewashed brick ceiling, a large room is filled with a fervour of communal creativity. People of all ages are clustered around long trestle tables overflowing with soaked willow stems, over 150cm high, and sheets of white tissue paper. There is a babble of consultation and congratulation as lantern-makers bend their willows (withies) this way and that and hold up nearly completed lanterns – encased in paper – for final inspection. Some have already attached their finished lanterns to long poles and are proudly parading them to whoops of admiration from enthusiastic onlookers. And as giant spiders and huge strawberries tower over us, in my head I readjust the scale of our proposed thistle.

A workshop leader welcomes us and furnishes us with essential materials: withies, sheets of tissue paper, masking tape, PVA glue and a sponge. We clasp them tentatively and scan the room for an available table. But every table seems occupied. For a nanosecond I feel a twinge of relief. Perhaps, if there is no space, we will have to forgo the challenge of crafting a huge three-dimensional thistle and instead scuttle off in search of food. But, just then, a woman beckons us with a cheery wave and, scooping up the large, concertinaed caterpillar that lies basking on her table, gestures for us to take her place.

We thank her, plop down our materials and consult my sketch. I talk Charlie through my plan, how eight small, curved struts will be joined to top and bottom circles for the thistle's sphere; how ten longer struts will become a framework for its flower head. A bunch of withies will act as the thistle's stem, to which we will attach leaves spined with long withies and veined with a series of gradated ones. We just need to cut the withies to size, tape them to their relevant parts, cover the emerging structure in paper and our thistle lantern will materialise before our very eyes. Charlie looks dubious. But he dutifully measures out the struts while I begin to curl withies into circles. When I start to tape the shortest withies to the top and bottom circles they prove wayward. A few bend to a natural curve but others stay stubbornly straight. Ever optimistic, I reassure Charlie that the tissue paper shell will coax them into shape, but I can see that he remains unconvinced.

Charlie smears a sheet of tissue paper with PVA and I smooth it over my misshapen sphere, but the perfect globe eludes me. The withies turn rebellious under my pressing hands, spring free from their taped captivity and puncture the fragile paper. I try again with the same result. Maybe, I suggest, we should leave that particular challenge and tackle the easier task of the leaves. Withies are duly cut to size, attached to their central spines, more glue is spread, more tissue paper patted down over them. The paper sticks in parts but stretches in others and creases as I try to smooth it. All around us the chatter is convivial, the crowd companionable, creativity and enjoyment abounds. While everyone else seems to be making progress and having fun, we tussle, prod ineffectually at our tissue membrane, poke each other inadvertently with our long stems of willow and grow irritated. We alone seem marooned in petulant frustration.

I proffer a solution: two sheets of paper instead of one: more strength, greater control. I watch as Charlie grimly sweeps another layer of glue across yet another sheet of tissue paper. I press the double layer over the leaf frame and lift it up. The paper buckles, slips a little, curls away from the edges. I realise that I have been reckless in my confidence, too reliant on my established craft credentials and too sure that I could conquer a simple lantern in half the time it would take other people. Making takes time. It needs patience. To make something well demands consideration and thought. As Charlie curses under his breath I fold away my sketch and suggest we leave. We will take the withies back to our accommodation and tomorrow morning – away from the banter of community camaraderie and out of sight of weathered lantern-makers – we will triumph, go more slowly and make something simpler, a slug perhaps, still suited to the garden theme.

We skulk into the night clutching our assignment of withies and go back to where we are staying. I google local shops, searching out suppliers of PVA glue and masking tape, of slug-coloured tissue paper. Then I look across to Charlie, relaxing over a beer now that he has been released from artistic endeavour, and propose that we forget about the lantern, that we content ourselves with being spectators rather than participants. He nods. We smile at each other. 'We can always make a thistle lantern back home,' I say. And, as I say it, I know that this will never happen, and Charlie knows it too, but it comforts us to feel that we have a fallback position, that our creative zeal has not been completely quashed and that we still have a small hold on our artistic pride.

The following evening we go, lantern-less, to the procession. We discover the quiet town of Ulverston overrun, rivered by hundreds of eager spectators who move in a murmuring current of excited anticipation towards the centre's cobbled streets. This is, palpably, a community gathering: local people coming to an event of their own making, held on their home turf. The majority have come in family groups. There are parents pushing babies in prams and toddlers in pushchairs, teenagers propelling grannies and grandads along in wheelchairs and daughters and sons holding steadying hands under the elbows of elderly parents: local people moving in a steady stream, confident of a night's entertainment.

Spectators are already settled on the narrow pavements. Some have brought blankets to spread along the kerbside for family members to share, others are sitting on the folddown chairs they have carried from home. Hawkers are peddling their LED novelties and the dark of the night is punctuated with the quiver of flashing sabres and glow sticks. Over the next half-hour, as we wait for the procession to begin, the streets become thronged and more thronged with onlookers and yet, despite the size of the crowd and the push of people, the atmosphere feels intimate, more like a neighbourhood street party than a public spectacle. After nearly forty years of lantern processions the event is embedded in community memory as an annual reassertion of Ulverston's spirit.

There is a communal sigh of pleasure from the crowd as the rumble of an approaching percussion band sounds in the still of the night and the first of what is to be four processions – each emerging from the cardinal points of the town – comes into view. People cheer, clap, shout out hellos and hold up their phones to snap photos of passing lanterns. And the lanterns themselves are wondrous, seeming even more spectacular to me and Charlie because we can appreciate the difficulty in their making. There are magic mushrooms studded in fairy lights with fairies skipping around their fungi caps. Huge daffodils are petalled in glimmering yellow and enormous carrots glow in iridescent orange. Insects proliferate, spiders, bees, caterpillars and ladybirds dancing around a carnival of birds and a hunch of hedgehogs. There are snails of ghostly white and multi-coloured butterflies with their sparkling wings fluttering from swaying poles. One participant carries a lanterned wishing well, another a garden shed, and there are a plethora of outsized watering cans. A giant peapod has each pea gleaming in a bauble of light. When a small girl passes carrying a single huge leaf, Charlie and I trace its internal withy structure with a keen eye and a pang of envy.

By the time the last procession wends its way down the street, the audience has become sated and its applause is more desultory: excitement waning in the evening's chill. Just as the smallest children start to become restless and dogs begin to bark, the procession ends. Blankets are gathered up, chairs folded away and people begin to move en masse towards the park for the grand finale, the fireworks display, but Charlie and I resist the pull of the crowd and the lure of sky explosions and turn for home.

The first lantern procession took place in Ulverston in September 1983. It was organised by Welfare State International, an internationally acclaimed arts company that was founded in the 1960s. This was the time in Britain when establishment culture clashed with the burgeoning, more anarchic ambitions of young artists. Those emerging from art schools, drama colleges and media courses were intent on diverging from the mainstream. Traditional art forms and venues were being rejected in favour of more radical ways to make affordable art that was more accessible to all, art that had more relevance to increasingly diverse and marginalised communities. Amongst that band of cultural radicals were Sue Gill and John Fox, a husband-and-wife team, who founded their company in 1968 (tagline: 'Engineers of the Imagination') and set about devising large-scale, street-based extravaganzas. Universal themes such as good versus evil, power and oppression were revisited in allegorical dramas that referenced a dysfunctional Britain: old myths reimagined, their morals and values distilled through an ironic social and political visual commentary that carried local resonance.

Welfare State adopted the age-old mantle of the Lord of Misrule – the peasant-cum-master of ceremonies of the Christmastide Feast of Fools – to produce subversive entertainment. Its repertoire consisted of street carnivals exuberant with enormous articulated satirical puppets made from found materials, bizarre pageants with players costumed as grotesques, and spectacular fire shows such as 'Parliament in Flames' on Guy Fawkes Night when, for a decade, a replica of the Houses of Parliament was set ablaze as giant caricatures of establishment figures and recognisable radicals played out themes of liberty and suppression. In 1983, their mesmerising, allegorical 'Raising of the *Titanic*' saw a reconstruction of the vast doomed liner being dragged from the depths of the Canal Dock Basin in London's Limehouse as a symbol of the current social decay. These were events purposed to be ephemeral. The essence of a Welfare State show lay in its immediacy, in the live performance. You had to be there to be snared by its energy, to feel transported by its extraordinariness. Mood and atmosphere were captured in the visceral bash and blare of street music, the sudden and surprising appearance, alongside the visual mayhem, of something unexpectedly tender: a white bird silhouetted against the moon; a thousand paper hearts falling from on high; a baby lying cocooned in a cradle. Their shows had a wild, palpable beauty. And there was always fire, always flame: a living spark that, in the night juxtaposed with the tumult of strange imagery and swelling music, brought the audience back to something more elemental than all the fabricated spectacle: the flicker of hope, the glimmer of revolt.

John and Sue moved to Ulverston with their young family in 1979. They put down roots and became part of the community. And it was that move that prompted a change of focus for them. They began to develop more participatory work, shows and events *with* rather than *for* local residents, events that responded more insightfully to what needed to be shown and expressed to boost community cohesion and confidence. They wanted to find a different way to articulate 'community', to nurture events through which people could discover their innate creativity and experience a more connected, more joyous sense of belonging to the place they lived in and those they lived amongst.

The Lantern Festival was inspired by a visit the company made to Japan when it was invited to participate in the first Japanese International Theatre Festival. One night, while they were there, John and Sue were taken to watch an event in a village by the sea. They stood transfixed as a large group of men, wearing only loincloths, descended wooded paths from the high rim of a forested volcano. On their hunched shoulders they bore thirty lit lanterns, each carried by ten men, each accompanied by twenty drummers. The lanterns, nearly five metres high, translucent and intricately painted, emerged in the gloom of night like glorious stained-glass windows. Atop each lantern sat a small boy ringing a plaintive bell, swaying precariously in a rites-of-passage ritual, as the men made their way down the hill to the harbour. There, in a Shinto Buddhist ceremony, the lanterns were taken out to sea in local fishing boats as blessings. The villagers held vigil until their vibrant colours had ebbed away and all that was left was a lingering distant trill of bells. It was, John later said, 'a chance vision'. The juxtaposition of the strength of the men, the majestic presence of their lanterns and the fragility of the small boys and their tinkling bells was spellbinding.

In the years to come, looking for a way to bring together the Ulverston community, to offer a moment of delight amidst the travails of rising unemployment and community malaise, they introduced the annual lantern parade. What began as a modest celebration, involving a hundred local people, has expanded, over forty years, to become a procession involving more than a thousand participants. And, while Welfare State provided the initial impetus and has nurtured local know-how in lantern-making, the event is now entirely in community hands.

The emphasis of the Ulverston Lantern Procession is not on its effect but on its purpose. It is designed to be inclusive, to be large-hearted. As well as people creating their own lanterns, lanterns are made for the babies born each year, while others are made as 'surrogate' lanterns for those unable, because of age or infirmity, to take part in the procession. Neighbourhoods exchange lanterns and every year 'gift' lanterns are bestowed on local individuals as an acknowledgement and thank you for the contribution they have made to the town's wellbeing: a gift that is given privately and subsequently carried by its recipient or their representative in the procession. This collective making and gifting, the gathering together as participants and audience, offers the Ulverston community the means to reground itself, to express, display and celebrate its imagination in an annual affirmation and evocation of its spirit.

Lanterns have been lit through millennia and across cultures for ceremonial events, festivals and religious rituals. And today they are still being hung along city streets, sent soaring into the dark of the night sky, set drifting on the waves of lapping water and carried, as in Ulverston, in community processions. Their universal appeal persists. While their origins lie in diverse and ancient beliefs – Chinese Buddhism, Slavic paganism, Hindu astrology, Christian veneration to name but some – and they are despatched with myriad motives – to honour ancestors, commemorate loss, heal emotional and physical wounds, release personal hopes or atone for past misdeeds – they all manifest a yearning for a better self, a better world, a better future. Making and lighting a lantern, bringing it to take its place among the others already assembled in a village, town or city, challenges nature's curfew. It confronts the dark of night with light conjured by a human hand. Metaphorically, it banishes evil to allow goodness to prevail. Individual and collective lanterns represent human resilience. Through them personal emotions can be released in a public performance to manifest a collective longing for renewal.

The ritualistic use of lanterns is thought to be rooted in Iranian Zoroastrianism, one of the world's most ancient religions. Its central deity, Ahura Mazda, the god of the sky, was venerated as the bringer of the light of wisdom, a light that could dispel the shadow of chaos; because of him, Zoroastrians chose fire and flame as the focus for their devotional practice, with lamps of clay continuously burning in their temples. When Zoroastrianism spread, reaching central Asia in the sixth century BC, elements of its spiritual culture, including the practice of the lighting of lamps, became entwined with those of other religions. So it was in China. Even before Zoroastrians began to settle in China, sky lanterns were already employed as expedient forms of long-distance communication, particularly useful in warfare, and lanterns also adorned Chinese temples. But the fusion of Zoroastrianism and Buddhism saw lanterns garnering a deeper significance, to become viewed as agents of human hope. Now lanterns are ever-present in Chinese life. They have been embraced as a national talisman: both auspicious and protective.

There are multiple stories and legends surrounding the source of the display of lanterns in China. Alongside the theory of Iranian descent is the claim that their popularity was fanned by a 2,000-year-old Buddhist dictat that the darkness of ignorance and prejudice was to be eradicated, symbolically, by the lighting of lanterns when the moon was at its fullest. Others tell of ancient times when a Chinese emperor threatened to burn down a village, a fate only averted when local people swathed the village in red lanterns to dupe the emperor into believing that the deed was done. Whatever the origin, China is a land of lanterns. Made of bronze, clay, stone, bamboo, silk or mulberry paper; decorated with carvings, paintings and calligraphed poems; lanterns punctuate China's physical world, indoor and out, constantly on display in public places and family homes. And they serve myriad purposes in the everyday emotional life of the Chinese. Red lanterns, embellished with Chinese knots or symbolic flowers and birds, are gifted to newlyweds as blessings for a harmonious and happy future. Blue and white lanterns, carrying written memorials and condolences from family members, friends and neighbours, are part of traditional funeral rites. Lanterns brought by children on their first day of school are lit by their teachers as a tangible commitment, on both sides, to follow the light of knowledge. And in public venues, local restaurants, houses and factories, they frame doorways and entrances in pairs, in even numbers, as a symbol of togetherness.

This is a culture that, despite increasing consumerism, still values the deeper significance that meaningful objects can bring to the spirit of a place and a community. It is the antithesis of the Scottish culture I grew up in, where the sixteenth-century Protestant Reformation and its ensuing Calvinist zeal removed all vestiges of superstitious iconography and erased any dependence on the agency of objects to mediate salvation. It left a people bereft of spiritual props. The crafting of objects that harboured emotive expression, the sacred rites that employed inanimate objects as spiritual agents – statues and relics, sacred cloths and holy medals – as well as ritual festivities were all but banished. Scotland became a country of functionality, a nation robbed of its emotional and spiritual connection to beauty beyond its natural world.

For key traditional Chinese celebrations – the New Year Spring Festival and the Mid-Autumn Moon Festival – lanterns proclaim a time of hope, purification and revival. Through their flickering flames, their ritual lighting and their display, the failures and hurts of the past can be set aside and new possibilities embraced. Lanterns provide an immersive frisson of optimism. At festival time they line city streets, are looped around civic squares and hoisted up outside homes, shops, hotels and supermarkets to ensure that China is ablaze, gloriously illuminated with the portents of good fortune. More lanterns inscribed with wishes carpet lakes and rivers or drift heavenwards to stud the sky like newly formed stars. Children process, door to door, carrying home-made lanterns on which they have written age-old riddles, as Chinese children have done generation upon generation. And public parks and city temples are transformed into fantastical wonderlands of light with vistas of illuminated mythical creatures, zodiac signs, flowers, pagodas, birds and butterflies, and, more recently, cartoon characters.

The scale of these Chinese events is extraordinary. In the village of Tuntou in Hebei Province, 100 million pairs of red lanterns, large and small, decorated with gold, are made each year to supply a domestic and wider market. Over a million people descend on the city of Chengdu after sundown each February to meander through its lantern parks and create their own hand-decorated lanterns.

And millions more visit Nanjing, one of the ancient capitals of dynastic China, for its annual Qinhuai Lantern Festival, where they wander among the 400,000 lanterns that light up the city's temples, riverways and parks. This is an age-old festival whose charm was captured in Cao Xueqin's classic eighteenth-century novel *Dream of the Red Chamber*:

> Due to the season, the willows and apricot trees were bare and leafless; but instead of leaves, they were adorned with hundreds of tiny lanterns ... other lanterns made from shells and feathers, shaped like lotus flowers, water lilies, ducks, and herons floated on the water's surface... Together they formed a fairyland of jewelled light.[1]

In the 1960s, the Qinhuai Lantern Festival came to an abrupt end, falling victim to the sweeping changes that the Chinese Cultural Revolution had instigated with the erasure of the Four Olds: old customs, old cultures, old habits and old ideas. After Mao's death in 1976 and with the decline of revolutionary ideology, Nanjing was quick to reclaim its heritage. Over subsequent decades it has revived its lantern festival, reopened its lantern market and renovated its famed Confucius Temple, the traditional centre for its lantern festivities. In 1984 the Qinhuai Lantern Craft Association was formed and a museum of lantern arts established in the city. The city's sights, however, are not set on just recapturing past traditions but on investing in economic and cultural profit for the future through becoming recognised internationally as a centre for innovative lantern-making and display. It is the fusion of the familiar and traditional with contemporary ingenuity and imagination in lantern design that makes the Qinhuai Lantern Festival so magnetic.

Chinese lantern festivals are enthusiastically replicated throughout the world by a Chinese diaspora eager to exercise a distinct identity and honour a rich visual and symbolic heritage. But the use of hanging lanterns, floating lanterns and sky lanterns has universal appeal as a magical way to mark a diversity of cultural, historical and religious celebrations, and different communities have nuanced their lantern festivities in different ways to intensify their visual drama.

In the small railway village of Shifeng in Taiwan, 30,000 sky lanterns, inscribed with visitors' individual names and wishes, are released every month. These are colour-coded: red for health and peace, blue for better career prospects, orange for love, green for vigour. Each collective release sees people scanning the skies to watch the thousands of lanterns gently drift up in a heavenly rainbow of hope. The city of Hoi An in Vietnam, dubbed 'lantern city', switches off all its electricity every month for an hour when the full moon is in full glow. The hanging and floating lanterns that fill the city turn its streets and rivers into sites of iridescent wonder, crowded with illuminated iconography and illustrations of age-old stories. Symbolic flowers, mythical creatures and auspicious deities jostle for attention amidst lanterns of every imaginable shape and size, their colour and imagery spilling in reflected glory over the Mekong River and canopying Hoi An's skyline.

The *Laylat al-Qadr*, or Night of Power, when the Koran was sent to Earth by Allah, is celebrated in Freetown,

Sierra Leone, with street processions that teem with elaborate lantern floats featuring ships, animals, airplanes, mosques, biblical narratives and Islamic iconography such as Muhammad's winged horse or the tomb of the martyr, Husayn. And thousands of people gather for the Nagatoro Funadama festival in South Korea, to follow the progress of large boats as they sail down the Arakawa River, each one stacked with hundreds of lit paper lanterns, in a ritual that is both a salutation and a supplication to local water deities, in gratitude for their past protection and as entreaties for its continuance. It is similar to the offerings of small lit lanterns that people in India launch on the Ganges each day to carry blessings to Ganga, the Hindu goddess of water, and petition her for their future happiness. Ganga is also venerated in Thailand where, for its Loi Krathong Festival, people make floating lanterns, shaped and coloured like lotus flowers, the symbol of purity and rebirth, to despatch in sacred homage to the goddess. These delicate floating vessels appear like luminous flowers, bobbing on a gentle lap of waves, to make a light-filled garden of spiritual devotion.

Such floating lanterns have their own mesmeric, haunting beauty. Stilled and silent on a dark stretch of water, it is the flicker of their flame that imbues them with the glimmer of life, that evokes a sentinel spirit. Because of this, floating lanterns are eloquent expressions of commemoration, emblematic of loss. The memorial floating lanterns that are lit annually on the Namgang River in the South Korean city of Jinju have historical resonance. During the 1592 Imjin War against the Japanese, its South Korean population filled the river with lanterns to impede the progress of the enemy troops advancing on the city. And when, despite their efforts, the city fell under siege, those trapped there used lanterns to send messages to families living across the river, while others tried to flee in its waters. So many of those who tried to escape were cut down by samurai soldiers that it was reported that the river ran red with their blood. Now floating lanterns are lit each October in memory of the 70,000 who died in the conflict. And more, many more, are lit around the river and in the city itself, including a grand sculptural arcade composed of over 20,000 lanterns, replaced each year, on which local people write their individual wishes in a tangible, communal display of future dreams.

But the most poignant of floating lantern events must surely be that which takes place each August in the Japanese cities of Hiroshima and Nagasaki. It was there that, on 6 and 9 August 1945, atomic bombs were used for the first – and so far only – time in conflict, decimating their populations and destroying their cities. It is estimated that over 120,000 people died in the initial blast in Hiroshima alone – a third of its people – and thousands more succumbed to the effects of radiation poisoning in its aftermath. Each year, the communities of both cities create memorial lanterns to float out to sea. In doing so they are following a traditional Japanese ritual of connection, that of Toro Nagashi. It occurs at the end of the Obon festival, a period of ancestral worship when it is believed that the gates of heaven and hell are opened for a short while to allow the spirits of the dead to be reunited with their families. Toro Nagashi marks the time of parting, when the souls of the departed have to return to their afterworld and families make a floating lantern to accompany them and act as their guide: some inscribed with text and imagery as personal testimonials to ensure acceptance when they reach their final destination.

In Hiroshima and Nagasaki the lanterns of Toro Nagashi encompass individual and collective grief. Some are made as visual biographies bearing pictures of lost loved ones, the children or relatives who have died. They are decorated with family emblems and illustrated with motifs that record unfulfilled potential and possibility – motifs that convey a personality, that document an occupation, a hobby or a talent. Others are left blank to emphasise absence: a story untold, a life not fully lived. To scan the rivers of these cities glowing with the lights of thousands of kindled ghost spirits, a shimmering of souls drifting back to their place of rest, must be so extraordinarily moving: lanterns made not only to commemorate but to lament, guardians of sorrow, of memory and of continuing familial care.

Some lantern rituals are rooted in religious faith. Sikhs and Jains mark Diwali, the Festival of Light, by lighting small *diyas* or oil lamps to signify the victory of light over darkness, good over evil and knowledge over ignorance. Muslims traditionally light ornate glass lanterns, *fawanees*, to celebrate the holy month of Ramadan, a period of fasting. Hung at the entrances to neighbourhoods, in the doorways of people's homes, outside public buildings and in street markets, they herald the coming of night and the time when families can gather to eat together. There is also a tradition of children making their own Ramadan lanterns, often in the shape of a mosque, which they take to neighbours' houses as a gift or hang in their own homes as devotional decoration.

Buddhists mark *Pavarana*, the end of the Buddhist lent, when monks leave their three-month period of seclusion, by the lighting of sky lanterns in a ritualistic release of appeals for forgiveness and purification. While in Java, at the Borobudur Temple, one of the largest Buddhist temples in the world, they launch sky lanterns for Vesak Day in commemoration of the three most significant moments in Buddha's life: when he was born, reached enlightenment and died. These lanterns are beacons of entreaty, sent as seekers of Buddha's spiritual guidance: each person's desire for enlightenment manifested in the kindling of their lantern's flame. This is a sacred and solemn ceremony. Monks dressed in saffron robes process with torches across a ground patterned with votive nightlights; scriptures are recited, mantras chanted, participants are sprinkled with holy water; and each lantern is lit with consecrated fire. Only then are the thousands of 'puja' (ceremonial) lanterns released, lifting to the sky as individual petitions and conveyors of collective faith, to discharge the prayers of those present.

Christian communities have also embraced lantern display as a sacred rite. In the municipality of Mendrisio in Switzerland, on the days preceding Easter, 10,000 people join locals for a dramatic re-enactment of the passion and crucifixion of Christ. In an event that began in the sixteenth century as a counter-Reformation assertion of Catholic faith, over 300 large lanterns of transparent cloth called *i trasparenti* are processed on poles, each painted with illustrations of Christ's passion, the instruments of his torture and other Catholic symbols. Funeral dirges sound out as forty horsemen and costumed torchbearers lead 700 participants, walking behind a large crucifix, through streets thronged with onlookers. And in Poland and Portugal the feast day of John the Baptist is observed with lantern processions and the releasing of sky lanterns; while, in Germany and Czechoslovakia, it is St Martin's feast day that is celebrated, with children making paper lanterns to process through their local neighbourhoods, accompanied by the singing of songs and visits to people's homes in the hope of being rewarded with sweets.

St Martin's Day is also celebrated with lanterns in Switzerland but, rather than being made from paper, these are lanterns created from hollowed-out turnips that are intricately carved in delicate designs. Turnips crowd together on balconies, pattern neighbourhood gardens and sway from overhead wires. Hundreds more are used to construct enormous lantern floats to swell spectacular street parades in a traditional thanksgiving event that is rooted in agricultural folklore, when the lighting of turnips was thought to augur a good harvest.

In other parts of the world, it is pumpkins that are hollowed out to fashion lanterns for Halloween, the All Hallows' Eve festivities at the end of October, which some say emanated from age-old Celtic harvest festivals and others from Christian holy days. Most probably, they owe their origin to a combination of both. Unlike the exquisite filigree lanterns of Switzerland, British and American Halloween lanterns, made from pumpkins, are designed as grotesques, caricatured with gaping mouths baring teeth, triangular noses and holed slits for eyes. They are purposed as protective talismans to frighten off evil spirits. The gouging out of the dense flesh of a pumpkin is not for the faint-hearted, nor the impatient, as I know from personal experience, when we had a French family visit us one Halloween. Over-eager to induct their children in our traditions, I bought an enormous pumpkin and set to work on the kitchen table to demonstrate its transformation from vegetable to demonic lantern. I plunged my knife into the pumpkin's innards and began to slice off chunks of its flesh, but the children's interest soon turned to boredom as the minutes ticked by. Despite using the sharpest knife I could find, the pumpkin proved reluctant to relinquish enough of its contents to enable the carving of its grimacing features to begin. While the children drifted away in search of better entertainment, I wrestled on until a lantern did eventually emerge. My efforts were applauded, somewhat half-heartedly, by our French guests and the lantern took its place on our doorstep, where its snapping jaws seemed to grimace at me resentfully whenever I passed.

Today, around the world, lantern events proliferate. In Britain in 2024, community lantern processions took place not just in Ulverston but in Derby, Leeds, Arbroath, Helston, Okehampton and many more villages, towns and cities throughout the country. But the spiritual beliefs that lay at the heart of their origin are in danger of being forgotten. The larger these events grow, the further they move away from the quietude and reflective quality that once characterised them and the more they lose what made them special, what made them unique. And with that loss, the heartfelt salve they once inculcated is diminished. But, perhaps, for those who participate in them, these increasingly secular events still offer a different kind of comfort in their collective, celebratory energy. Their growing popularity and the seismic increase in their visitor numbers, however, have brought new challenges. Emergency services and local authorities are facing more pressure to provide better crowd control and safety measures and to find the financial resources such provision entails. It leaves organisers with an unenviable dilemma. How best to maintain visitor appeal while conserving the qualities that make such events special: a sense of intimacy, of ancestral connection, of emotional and spiritual release.

The impact on ecological sustainability lantern celebrations engender is also being questioned. While traditional lanterns were home-made from natural materials, as demand for them has grown, many are now mass-manufactured from unrecyclable components. The remains of sodden lanterns pollute our waters. Sky lanterns can cause danger to birds and air traffic and, if their flame has not been extinguished, they can start forest fires and harm wildlife. All over the world steps are being taken to avert their damage. Sky lanterns are now banned in many countries, while others have restricted their sale. Teams of volunteers are being recruited to retrieve the debris of floating lanterns and the use of sustainable materials for lantern-making is being more actively encouraged.

It is curious that, despite their popularity and the apparently enthusiastic participation they attract, despite their rich and multifaceted history, their spectacular presence and the spellbinding visual experience they offer, lanterns – their making and their display – is little documented. Researching them has proved surprisingly challenging.

There seem to be very few books devoted to the subject and little in the way of scholarly attention paid to their genesis and evolution. Outside of tour agencies' websites, travel blogs and event promotions, they have scant mention. Even then, most of what is featured are photographs that capture their collective visual impact. There is rarely any mention of their purpose, few descriptions of the lanterns themselves, and even less information on the various techniques used by lantern-makers. That said, it is interesting, and reassuring, to discover that even the largest lantern festivals and processions host lantern workshops, that there is still a recognition that these events need the spirit that personal investment brings. Many festivals now provide kits that can be bought in advance for you to make your own lantern; others offer materials on site so that participants can personalise their lanterns with illustrations and private memories and messages. And many of the most recently established lantern events emphasise their role as a memorable, beautiful and thoughtful way to experience a sense of community.

When the Atlanta spa shootings in 2021 fanned anxiety about anti-Asian acts of violence and the surge of racial hate crimes the pandemic had fostered, concerned Americans responded by organising an annual Festival for Justice and Remembrance that has lanterns at its heart. Taking place each year at Edgemont National Park in New Jersey, it is publicised as a time for interfaith reflection and as an 'illuminated memorial for all souls lost to racial violence and inequality'.[2] Another festival, RISE, held in the flat Mojave Desert, a mere 25-minute drive away from the neon lights of Las Vegas, promotes a 'place for reflection and introspection' and invites its 20,000 participants to write their own thoughts on 100 per cent biodegradable paper lanterns. Encouraging its participants to recreate responsibly, this event is not based on any religion or tradition but responds to the human impulse in a fast-changing and distressing world to find a 'mellow, serene, soulful space'.[3] And, across America, there are now over fifty newly established, annual lantern events organised by the Water Lantern Festival, with visitors invited to inscribe their hopes or memories of loved ones on lanterns made from sustainable materials. Promising an experience for 'emotional healing and rejuvenation', the organisers emphasise the potency of a collective release of lanterns to 'share positive energy, spread love and kindness, and find comfort and strength'. Over a million people respond each year to its call.[4]

The day after the lantern procession in Ulverston, I met up with John Fox. We talked about the event's genesis, about his 'chance vision' in Japan. For John, while the Ulverston event is secular and not imbued with the spiritual significance of the Japanese ritual he witnessed, it still has spirit at its heart: the spirit of a community exercising its creativity and its own sense of possibility. We talked of what the people of Ulverston gained from being involved. John felt that the preparations for the procession brought local people together with a common goal in an imaginative challenge that demanded co-operation. Its workshops offered participants the opportunity to be surprised, to discover their own innate talents and each other in a different way. Moreover, taking part in the procession was exciting.

It allowed people to escape the mundane and invest in something extraordinary: to become begetters of wonder. He believes in the potency of strange images, images that offer a different dimension, that encourage people to experience the world in an unexpected way. And for this, scale is important: the size of the lanterns themselves, the hundreds that sway together above people's heads, the swell of the crowds who gather to watch them pass.

But John also wondered if the event's increasing popularity has seen it become more of a spectator sport rather than, as intended, an event to bolster community confidence and cohesion. It is a danger inherent in other such events when they are loosed from their origins. The Ulverston Lantern Procession was first conceived, first experienced, in the throes of Thatcher's Britain when communities felt that their way of life, their stability, was under threat. It was born out of an urgent need to assert Ulverston's community identity. While it continues in tough times, the response by many communities to economic frailty is to garner tourist interest, to scale up local events to attract increased outside support. But, in doing so, there is a danger that it is the spectators who become the focus, who appropriate the emotional agenda. It is the audience's engagement, expectation and response that drives the atmosphere, the spirit. What the Ulverston Lantern Procession has retained, however, and what can never be erased from its essence, is its human legacy. After forty years, it binds generation to generation and provides the comfort of continuity. People who made lanterns for the procession in the past, then helped their children make theirs, now watch their grandchildren carrying their own creations. The procession has become so ingrained in the local psyche that it is now considered a time-honoured tradition.

Later John sent me one of his essays, 'A New Role for the Artist', and in it I found an extract that seemed to sum up the reason why so many thousands, so many millions of people across the world make lanterns and take part in lantern events: 'In this unsettling time of enforced hysteria it could be useful to lay down the initial ground rules of a culture which may be less materially based, but where more people will actively participate and gain the power to rejoice in moments that are wonderful and significant.'

He ends with a call to creativity, where every generation and every community 'is given freedom to participate and collaborate. Where re-generation is of the soul and not of economics. Where a holistic way of being is given credence and where making art is a daily experience for everyone.'[5]

An Ending

> *Imagination is the beginning of creation. You imagine what you desire, you will what you imagine, you create what you will.*
> George Bernard Shaw

All over the world there are people sitting at home folding and refolding paper to fashion origami birds or boats. They are snipping out small paper shards to create delicate paper-cuts or ingenious pop-up pictures. Some are gluing wooden struts to fabric to construct a kite decorated with symbolic motifs and inscribed with personal messages. Others are holding up a home-made cylinder to their eye to watch as their familiar world fragments and its detail becomes kaleidoscopic, segmented in ever-changing symmetrical patterns. And still more are out in the cold, rolling up snow with numbing fingers to build a snowman or basking in a summer's sun as their children spade up sand, heaping and moulding it into a moated castle that, like the snowman, will all too soon be gone. And I am making a lantern.

On my kitchen table I have laid out its requirements: some coloured remnants of rib stock nylon – a fabric that might seem to lack charm but, once lit, acquires a vivid luminosity that is entrancing – glue, scissors, and needle and thread: all that I need to make something that, hopefully, will be beautiful. I have discarded the idea of making a thistle lantern. In the gloom of a winter's afternoon something cheerier, less soulful than my national emblem seems more appropriate. Instead, I have decided to make a bird: the symbol of freedom, the harbinger of spring, a beckoner of hope. I have at my disposal a template, the wire frame of a bird that I bought in Manchester's Chinatown years ago that was once covered in coloured paper – paper that has long since disintegrated. It is this that I will now repurpose as a lantern.

My bird will not be realistic. Rather it is to be a bird of fantasy, of fairy tales and myths, its plumage bright in orange and green, turquoise and yellow, a bird that might be glimpsed in a dream flying in a blur of rainbowed hues. I cover its frame, piece by piece, in a patchwork of bright fabric, sewing each scrap taut along the ribs of wire. I have sewn since I was a child and made needlework my profession in later life. Armed with a needle and thread I am a confident maker, well-practised in how to tease out frustrating knots and coax my fabric to my will. I begin with the wings, cutting out scallops of green rib stock nylon and underlaying them with orange, stitching them tightly onto the frame. I repeat the process with turquoise for the body, fans of yellow and green for the tail. I sew on sequins to ape the bird's glimmering eyes and a morsel of vivid orange for its beak. Then I root around in my hoard of ribbons and braids, leftovers from my days of community textile-making, searching out some further embellishment and discovering a skein of glistening gold braid. With the

An Ending

fabric now clinging to the bird's surface like a skin, I stitch the braid around its wings and tail, sew it along its turquoise body. And it is done.

Outside the world is dimming, the sky is turning black and I turn off the light and switch on the LED bulb I have placed inside the bird. It is a moment of quietude. It seems that the only things alive are me and the glowing, fantastical bird now nesting on my table. And, as we sit in the calm of the darkened room, my task complete, the bird seems to demand a role beyond being merely decorative. So I whisper it a wish and settle it at the kitchen window so it can transmit its light and my hope to the world beyond. And this small act makes me feel connected to generations of other makers, those I have researched who, through centuries and across cultures, have made things with a purpose in mind – to honour their ancestors, protect their homes, convey their dreams, or commemorate those they have loved: people making a small delight that matters to them, that manifests some longing that lies deep within their hearts.

Notes

CHAPTER I. PAPER BOATS

1 David Mitchell's Origami Heaven, https://origamiheaven.com/historyofthepaperboat.
2 Known on the continent as Johannes De Sacrobosco, Thorndike, L., *The 'Sphere' of Sacrobosco and Its Commentators* (Chicago: University of Chicago Press, 1949).
3 S. Chauncey Woolsey, *The Letters of Jane Austen*, Monday, 24 October 1808, pp. 61–2, https://www.gutenberg.org/files/42078/42078-h/42078-h.htm.
4 Thomas Medwin, *The Life of Percy Bysshe Shelley* (London: Thomas Cautley Newby, 1847), p. 152.
5 Thomas Jefferson Hogg, *Shelley at Oxford* (London: Methuen & Co., 1904), pp. 50–1.
6 Neil Fraistat and Donald H. Reiman (eds), *Shelley's Poetry and Prose* (New York: W.W. Norton & Company, 2002), pp. 328–9.
7 Collins Classics, *Rabindranath Tagore, Selected Poems* (London: Harpers Press, 2013), p. 138.
8 http//www.paperboatcharity.org.uk.
9 https://timesofindia.indiatimes.com/city/cuttack/cuttack-2000-students-set-guinness-record-with-23000-paper-boats-in-35-mins/articleshow/95548761.cms.
10 https://indiabookofrecords.in/smallest-paper-boat-made-by-a-child/.
11 Maggie Browne, *Pleasant Work for Busy Fingers* (London: Cassell and Company Limited, 1896), p. 18.

12 Adam Smith, *The Theory of Modern Sentiments* (London: Henry G. Bohn, 1855) p. 1.
13 Louise Wylie and Jan Patience, *Arrivals and Sailings: The Making of George Wylie* (Edinburgh: Birlinn, 2015), p. 149.
14 https://paperboats.org/about/.
15 ©Karine Polwart. *Making Ready*, https://www.karinepolwart.com/.

CHAPTER 2: PAPER-CUTS AND POP-UPS

1 https://collection.museeyslparis.com/ws/collection/app/plugin/museum/series?id=31.
2 https://museeyslparis.com/stories/new-entry-1.
3 https://www.nytimes.com/2014/07/19/arts/tom-tierney-who-made-paper-dolls-an-art-form-dies-at-85.html.
4 Scottish Poetry Library, *The Tale of 10 Mysterious Book Sculptures GIFTED to the City of Words and Ideas* (Edinburgh: Polygon, 2013).
5 Peter Apian (1495–1552), *Astronomicum Caesareum*, New York Public Library, Schwarzman Building – Rare Book Collection Room 328, available online, https://www.nypl.org/events/exhibitions/galleries/explorations/item/5392.

CHAPTER 3: PAPER THEATRES

1 George Speaight, *The Toy Theatre*, Harvard Library Bulletin, vol XIX, no. 3, July 1971, p. 308.
2 Charles Dickens, *A Christmas Tree* (London: Book Cub Associates/Michael O' Mara Books Ltd,1969) pp. 19–21.
3 Robert Louis Stevenson, *Memories and Portraits* (London: Chatto & Windus, 1887), p. 232.
4 John Oxenford, 'The Toy Theatre', *The Era Almanack* (London: Frederic Ledger, 1871), pp. 67–8.
5 Jean Cocteau, *La Difficulté d' être* (Editions du Rocher, 1989) p. 51.
6 Peter Brook, *Threads of Time* (London: Methuen, 1998), p. 4.
7 John Foster, *The Life of Charles Dickens* (London: Chapman & Hall Ltd, 1875), p. 84.
8 E. Routledge (ed.), *Every Boy's Book: A Complete Encyclopaedia of Sports and Amusements* (London: George Routledge and Sons, 1869) p. 768.

Notes

9 https://lemonde.fr/archives/article/1983/12/08/portrait-de-l-artiste_2851250_1819218.html, 2/7.
10 A.E. Wilson, *Penny Plain, Two Pence Coloured: A History of the Juvenile Drama* (London: George F. Harrap & Co. Ltd, 1932), pp. 47–8.
11 Edward Draper, 'Calendar & Scenes', in *The Savage Club Papers 1869*, cited by George Speaight in *The History of the English Toy Theatre* (Massachusetts: Plays, Inc., 1969) p. 43.
12 Wilson, *Penny Plain, Two Pence Coloured*, p. 65.
13 Marisa Hayes, 'The Magic Is in the Miniature: Toy Theatre Thrives Online During Quarantine', https://thetheatretimes.com/the-magic-is-in-the-miniature, 26 April 2020.
14 Clive Hicks-Jenkins Artlog, 'Down the Rabbit Hole: picturing Alice', 6 September 2014, https://clivehicksjenkins.wordpress.com.

CHAPTER 4: SNOW AND SAND

1 Robert Macfarlane, *Landmarks* (London: Penguin, 2016), pp. 87–9.
2 Mika Hannula, *The Politics of Small Gestures: Chances and Challenges for Contemporary Art* (Istanbul: Art-ist, 2006).
3 Bob Eckstein, *The History of the Snowman: From the Ice Age to the Flea Market* (New York: Simon Spotlight Entertainment an imprint of Simon & Schuster, 2007).
4 Carol Ann Duffy, *The Wound in Time*, published online 2018.
5 YouTube, Jessica Langford Animator, THE GIFT, 8 August 2022.
6 Andy Goldsworthy, *Midsummer Snowballs* (London: Thames & Hudson 2001), p. 35.

CHAPTER 5: BUBBLES, BLOW BOOKS AND KITES

1 Marcus Terentius Varro, *De Re Rustica*, trans. F.H. Belvoir.
2 Hendrik Goltzius, *Allegory of Transience ('Homo Bulla')*, 1594, National Gallery of Art, Washington Accession No. 2000.55.1.
3 David Bailly, *Self Portrait with Vanitas Symbols*, 1651, Stedelijk Museum De Lakenhal, Leiden.
4 Jan Steen, *The Dancing Couple*, 1663, National Gallery of Art, Widener Collection, Washington Accession No: 1942.9.81.
5 John Everett Millais, *Bubbles*, 1886, Lady Lever Art Gallery, Port Sunlight, UK, Accession Number: L916.

Notes

6   Gerolamo Cardano, *De Subtilitate*, ed. John M. Forrester, Arizona Centre for Medieval and Renaissance Studies Tempe, Arizona, 2013.
7   Reginald Scot, *Discoverie of Witchcraft* 1584, Book xiii, Chapter xxxiii (London: Elliot Stock, 1886) p. 343.
8   Ibid.
9   Ibid.
10 Ibid.
11 Louise George Clubb, 'A Magic Book of Renaissance Shows', *Artibus et Historiae*, vol. 28, no. 55, 2007, pp. 37–52, JSTOR, http://www.jstor.org/stable/20067138.
12 Clive Hart, *Kites: An Historical Survey* (London: Faber & Faber, 1967), plate 17.
13 Giambattista della Porta, *Magia Naturalis*, chapter 5, 'Chaos', p. 407.
14 Khaled Hosseini, *The Kite Runner* (London: Bloomsbury, 2018).
15 George Pocock, *The Aeropleustic Art, or, Navigation in the Air by the use of Kites or Buoyant Sails*, 1827, p. 1, https://books.google.co.uk/books/about/The_Aeropleustic_Art_Or_Navigation_in_th.html?id=It5eAAAAcAAJ&redir_esc=y
16 Feb. 1828, A London Newspaper, Notice of an attempt to Navigate the air by means of Kites, p. 95 as cited in http://www.energy/kitesystems.net
17 George Pocock, *The Aeropleustic Art, or, Navigation in the Air by the use of Kites or Buoyant Sails*, p. 31.
18 https://www.rafmuseum.org.uk/documents/online_exhibitions/rfc/cody_kite.pdf.

CHAPTER 6: DRESSING UP

1   Verity Wilson, *Dressing Up: A History of Britain in Fancy Dress* (London: Reaktion Books Ltd, 2022), p. 256.
2   Ibid., p. 259.
3   Milla C. Riggio, 'Introduction: Resistance and Identity: Carnival in Trinidad and Tobago', *TDR* (1988–), vol. 42, no. 3, pp. 7–23, JSTOR, http://www.jstor.org/stable/1146676.
4   https://www.theguardian.com/commentisfree/article/2024/aug/27/notting-hill-carnival-crime-cop-critics-met-police.
5   Phyllis Galembo, *Maske* (New York: Aperture Foundation, 2016), p. 79.

Notes

6 Roy Strong, *Art and Power: Renaissance Festivals 1450–1650* (Suffolk: The Boydell Press, 1984), p. 3.
7 'THE BRADLEY BALL PREPARATIONS Nearly Competed for an Entertainment Which Promises to be Historic' (*New York Times*, 7 February 1897), https://halfpuddinghalfsauce.blogspot.com/2013/02/the-bradley-martin-ball-preparations.html, 7 February 2013.
8 *Julia Margaret Cameron: by Herself*, Virginia Woolf and Roger Fry, (Pallas Athene 2023), p. 20.
9 Wison, *Dressing Up: A History of Fancy Dress in Britain*, p. 268.
10 Tara Mayer, 'Cultural Cross-Dressing: Posing and Performance in Orientalist Portraits', *Journal of the Royal Asiatic Society*, vol. 22, no. 2 (April 2012). pp. 281–98, JSTOR, http://www.jstor.org/stable/41490100.
11 Arden Holt, *Fancy Dresses Described: A Glossary of Victorian Costumes* (London: Dover, 2017), pp. 23, 54, 95, 124, 135, 206, 244, 257–8, 276, 279.
12 Eliza Davis Aria, *Costume, Fanciful, Historical and Theatrical* (London: Macmillan and Co., 1906), p. 185.
13 J. Stevenson (ed.), *Selections from Unpublished Manuscripts in the College of Arms & the British Museum, illustrating the Reign of Mary, Queen of Scots* (Glasgow: Maitland Club 42, 1832), pp. 119–20.
14 Rictor Norton (Ed) "Hulme Fancy Dress Ball, 1880" *Homosexuality in Nineteenth-Century England: A Sourcebook*, 1 December 2018, updated 5 December 2018, https://rictornorton.co.uk/eighteen/1880ball.htm.
15 Rictor Norton (ed.), 'Jonathen Wild Exposes Charles Hitchin, 1718', *Homosexuality in Eighteenth Century England: A Sourcebook*. 29 April 2000, updated 16 Jun 2000, https://www.rictornorton.co.uk/eighteen/hitchen 2.htm.
16 Charles H. Hughes, "Postscript to paper on 'Erotopaths' – An Organization of Colored Erotopaths, "*Alienist and Neurologist (St Louis, Mo.)*, vol 14, no 4 (Oct. 1893) pp. 73–32

CHAPTER 7: PUPPETS

1 Burr Tillstrom, *'Berlin Wall'*, YouTube -Nataloff.
2 Officially called *Ningyo-Joruri Bunrakuza*, https://www2.ntj.jac.go.jp/unesco/bunraku/en/theatre/index.html.

Notes

3 Didier Plassard, 'Puppetry for a Total War: French and German Puppet Plays in World War 1', *Representing Alterity through Puppetry and Performing Objects*, edited by John Bell, Mathew Isaac Cohen, and Jungmin Song, https://digitalcommons.lib.uconn.edu/ballinst_alterity/6, pp.2–3.
4 Eileen Blumenthal, *Puppets and Puppetry: An Illustrated Word Survey* (London: Thames & Hudson, 2005) p. 174.
5 C.L. Dretel, *The Gift of Happy Memories: A World War II Christmas Play at Ravensbrück*, Open Library of Humanities, 8 (2), pp 1–31, DOI, https://olh.openlibhums.org/article/id/6379/.
6 Jan Malik, *Puppetry in Czechoslovakia* (Prague: Orbis, 1948), p. 36.
7 Blumenthal, *Puppets and Puppetry*, p. 163.
8 *World Encyclopaedia of Puppetry Arts*, https//wepa.unima.org/en/reichsinstitut-fur-puppenspiel/.
9 Blumenthal, *Puppets and Puppetry*, p. 163.
10 Fan Pen Li Chen and Bradford Clarke, 'A Survey of Puppetry in China (Summers 2008 and 2009)', *Asian Theatre Journal*, vol. 27, no. 2 (Fall 2010), copyright 2010 by University of Hawai'i Press.
11 https://thejudyproject.exeter.ac.uk.
12 Alissa Mello, Claudia Orenstein and Cariad Astles (eds), *Women and Puppetry: Critical and Historical Investigations*, (Abington, New York: Routledge, 2019).
13 Ibid., Claudia Orenstein, 'Class, gender and ritual puppetry: negotiating revival for the hakomawashi puppeteers of Tokushima, Japan', pp.105–111.
14 V.K. Karthika, 'Girl Power in Puppetry', *India Art Review*, 30 September 2022, https://indiaartreview.com/stories/tholppavakkooth-shadow-puppetry-rajitha/.
15 Mello, Orenstein and Astles, *Women and Puppetry*, Heather Jeanne Denyer, 'Werewere Liking Vicky Tsikplonou, and Adama Lucie Bacco: female artists appropriating puppetry to empower women in West Africa', pp. 85–100.
16 Ibid., Salma Mohseni Ardehali, 'Whispering women, shouting puppets: women and puppetry in Iran', pp. 121–2.
17 Ibid., Daniz Basar, 'Modes of Pleasure: contemporary feminist erotic puppet theatre from Istanbul with love', pp. 35–49.

Notes

CHAPTER 8: PINHOLES AND PEEPSHOWS

1. Leonardo da Vinca, *Codex Atlanticus*, 1502, folio 357, Ambrosian Library, Milan, Italy.
2. David Hockney, *Secret Knowledge: Rediscovering the Lost Techniques of the Old Masters* (London: Thames & Hudson, 2001).
3. Giambattista della Porta, *Magia Naturalis*, 1558.
4. Joscelyn Godwin, *Athanasius Kircher's Theatre of the World* (London: Thames & Hudson, 2009), pp. 212–3, plates 11, 32 & 33.
5. Samuel van Hoogstraten, *Interior of a Dutch House*, the National Gallery, London, NG3832.
6. Cited by Richard Balzer, *Peepshows: A Visual History* (New York: Harry N. Abrams, Inc., 1998), p. 21.
7. 'Wooden Moonlight Landscape with Pool and Figure at the Door of a Cottage', https://collections.vam.ac.uk/item/O17300/, accession no: P33–1955.
8. Cited in Cozy Baker, *Kaleidoscopes: Wonders of Wonder* (California: C&T Publishing Inc., 1999) p. 11.
9. British Patent #4136 (July 1817).
10. *The Diary of Samuel Pepys*, '19 August 1666', https://www.pepysdiary.com/diary/1666/08/19.

CHAPTER 9: LANTERNS

1. Cao Xueqin, *Dream of the Red Chamber* (Honglou Meng), vol. 1 (Imprint: Daybreak Studios), p. 331.
2. https://aapimontclair.org/lantern-festival-2024.
3. https://risefestival.com.
4. https://www.waterlanternfestival.com.
5. John Fox, *A New Role for the Artist*, March 2013, published by Francois Matarasso, 29 March 2016, https://arestlessart.com/john-fox-a-new-role-for-the-artist

Acknowledgements

To Ewan Amstrong, Philip Dundas, Cathy Jeffries and Ginnie Smith for taking the time and trouble to provide feedback on my early scribblings. To Peter McCaughey and Lizzy O'Brien at WAVE particle, the puppeteer Andy Jones and film animator Jessica Langford, and the playwright and theatre director Patrick Sandford for lending me their stories. To John Fox and Sue Gill of Dead Good Guides (www.deadgoodguides.co.uk) for their help in describing the work of Welfare State International. To all those who have augmented my research so generously: the artist David Harding; the folklorist and singer Margaret Bennett; the art historian Barbara Maria Stafford, emeritus professor at the University of California; the archivist Annabel Valentine at Oxford Brookes University; the puppeteer Emily Goodwin of the Garvald Edinburgh Puppetry Workshop; the construction worker Connor Burns; the archivist Mark Manivong of the Rare Books and Special Collection Division of the Library of Congress in Washington; Sarah Wheale and Nicole Gilroy at the Bodleian Libraries University of Oxford; the multidisciplinary artist Yulya Dukhovny of Microscope Toy Theatre; Akemi Roy for information on Japanese kites; the Japan Arts Council for clarification on the *bunraku* performances in Japan; and my neighbour, Christine Merchant, for help with French translation. To the Bill Douglas Cinema Museum at the University of Exeter, in particular Dr Phil Wickham, for financial and research assistance for my study of its collection; to Olivier Flaviano of La Galerie Dior for providing invaluable insight into Yves Saint Laurent's dress-up dolls and toy theatre; to the book artist and print-maker Patricia Silva for her information on her *Paper Boats* publication with Lyall Harris; and to my neighbour, Adrian Squires, for helping me understand the mysteries of a blow book. To Scotland's Makar, Kathleen Jamie, for allowing me to use an extract from her poem 'What the Clyde said, after COP26', and to the singer-songwriter Karine Polwart for letting me quote from her paper-boat song. To all involved in the 2023 Preetzer Papiertheatertreffen in Preetz, Germany, for their warm welcome. Most especially to Juliet Brooke and Jo Dingley for their early editorial support and to my editor Charlotte Humphery of Sceptre at Hodder & Stoughton, who has stoically persevered in guiding this book through to its best conclusion. To Nico Parfitt and Ian Allen for their meticulous care of my prose and to Louise Court at Sceptre for her unflagging zeal in promoting my work. Thank you to Helen Musselwhite for her superb paper-cut artwork for the book's cover. And, of course, to my agent Jenny Brown, for her unfailing enthusiasm and support. Lastly, and never least, to my husband Charlie and my children Kim and Jamie for knowing not to keep asking how the book is coming along.

Bibliography

CHAPTER 1: PAPER BOATS

Rhodes, C., *Outsider Art; Spontaneous Alternatives* (London: Thames & Hudson, 2000)

Tagore, R., *Selected Poems* (London, William Collins Publishers, 2013)

Wyllie, L. and J. Patience, *Arrivals and Sailings: The Making of George Wyllie* (Edinburgh: Birlinn Ltd, 2016)

CHAPTER 2: PAPER-CUTS AND POP-UPS

Apotheloz, C., (introduction), *Paper Cuts*, by Johann-Jacob Hauswirth and Louis-Davd Saugy (London: Thames and Hudson, 1980)

Arquette K., Adrea Zocchi and Jerry Vigil, *Day of the Dead Crafts: More than 24 Projects that Celebrate Dia de Los Muertos* (USA, Cantata Books, Wiley Publishing Inc., 2008)

Heyenga, L., (compiler), *Paper Cutting: Contemporary Artists Timeless Craft* (San Francisco: Chronicle Books LL, 2011)

Kurlansky, M., *Paper: Paging through History* (New York, London: W.W. Norton & Company Inc., 2016)

Marsack, R., (introduction), *The Tale of 10 Mysterious Book Sculptures Gifted to the City of Words and Ideas* (Edinburgh: Polygon, Birlinn Ltd, 2013)

Pienkowski, J., *Haunted House* (London: Willam Heinemann Ltd, 1979)

Schlapfer-Geiser, S., *Traditional Papercutting: The Art of Scherenschnitte* (New York: Lark Books, Sterling Publishing Co. Ltd, 1996)

Smith, J., *Notes on the History of Origami* (London: British Origami Society, 2014)

Tierney, T., *New Attitude: an Adult Paperdoll Book* (USA: Schiffer Publishing Ltd, 2008)

CHAPTER 3: PAPER THEATRES

Baldwin, P., *Toy Theatres of the World* (London: A. Zwemmer Ltd, 1992)

Garfield, S., *In Miniature: How Small Things Illuminate the World* (Edinburgh: Canongate Books Ltd, 2018)

Nash, E.P., *Manga Kamishibai: The Art of Japanese Paper Theater* (New York: Abrams Comicarts, Harry N. Abrams Inc., 2009)

Powell, D., (introduction), *Robert Louis Stevenson A Penny Plain & Twopence Coloured* (London: Pollock's Toy Museum Trust, 2022)

Powell, D., and J.R. Piggott and Horatio Blood, *Printing the Toy Theatre* (London: Pollock's Toy Museum Trust, 2009)

Powell, D., *William West and the Regency Toy Theatre* (London: Sir John Soane's Museum, 2004)

Speaight, G., *The History of the English Toy Theatre* (London: Studio Vista Ltd, 1969)

Stewart, S., *On Longing: Narratives of the Miniature, the Gigantic, the Souvenir, the Collection* (USA: Duke University Press Books, 1992)

Wilson, A.E., *Penny Plain, Twopence Coloured: A History of the Juvenile Drama* (London, George G. Harrap & Co. Ltd 1932, reproduced as a facsimile of the original from Gale, Cengage Learning and the British Library)

Bibliography

CHAPTER 4: SNOW AND SAND

Eckstein, B., *The History of the Snowman* (New York: Simon Spotlight Entertainment, Simon & Schuster, 2007)
Goldsworthy, A., *Midsummer Snowballs* (London: Thames & Hudson, 2001)
Macfarlane, R., *Landmarks* (London: Penguin, 2016)
Whittell, G., *The Secret Life of Snow* (London: Short Books, 2019)
Wierenga, L., *Sandcastles Made Simple: Step-by-step Instructions on Building Sensational Sand Creations* (New York: Stewart, Tabori & Chang, Harry N. Abrams, 2009)

CHAPTER 5: BUBBLES, BLOW BOOKS AND KITES

Clubb, Louise George, 'A Magic Book of Renaissance Shows', *Artibus et Historiae*, vol. 28, no. 55, 2007, pp. 37–52, JSTOR, http://www.jstor.org/stable/20067138
Gode, P.K., 'Some Further Notes on the History of Kite-flying in India and Outside between BC 500 and AD 1956', *Annals of the Bhandarkar Oriental Research Institute*, vol. 37, no. 1/ 4 (1956) pp.111-119, JSTOR, http://www.jstor.org/stable/44082911
Hart, Clive, *Kites: An Historical Survey* (London: Faber & Faber, 1967)
Kent, S., *The Creative Book of Kites* (New York: Smithmark Publishers, U.S. Media Holdings Inc.,1997)
Modegi, M., *The Making of Japanese Kites: Tradition, Beauty and Creation* (Tokyo: Japan Publications Trading Co. Ltd, 2007)
Newman, L.S. and H., *Kite Craft: The History and Processes of Kitemaking throughout the World* (London: George Allen & Unwin Ltd,1974)

Making Matters

CHAPTER 6: DRESSING UP

Bullough, V.L. and B. Bullough, *Cross Dressing, Sex and Gender* (Pennsylvania: University of Pennsylvania Press, 1993)

Galembo, P., *Maske* (New York: Aperture Foundation, 2016)

Holt, A., *Fancy Dress Described: A Glossary of Victorian Costumes* (New York: Dover Publications Inc., 2017)

Liptak, A., *Cosplay: A History* (New York: Saga Press, 2022)

Mayer, Tara, 'Cultural Cross-Dressing: Posing and Performance in Orientalist Portraits', *Journal of the Royal Asiatic Society*, vol. 22, no. 2 (APRIL 2012) pp. 281–98. JSTOR, http://www.jstor.org/stable/41490100

Powell, T., (introduction), *Julia Margaret Cameron: By Herself, Virginia Woolf and Roger Fry* (London: Pallas Athene, 2023)

Riggio, Milla C., 'Introduction: Resistance and Identity: Carnival in Trinidad and Tobago', *TDR* (1988–), vol. 42, no. 3, pp. 7–23, JSTOR, http://www.jstor.org/stable/1146676

Roberts, Helene E., 'Victorian Medievalism: Revival or Masquerade?', *Browning Institute Studies* 8 (1986), pp. 11–44, JSTOR, http://www.jstor.org/stable/25057683

Wilson, V., *Dressing Up: A History of Fancy Dress in Britain* (London: Reaktion Books Ltd, 2022)

CHAPTER 7: PUPPETS

Blumenthal, E. *Puppets and Puppetry: An Illustrated World Survey* (London: Thames & Hudson, 2005)

Chen, Fan Pen Li, and Bradford Clarke, 'A survey of Puppetry in China (Summers 2008 and 2009)', *Asian Theatre Journal*, vol. 27, no. 2 (Fall 2010), copyright 2010 pp.333–65, JSTOR, http://www.jstor.org/stable/25782123

Dretel, C.L., 'The Gift of Happy Memories: A World War II Christmas Play at Ravensbrück', *Open Library of Humanities*, 8 (2) DOI, https://olh.openlibhums.org/article/id/6379/

Bibliography

Goodlander, J., *Puppets and Cities: Articulating Identities in Southeast Asia* (London: Methuen Drama, Bloomsbury, 2020)

Gross, K., *Puppet: An Essay on Uncanny Life* (Chicago, London: University of Chicago Press Ltd, 2011)

Hogarth, Anne and J. Bussell, *Fanfare for Puppets* (Australia: Macmillan,1985)

Hulburd, C., *Puppet-Assisted Therapy: Theory, Research and Practice* (London, New York: Routledge, 2021)

Jenkins, Clive Hicks, blog, https: clivehicksjenkins.wordpress.com

Jilin, L., *Chinese Shadow Puppet Plays* (Beijing: Morning Glory Publishers,1988)

Leach, P. *The Punch & Judy Show: History, Tradition and Meaning* (London: B.T. Batsford Ltd, 1985)

Malik, J., *The Puppet Theatre in Czechoslovakia* (Prague: Orbis, 1970)

Mello, A., and Claudia Orenstein and Cariad Astles, *Women and Puppetry: Critical and Historical Investigations* (Abington, New York: Routledge, 2019)

Millar, M., *The Horse's Mouth: How Handspring and the National Theatre made War Horse* (London: The National Theatre & Oberon Books Ltd, 2007)

Nelson, V., *The Secret Life of Puppets* (Cambridge, Massachusetts & London: Harvard University Press, 2001)

Orenstein, Claudia, 'Women in Indian Puppetry: Negotiating Traditional Roles and New Possibilities', *Asian Theatre Journal*, vol. 32, no. 2 (Fall 2015), pp. 493–517, JSTOR, http://www.jstor.org/stable/24737042

Plassard, D., 'Puppetry for a Total War: French and German Puppet Plays in World War 1', *Representing Alterity through Puppetry and Performing Objects* (edited by John Bell, Mathew Isaac Cohen, and Jungmin Song), 2023, https://digitalcommons. lib.uconn.edu/ballinst.alterity/6

Speaight, G., *The History of the English Puppet Theatre* (UK: George Harrap & Co. Ltd, 1990)
Von Boehn, M., *Puppets and Automata* (New York: Dover Publications Inc., 1972)
World Encyclopaedia of Puppetry Arts, https//wepa.unima.org/en
Yousef, Ghulam-Sarwar (ed.), *Puppetry for All Times: Papers Presented at the Bali Puppetry Seminar 2013* (Singapore: Partridge, 2015)

CHAPTER 8: PINHOLES AND PEEPSHOWS

Bake, C., *Kaleidoscopes: Wonders of Wonders* (California: C&T Publishing Inc., 1999)
Balzer, R., *Peepshows: A Visual History* (New York: Harry N. Abrams, Inc., 1998)
Cook, O., *Movement in Two Dimensions* (London: Hutchinson, 1963)
Dale R., and Rebecca Weaver, *Home Entertainment* (London: The British Library, 1993)
Freeman Sayer, P & C., *Victorian Kinetic Toys and How to Make Them* (London: Evans Brothers Ltd, 1977)
Godwin, J., *Athanasius Kircher's Theatre of the World* (London: Thames and Hudson 2009)
Hockney, D., *Secret Knowledge: Rediscovering the Lost Techniques of the Old Masters* (London: Thames & Hudson, 2001)
Humphries, S., *Victorian Britain through the Magic Lantern* (London: Sidgwick & Jackson Ltd, 1989)
Jewell, P., (foreword), *Bill Douglas Centre Museum Guide* (Exeter: University of Exeter, 2010)
Mogridge, G., *Sergeant Bell and his Raree Show* (London: Thomas Tegg, 1839)

Bibliography

CHAPTER 9: LANTERNS

Coult, T., and Baz Kershaw (eds), *Engineers of the Imagination: The Welfare State Handbook* (London: Methuen Drama, Reed Consumer Books Ltd, 1990)
Fox, John, *A New Role for the Artist*, March 2013, published online by Francois Matarasso, 29 March 2016, https://arestlessart.com/john-fox-a-new-role-for-the-artist
Xueqin, Cao, *Dream of the Red Chamber*, Honglou Meng, vol. 1 (Imprint: Daybreak Studios)

RELEVANT ORGANISATIONS

The Original Paper Doll Artists Guild: https://www.opdag.com
The British Puppet Guild: https://www.britishpuppetguild.com
Puppeteers of America: https://www.puppeteers.org
Pinhole Photography: https://www.pinholephotography.org
British Origami Society: https://britishorigami.org
The National Puppetry Archive: https://nationalpuppetry-archive.co.uk
Dressing Up Podcast: https://dressfancy.uk
The Kite Society of Great Britain: https://thekitesociety.org.uk
Bill Douglas Cinema Museum: https://www.bdcmuseum.org.uk

Index

Aboriginal Australian 108–9
Ackerman, Forrest J. 169
Adamson, Robert 160
Afghanistan 136–7
Al-Jahiz 134
Albers, Josef 58
Alberti, Leon Battista 212–13
Alice's Adventures in Wonderland 62
Allegory of Transience: 'Homo Bulla' (Goltzius) 117
Always Jolly (Meggendorfer) 61
Alyoshkina, Dariya 58–9
Amadeus (Shaffer) 205
Andersen, Hans Christian 59
Angola 109
Anthemius of Tralles 209
Apianus, Petrus 60
Aria, Eliza Davis 163
Aristotle 209
Armitage, Simon 90
Astronomicum Caesareum (Apianus) 60
Atwood, Margaret 171
Austen, Jane 12
Bacall, Lauren 43
Baker, Cozy 223, 224

Balaban, Candan Seda 192
Ballard, Frank 174
Barber of Seville (Rossini) 80
Beardsley, Aubrey 73
Beauty & the Beast 90
Beginner's Way, The (McCullough) 100
Bellifortis (Kyeser) 135
Benjamin Pollock's Toyshop 90
Bentley, Wilson A. 92–3
Berezowska, Maja 187
Bergman, Ingmar 73
Bersudsky, Eduard 19
Beuys, Joseph 19
Biju, Nesto 15
Bill Douglas Cinema Museum 219–20, 222–3, 224–5, 227
blow books
 author's experience of 122–6
 description of 119–20
 history of 120–2
Blundall, John 176–8
Bolter, Frank 26–7
Bonnet, Betty 39
Boyle, Danny 111–12
breath 118–19
Brewster, Sir David 221–2
Brewster, Margaret 222

Index

Brook, Peter 73
Browne, Maggie 16
bubbles 115–18
Bubbles (Millais) 118
Büchner, Georg 230
Buddhism 108, 126–7, 251
Bulwer-Lytton, Edward 169
bunraku 184–5
Caldwell, John 161
Callow, Simon 205, 206
camera obscuras 207–11
Cameron, Julia Margaret 160
Cannon Hill Puppet Theatre 176, 177
Čapek, Karel 88
Cardano, Gerolamo 121
Carnival of Cayenne 152
carnivals 149–55
Carroll, Lewis 73, 160
Chanel 44
Chardin, Jean Simeon 117–18
Charles Emmanuel II, Duke 155
Chelsea Art Club Ball 163–4
Chesterton, G.K. 73
China
  author in 31–2, 52–4, 127, 198–9
  kite flying in 133, 134, 137
  lanterns in 243–4, 245–7
  paper cutting in 50–4
  paper-making in 10
  prayer wheels in 127
  puppetry in 188–9, 198–200
Christmas Tree, A (Dickens) 66
Clap, Margaret 165–6
climate change 27–30, 32–3
Clubb, Louise George 125
Cocteau, Jean 73
Cody, Samuel Franklin 140

Collins Gallery 23
Comrie Parade 172–3
Conan Doyle, Arthur 50
Cooley, Mason 142
cosplay 169–72
Costume: Fanciful, Historical and Theatrical (Aria) 163
costumed balls 155–9, 163–4, 171
Coward, Noel 73
Craig, Edward Gordon 73
cross–dressing 164–9
cummings, e e 7
da Vinci, Leonardo 205, 208
Daguerre, Louis 226
Dalai Lama 45
Dancing Couple, The (Steen) 117
Danton's Death (Buchner) 230
Day of Broken Kite Strings 133
Day of the Dead 3, 55–6, 108
De Re Rustica (Varro) 117
De Subtilitate (Cardano) 121
Dean & Sons (publisher) 60
della Porta, Giambattista 135, 209–10
Demarco, Richard 19
Deneuve, Catherine 43
Denmark 80
Devonshire, Duchess of 158–9
Dickens, Charles 66, 74, 78
Dickinson, Emily 233
digital media 4–5
Dior 40, 42, 44, 167
dioramas 219–21
Discoverie of Witchcraft (Scot) 121–2
Diwali 250
Dorsey Swann, William 166

Index

Douglas, Bill 219
Douglas, Myrtle R. 169
dressing up
   author's experience of
     142–4, 147–9, 172–3
   carnival costumes 149–55
   in celebrations 144–7
   cosplay 169–72
   costumed balls 155–9, 163–4, 171
   cross–dressing 164–9
   tableaux vivant 159–61
   Victorian interest in 161–3
drones 140–1
Duffy, Carol Ann 112
Dukhovny, Yulya 85–7
Eckstein, Bob 97–8
Edinburgh Book Festival 27, 50
Edinburgh Central Lending Library 50
Edinburgh College of Art 46, 49
Eglinton, Earl of 156
Emerson, Ralph Waldo 92
Erté 44
Evelyn, John 214
Every Boy's Book: A Complete Encyclopaedia of Sports and Amusements 75
Exit Music (Rankin) 50
Fancy Dresses Described: A Glossary of Victorian Costume (Holt) 161–2
Fanny and Alexander 73
Farrer, Reginald 160–1
Festival for Justice and Remembrance 255
Finster, Howard 19
Flaviano, Olivier 40–1
Fo, Dario 73, 180–1

Fox, John 239, 240–1, 256–8
Francis I, King 155
Franklin, Benjamin 148
Fraser, George 160–1
French Guiana 152
Furse, Roger 83
Gainsborough, Thomas 214–15
Galembo, Phyllis 154
George IV, King 139
Germany
   paper cutting in 57
   paper theatres in 80
   puppetry in 187, 188
Gestetner Collection (V&A Museum) 220–1
Gielgud, John 73
Gift, The (Langford) 112–14
Gill, Sue 239, 240–1
Goethe, Johann Wolfgang von 181
Goldsworthy, Andy 103–5, 114
Goltzius, Hendrik 117
Graham, Maria 220
Great Small Works 89
Guatemala 133
Guignol in the Trenches 186–7
Halloween 145–6, 252–3
Hamlet (Shakespeare) 83
Hanauer Papiertheatermuseum 90
Handmaid's Tale, The (Atwood) 171
Hannula, Mika 94
Hansel and Gretel 90
Harris, Kamala 36
Harris, Lyall 25–6
Haunted House (Pieńkowski) 61–2
Haydn, Joseph 181

283

Index

Hayes, Marisa 89
Haytham, Ibn al 209
Heartbeats (comic) 40
Hemingway, Ernest 88
Herodotus 184
Hicks-Jenkins, Clive 90, 91
Hill, Octavius 160
Hiroshima 249–50
History and Adventures of Little Henry, The 38
History of the English Toy Theatre, The (Speaight) 83
History of Little Fanny, Exemplified in a Series of Figures, The 37–8
History of the Snowman, The (Eckstein) 97–8
Hockney, David 208–9
Hogg, Thomas Jefferson 13
Holt, Arden 161
Holywood, John 11
Hoogstraten, Samuel van 214
Hughes, Charles H. 166
Hunter, Clare
   at Bill Douglas Cinema Museum 219–20, 222–3, 224–5, 227
   and blow books 122–6
   in China 31–2, 52–4, 127, 198–9
   and dressing up 142–4, 147–9, 172–3
   experience of making 3–4
   and kite flying 128–31
   and lanterns 233–8, 253, 259–61
   and magic lanterns 229–31
   meetings with George Wyllie 22–3
   paper boat making 7–9, 17
   and paper cutting 46–9
   and paper dolls 34–6, 40–1
   and paper theatres 67–72, 83–8
   and peepshows 215–16
   and pinhole photography 205–6, 210–11
   and puppetry 176–9, 197–200, 201–4
   and sand sculptures 109–10
   working with snow 99–103
India
   lanterns in 248
   paper boats in 14–15
   puppetry in 191–2
Interior of a Dutch House (Hoogstraten) 214
International Circus (Meggendorfer) 60–1
Jamie, Kathleen 28, 30
Japan
   cross-dressing in 164
   kaleidoscopes in 224
   kite flying in 131–3, 134, 136
   lanterns in 240–1, 249–50
   Obon festival 2
   origami in 10–11
   paper boats in 10
   paper cutting in 59
   paper-making in 10
   paper theatre in 82–3
   peepshows in 218
   puppetry in 184–5, 191
Jarry, Alfred 180
Jay, Ricky 125
Jewell, Peter 219
Jewish paper cuts 54–5
John, Augustus 163

Index

John Paul II, Pope 45
Jones, Andy 179
Judy Project, The 189
kaleidoscopes 221–4
Kaleidoscopes: Wonders of Wonder (Baker) 223
kamikiri 59
kamishibai 82–3
Karim, Abdul 160
Kean, Edmund 72
Kemble, Charles 72
Kircher, Athanasius 210
kite flying
  in Afghanistan 136–7
  appeal of 127–8
  author's experience of 128–31
  in China 133, 134, 137
  and drones 140–1
  in Japan 131–3, 134, 136
  in Korea 2–3, 133, 136
  military applications of 134–6
  practical applications of 138–
  spirituality of 127, 128, 131–4
Koerten, Joanna 56–7
Kopijowska, Jadwiga 187
Kyeser, Konrad 135
LaBeija, Crystal 167
Ladies' Home Journal 39
Lampedusa, The (paper boat) 24–5
Landmarks (Macfarlane) 93
Landseer, Edwin 156
Lang, Robert 63
Langford, Jessica 112–14
Langtry, Lily 43
lanterns
  author's experience of 233–8, 253, 259–61
  in China 243–4, 245–7
  in Japan 240–1, 249–50
  popularity of 247–50, 253–5
  sky lanterns 254
  spirituality of 250–3
  symbolism of 242–5
  Ulverston Lantern Festival 238–42, 256–8
  in United States 255–6
Le Chat Noir 200, 201
Leach's Fancy Dress 147
Legend of the White Snake, The 54
'Letter to Maria Gisborne' (Shelley) 13
Li Ye 134
library closures 49–50
Little Tree Giant, The (Dukhovny) 85–7
Lochhead, Liz 23
Logan, Leroy 153
Lost World, The (Conan Doyle) 50
Macfarlane, Robert 93
Mackenzie, Colin 161
Mackintosh, Charles Rennie 4
Maeterlinck, Maurice 181
Magia Naturalis (della Porta) 210
Magic Flute, The (Mozart) 80
magic lanterns 227–31
Mahabharata 195
Mahatat (arts collective) 217–18
making
  author's experience of 3–4
  cultural significance of 2–3
  desire for 4–5
  and digital media 4–5
  physical and mental benefits of 4

Index

public purpose of 1–2
   therapeutics of 4
Malik, Jan 187
Manet, Édouard 117–18
manga 83
Marconi, Guglielmo 140
Marriage of Figaro, The
   (Mozart) 80
Mary, Queen of Scots 35–6, 164
Maryam (Moini) 192
Masako, Nakauchi 191
Maske (Galembo) 154–5
Matisse, Henri 58
McCall, Betsy 44
McCall's 44
McCannon, Olivia 90
McCaughey, Peter 93–7
McCord, Philip 110
McCullough, Jamie 100–2, 103
McQueen, Alexander 45
Meanwhile Gardens
   (McCullough) 100
Meggendorfer, Lothar 60–1
Mexico
   Day of the Dead 3, 55–6, 108
   paper cutting in 55–6
   and sand 107–8
Michelangelo 98
Mickey Mouse 43
migrant crisis 24–7
Millais, John Everett 118
Minamoto no Tametomo 132
Miracle of 1511 98–9
Modes of Pleasure (puppet
   show) 192–3
Moini, Maryam 192
Molly Houses 165–6
Monroe, Marilyn 43

Morgan, Edwin 50
Morpurgo, Michael 179
moveable/pop-up books
   history of 59–61
   and *Haunted House* (Pień-
      kowski) 61–2
   and Robert Sabuda 62–3
Mozart, Wolfgang Amadeus 80
Mozi 209
Mug Ruith 119
Muir, John 28
Muniz, Vik 24–5
Munnings, Alfred 163
Museum Odense 59
Nagasaki 249–50
National Library of Scotland
   50
Navajo people 107
Newton, Isaac 135–6
Northampton 99–103
Notting Hill Carnival 152–3
Obon festival 2, 249
Old Man and the Sea, The
   (Hemingway) 88
Oliver Twist (Dickens) 78
Olivier, Laurence 83
Ombres Chinoises 200, 201
origami 10–11, 63
Original Paper Doll Artists
   Guild 45
Ormes, Jackie 'Zelda' 40
Oxenford, John 73
Paper Boat charity 14–15
paper boats
   author's experience of 7–9,
      17, 27–33
   and climate change 27–30,
      32–3

Index

and Frank Bolter 26–7
and George Wyllie 21–2, 24–5
in India 14–15
instructions for making 16–17
in Japan 10
and migrant crisis 24–7
in Millenium celebrations 7–9
origins of 10–11
and *Paper Boats* (Silva & Harris) 25–6
popularity with literary figures 12–14
symbolism of 9–10, 13–15, 24–33
and Vik Muniz 24–5
world records in 15
Paper Boats (Silva & Harris) 25–6
paper cutting
  as artistic form 56–9
  author's experience of 46–9, 52–4
  in China 50–4
  and Dariya Alyoshkina 58–9
  as folk art 56
  history of 50–1
  in Japan 59
  in Jewish culture 54–5
  and Joanna Koerten 56–7
  and library closure campaign 49–50
  in Mexico 55–6
  in Switzerland 57–8
paper dolls
  author's experience of 34–6, 40–1
  of celebrities 36, 43, 45
  history of 37–40, 43–4
  popularity of 36–7, 45–6
  and Tom Tierney 44–5
  and Yves Saint Laurent 40–3
paper-making
  in China 10
  in Japan 10
  mass production of 11–12
  in medieval Europe 11
paper theatres
  authenticity of 72
  author's experience of 67–72, 83–8
  as boys' pastime 72–6
  as diversion 76–7
  in Germany 80
  in Japan 82–3
  popularity of 64–7, 76–83, 89–91
  and *Preetzer Papiertheatertreffen* 83–5, 87–8
  and *Sarah's Paper Theatre* 87–8
  and Yulya Dukhovny 85–7
Paterson, Kim 23
Pearl, Louis ('the Bubble Man') 115–17
Peasgood, Sarah 87–8
peepshows
  in art 213–15
  author's experience of 215–16
  description of 211–12
  eroticism 217
  history of 212–13, 216–17
  in Japan 218
  popularity of 217–19

287

Index

Pellerin, Jean-Charles 79
'Penny Plain, Tuppence Coloured, A' (Stephenson) 66–7
Pepys, Samuel 227
Peter Pan 62
Picasso, Pablo 73
Picasso, Paloma 43
Pickford, Mary 43
Pieńkowski, Jan 61–2
pinhole photography
  author's experience of 205–6, 210–11
  camera obscuras 207–11
  in community arts 206–7
  history of 207–10
Pleasant Work for Busy Fingers; or, Kindergarten at Home (Browne) 16
Pocock, George 138–40
Poire, Emmanuel 200
Poland 56
Politics of Small Gestures, The (Hannula) 94
Pollock's Toy Museum 67, 82, 90
Polwart, Karine 24, 30–1
Poulter, Robert 88
Preetzer Papiertheatertreffen (festival) 83–5, 87–8
Procida Paper Fleet 27
Protean Views 226–7
Pulavar, Rajitha Ramachandra 191–2, 193
Punch and Judy 185–6, 189–90
Puppet and Model Theatre Guild 90
puppetry
  as art form 181
  author's experience of 176–9, 197–200, 201–4
  in China 188–9, 198–200
  in Germany 187, 188
  history of 183–4
  in India 191–2
  in Japan 184–5, 191
  manipulation of 182–3
  politics of 174–5, 180–1
  Punch and Judy 185–6, 189–90
  in Second World War 187–8
  shadow puppetry 193–201
  as therapeutic tool 181–2
  in *War Horse* 179–80
  women in 189–93
Queen Charlotte's Ball 171
R.U.R. (Čapek) 88
Ramadan 250–1
Ramayana 195
Rame, Franca 180–1
Rankin, Ian 50
Reinhardt, Max 181
Reiniger, Lotte 57
Rencontres Internationales de Théâtre de Papier 90
Ring Cycle (Wagner) 80
RISE festival 255–6
Riviere, Henri 200–1
Rob Roy (Scott) 70
Robert, Etienne Gaspard 194
Rock, Joseph 160–1
Rossini, Gioachino 80
Royal Shakespeare Company 3
Runge, Philipp Otto 57
RuPaul's Drag Race 168–9
Sabuda, Robert 62–3
Saint Laurent, Yves 40–3
Salis, Rodolphe 201

Index

sand
  author's experience of 109–10
  and *The Gift* (Langford) 112–14
  joy of 114
  sculptures from 109–12
  symbolism of 107–9
  writing on 106–7, 108–9
Sand, George 181
Sandford, Patrick 76
Sarah's Paper Theatre 87–8
Schumann, Peter 181
Scot, Reginald 121–2, 123
Scott, Judith 19
Scott, Walter 70, 78
Scottish Poetry Library 49, 50
Scottish Storytelling Centre 50
Secret Knowledge: Rediscovering the Lost Techniques of the Old Masters (Hockney) 208–9
Seeger, Pete 180
Sertdemir, Yigit 192
Seuss, Dr. 64
shadow puppetry 193–201
Shaffer, Peter 205
Shakespeare, William 68
Shaw, George Bernard 73, 181, 259
Shelley, Percy Bysshe 12–13
Siddons, Sarah 72
Sierra Leone 247–8
Silva, Patrici 25–6
Skupa, Josef 187
sky lanterns 254
Slack, David W. 90
Smith, Adam 22
snow
  and Andy Goldsworthy 103–5
  author's experience of 99–103
  joy of 114
  and Miracle of 1511 98–9
  and Peter McCaughey's bag of snow 93–7
  snowflake structure 92–3
  and the snowman 97–9
  vocabulary of 93
South Korea
  kite flying in 2–3, 133, 136
  lanterns in 248–9
Spain 79–80
Speaight, George 83
Spencer Ms.180 125
Spooner, William 226
Steen, Jan 117
Stevenson, Robert Louis 66–7
Stonewall riots 166–7
Stowe, Harriet Beecher 78
Stuart, Charles Edward (Bonnie Prince Charlie) 35
Styles, Harry 36
Swift, Taylor 36
Switzerland 57–8, 251–2
tableaux vivant 159–61
Tagore, Rabindranath 14
Taiwan 247
Taylor, Elizabeth 43
Temperance Society 229–30
Terry, Ellen 43, 72
Thailand 136, 248
That Was the Week That Was 174
Theory of Moral Sentiments, The (Smith) 22
Tierney, Tom 44–5

Index

Tillstrom, Burr 174–5
Times, The 73
Tintin 43
To the World's End project (Bolter) 26
Toy Theater of Terror as Usual 89
'Toy Theatre Thrives Online during Quarantine' (Hayes) 89
'Trace of Wings, A' (Morgan) 50
Tractatus Sphaera Mundi (Holywood) 11
Trinidad and Tobago 151–2
Trump, Donald 36
Twelfth Night (Shakespeare) 68, 70–1
Ubu Roi (Jarry) 180
Ukraine 56
Ulverston Lantern Festival 238–42, 256–8
Uncle Tom's Cabin (Stowe) 78
United States
 costumed balls in 157–8
 lanterns in 255–6
 paper theatres in 80
Up Helly A 165
Vagabond Puppeteers 180
Valentino, Rudolf 43
van Gogh, Vincent 1
Vanuatu 109
Varro, Marcus Terentius 117
Venice 149–51
Verne, Jules 169

Victoria, Queen 43, 156–7, 158, 159–60, 221
Vietnam 247
Vladimirovich, Andrei 159
Vril: The Power of the Coming Race (Bulwer-Lytton) 169
Wagner, Richard 80
Walker, Kara 34
War Horse (Morpurgo) 179–80
Water Lantern Festival 256
wayang 194–8
Webb, H.J. 75, 82, 87
Webber, Andrew Lloyd 73
'Wee Multitude of Questions for George Wyllie, A' (Lochhead) 23
Welfare State International 238–40
Welles, Orson 73
West, William 78, 81
Wickham, Phil 219, 226
Wilde, Oscar 73
Wilkinson, Norman 163
Williams, Gareth Patrick 24
Wilson, Orme 157
wind, spirituality of 126–7
Women and Puppetry: Critical and Historical Investigations 190–1
Worth (House of) 44
Wu, Emperor 134
Wyllie, George 18–24
Yitao Liu 52–4
zoetropes 224–5
Zoroastrianism 243